"[L]istening and talking skillfully can be acts of love. In *Let's Talk* Mudita Nisker and Dan Clurman offer practical ways we can communicate at our best. Parents, lovers, teachers, leaders—everyone—can benefit enormously from their kindly guidance."

—Daniel Goleman
bestselling author of *Emotional Intelligence* and *Altered Traits*

"Mudita and Dan's teaching has changed my life. More than that, the skills have changed the lives of everyone around me, because I am so much easier to live with. Long way of saying: read this book. Your communications, and therefore your relationships, with everyone in your orbit will improve. You'll get into fewer fights. And when you do have conflict, you'll navigate it more smoothly."

—Dan Harris
bestselling author of *Ten Percent Happier* and
co-founder of the Ten Percent Happier app

"Every teacher, parent, partner, manager, and leader needs to read *Let's Talk*! Mudita Nisker and Dan Clurman brilliantly combine theory and decades of real-world experience to educate us in critical skills and tools that will enhance how we communicate and relate to others (and ourselves), which will dramatically transform our personal, social, and professional lives."

—Marc Brackett
bestselling author of *Permission to Feel* and founding director
of the Yale Center for Emotional Intelligence

"Have you ever walked away from a conversation wondering how it had gone so off track? *Let's Talk* is a great book to help hone the skills for healthy communication with others—be it work related, with family, or with friends. . . . Written in an engaging way, it is a perfect book for venturing into social situations."

—Sharon Salzberg
author of *Lovingkindness* and *Real Happiness*

"*Let's Talk* is a powerful and moving tool. It guides us to understand the complex and dynamic web of factors that influence how we experience the world and how that impacts our connections to those around us. It may seem that there are some people who are 'just good communicators,' but this refreshing, detailed, action-based book underlines that clear, meaningful communication is a learnable skill. It integrates foundational concepts of compassionate conversation and also looks squarely at the complexities of diversity, differing positions of power and privilege, and the multitude of modes of communication available to us—in a way that is clear and supportive. In times when we can seem more and more polarized, *Let's Talk* truly gives me hope."

—Emiko Susilo
author of *Good to Know about Bali: A Friendly Guide to Arts and Culturally Sustainable Travel in Bali*, actor, and associate director of the Balinese music and dance performing ensemble Çudamani

"In this beautiful, astonishing, and useful book, Clurman and Nisker distill decades of research on the art of talking and listening. Communication, they remind us, is not just the transmission of ideas. We establish trust, enter into productive and satisfying relationships, and discover ourselves when we use language skillfully. With striking precision, and a light touch, *Let's Talk* provides the tools many of us need to do just that. This book is an opportunity and a revelation."

—Alva Noë
professor of philosophy, University of California Berkeley, and the author of *Out of Our Heads: Why You Are Not Your Brain and Other Lessons from the Biology of Consciousness.*

"Mudita Nisker and Dan Clurman gently guide us through our language in a way that clarifies how our communication breaks down and how making some simple adjustments can help us skillfully navigate our way through conversations, improving relationships of all kinds."

—Tara Bennett-Goleman
New York Times bestselling author of *Emotional Alchemy: How the Mind Can Heal the Heart*

"Mudita Nisker and Dan Clurman have been two primary teachers helping me to grow in skillful communication. In *Let's Talk* their clarity and wisdom shine through, illuminating a path to true connection and intimacy for anyone serious about embodying 'wise speech.' This is a valuable resource that I highly recommend."

—James Baraz
co-author of *Awakening Joy: 10 Steps to Happiness* and co-founding teacher of Spirit Rock Meditation Center

"Mudita and Dan have written a timely book that articulates powerful communication strategies that I use in multiple contexts. It is as relevant in my professional work in cultural diplomacy as it is in my personal life. I believe these principles are core to successfully communicating across nations."

—Rachel Cooper
director, Culture as Diplomacy, Asia Society

"*Let's Talk* can serve both as a self-and-other teaching text as well as an encyclopedia about communication skills. For me it is a treasure-trove of life wisdom, resting upon a foundation committed to maintaining the deepest respect for self and others."

—Marlys Mayfield
author of *Thinking for Yourself: Developing Critical Thinking Skills Through Reading and Writing*

"*Let's Talk* is the perfect blend of theory and practice. As a clear and easy-to-follow guide to improve your capacity to communicate when it matters, it is a true gem."

—John Ford
professor of negotiation, University of California (Hastings) Law School; author of *Peace at Work*; and creator of *The Empathy Set*

"I've been looking for a book like this for years. . . . Mudita Nisker and Dan Clurman encourage us to reflect deeply on how we communicate and show us how to become more skillful at it. The philosophy and techniques presented here have the power to improve our relationships with our partners, children, colleagues, community, and most importantly ourselves. These skills are life changing. What a gift!"

—Jane Baraz
Mindfulness-Based Stress Reduction (MSBR) instructor, University of California San Francisco Medical Center

Let's Talk

To Roger
with metta,
Du & Michek
♡ June 2023

Also by Mudita Nisker
and Dan Clurman

Deanne Stone, Mudita Nisker, and Dan Clurman, *Money Disagreements: How to Talk About Them* (n.p., 2019)

Dan Clurman, *You've Got to Draw the Line Somewhere* (Lulu, 2006)

Dan Clurman, *Floating Upstream: Poems and Drawings* (Sunyata Press, 1996)

Dan Clurman and John Esterle, eds., *Conversations with Critical Thinkers* (The Whitman Institute, 1991)

Let's Talk

an essential
guide to skillful
communication

MUDITA NISKER
AND DAN CLURMAN

Foreword by Joseph Goldstein

Let's Talk Method
2022

Let's Talk Method
398 61st St.
Oakland, CA 94618
letstalkmethod.com
letstalkmethod@gmail.com

First edition April, 2022.

Cover design by Karen Polaski
Book design by Meredith March
Back cover photo by Aidan Fraser
Developmental editing and writing by Amy Rost

ISBN 979-8-9851995-0-5 (book)
ISBN 979-8-9851995-1-2 (e-book)

The content of this book is for informational purposes only and is not intended to diagnose, treat, cure, or prevent any condition or disease. This book is not intended as a substitute for consultation with a qualified, licensed expert. The publisher and the authors make no guarantees concerning the level of success you may experience by following the advice and strategies contained in this book. The authors and publisher shall have neither liability nor responsibility to anyone with respect to any loss or damage caused, or alleged to be caused, directly or indirectly by the information contained in this book.

All the characters in examples used in this book are fictitious. Any resemblance to actual persons, living or dead, is purely coincidental.

Mudita:
To the memory of Lily Livon Ostrin,
my mother and most loving teacher.

Dan:
To the memories of my mother, father, and sister.
And to the memory of my dear friend Bob Morrison.

With thee conversing I forget all time.

—John Milton, *Paradise Lost*

Contents

Contents

Communication Skills Master List

- Discerning whether to talk or listen (chapter 4)
- Balancing talking and listening (chapter 4)
- Calming down when emotionally triggered (chapter 4)
- Loop communication (chapter 4)
- Chunking (chapter 4)
- Reflective listening (chapter 5)
  - Identifying and reflecting implicit meanings
  - Understanding without agreeing or disagreeing
- Recognizing the influence of absolute and relative beliefs (chapter 6)
- Provisional language (chapter 6)
- Detecting and assessing assumptions (chapter 7)
- Distinguishing between cause and influence (chapter 8)
- Shifting out of a blame mindset (chapter 8)
- Plan A versus Plan B (chapter 9)
- Adjusting your self-talk (chapter 10)
- Recognizing and addressing cognitive distortions (chapter 10)
- Reporting (chapter 10)
- I-language (chapter 11)
- Four-part messages (chapter 12)
- Framing (chapter 13)
- Identifying your goals in a conflict (chapter 14)
- Choosing a conflict-management strategy (chapter 14)

Foreword

By Joseph Goldstein

In any art, there are many levels of mastery. And in the profoundly rich art of communication, Mudita Nisker and Dan Clurman are adepts in their understanding of what brings people together and what pushes them apart. I've been familiar with their work over many decades and have been inspired and helped by what they have uncovered, explored, and understood in so many habitual communication patterns.

An obvious but frequently overlooked truth is that the words we use affect every aspect of our lives. Whether the arena is the intimate relationships of partners, children, or parents; our social network of friends; the complexities of our work situation; and even the larger societal context in which we live, *Let's Talk* examines the many pitfalls and possibilities in our daily life interactions. Proving ourselves right can be so seductive that we miss the opportunity to see what words we might use that would actually further our highest values.

In reading this book, I was struck so often by how both the theoretical frameworks and their pragmatic applications addressed real-time experiences in my own life. There were many aha moments when I saw a new opening in particularly sticky situations that had bogged down through less-than-skillful speech, even as I thought I was communicating in a very straightforward way.

The depth and subtlety of Mudita and Dan's work make clear the underpinnings of both the skillful and unskillful patterns that are woven into our interpersonal communication. Their many suggestions and practices open possibilities of greater interpersonal harmony, as well as our own deepening peace of mind. Even when boundaries need to be set or different conflicts need to be resolved, the art of communication can rest on the foundation of love and care. This illuminating book has the potential to transform one of the most important activities of our lives.

Joseph Goldstein has been leading insight and lovingkindness meditation retreats worldwide since 1974. He is a co-founder of the Insight Meditation Society and the Barre Center for Buddhist Studies in Barre, Massachusetts. His books include *Mindfulness: A Practical Guide to Awakening; One Dharma;* and *Insight Meditation: The Practice of Freedom,* among others.

A New Approach to Person-to-Person Communication

When you think about it, there's little in our lives more important than communicating clearly and effectively with our family, friends, and people we work with. For most of us, communicating with others is like walking and breathing: we do it practically all the time, every day, and it seems natural to us. For the most part, we don't even think about how we communicate—until things start to go wrong. For example, you might think your communication ability is solid until one day you and your partner are having a disagreement, and they suddenly say, "You never listen to me!"

Unfortunately, many people don't recognize that there are shortcomings in their communication, much less what those shortcomings are. So they simply struggle along, perpetuating cycles of poor communication and feeling frustrated, annoyed, or disheartened when their colleagues don't seem to listen to their ideas, when too many conversations with their loved ones turn contentious, when they can't find support from their friends, or when they can't seem to make genuine connections with new people.

In many circumstances, you don't have to be particularly conscientious about how you communicate with others. Discussing where to have dinner with your partner, making arrangements to carpool to work with a colleague, or telling your friend what you did on your vacation are pretty straightforward conversations. The person you're talking with doesn't need to make much of an effort to interpret the information you're sharing. But when the conversation is more consequential—such as when you're making up with a friend after an argument or negotiating your salary with a new employer—careful communication is crucial.

Communication is the foundation of any interaction between you and another person, whether that conversation is a onetime event or part of an ongoing relationship. All too often, communication mishaps lead to misunderstandings, which in turn can impair your relationships and create disruptions in your professional and personal lives.

In professional settings, people who can't communicate well often have difficulty collaborating, coordinating necessary tasks, and getting buy-in for their ideas. In a 2015 survey conducted by the Pew Research Center, 90 percent of respondents said communication is the most important skill people need to succeed in their professional lives. [1] Communication is also vital for intimate relationships. We've coached couples for decades. Over the years, they've consistently told us that the communication skills we teach promote mutual understanding, trust, and goodwill between them. They're able to discuss important or sensitive subjects with less stress. Conflicts are often diffused before they can blow up, and when disagreements do arise, couples are able to address them in a more constructive way.

Our approach to communication can open new and unexpected possibilities.

What This Book Can Do for You

This book can help you improve your interactions with others by changing the way you communicate with them in conversations—formal and informal. Our approach addresses two primary aspects of interpersonal communication: *what* you talk about (your content) and *how* you talk and listen (your process).

The content of any conversation needs to be understandable to both you and the person you're talking with. We offer specific skills to help you improve the clarity of *what* you say. However, no matter how compelling your content is, you can't overlook *how* you talk with others—the process. If you do, others might be less interested in listening to you, or they might have a hard time understanding you. So we're also giving you practical skills to help you get your message across to others more successfully and receive what they have to say with more accuracy.

Having a toolbox of new skills to draw on is truly helpful, but it's not all you need to shift your everyday conversation habits. How people communicate is intertwined with how they think, what they assume to be true, and what they value. Unless you look at the beliefs, assumptions, and values underlying what you say and how you say it, your ability to modify your communication is limited. So in addition to showing you effective new skills, we will help you develop the critical-thinking tools you need to improve your communication, including:

- how to observe your thoughts, feelings, and communication
- how to separate facts from opinions
- how to recognize and change your limiting beliefs and self-talk
- how to identify your underlying assumptions and values
- how to use specific, accurate information and precise language

As you try out the skills presented in these pages, we think you'll be pleasantly surprised to discover that conversations you once found difficult can become easier—and even more enjoyable. You'll avoid making inaccurate assumptions and saying things that can lead others to accuse you of ignoring or bruising their feelings. You won't need to put as much time and energy into cleaning up messy conversations and repairing relationships damaged by misunderstandings, thoughtless words, and unintended outbursts. You'll have fewer problematic conversations with your family, friends, colleagues and coworkers, and others, eliminating a lot of stress for both you and them. Overall, you'll likely find yourself living in greater harmony with the people in your life.

Who We Are and Why We Care So Much About Communication

We have been coaching individuals and couples and co-leading communication workshops for more than thirty-five years. Our approach combines communication skills with wisdom teachings from Buddhism and Taoism. We also use systems theory and critical-thinking principles to help people examine the beliefs and assumptions that shape their communication and behavior.

We know just how effective and life changing our approach is. Not only do our clients and workshop participants consistently tell us so, but each of us has also seen our own relationships and outlook transformed as we use them.

For my (Dan's) part, I've found the communication skills and principles in this book particularly useful in conversations with my father. An inventor and pioneer in the development of color television, he was accustomed to being seen as an expert, even in areas outside his expertise. In our conversations, I often had to struggle to voice my ideas and confirm their worth. Over time, the skills helped me advocate my perspective, especially when it differed from his. I also felt less reactive when he criticized me. It became easier to listen to his "expert" advice without getting defensive. In his old age, he seemed to find my presence comforting and relaxing. When I visited him shortly before he died, he asked me if there was anything I wanted to talk about with him. This invitation would have been highly unusual earlier in our relationship.

Had I (Mudita) not practiced the skills detailed in this book, I don't know if I could have had a harmonious relationship with my ex-husband. I've often felt grateful that I learned these skills before I got divorced. Without them, I most likely would have carried resentment and become estranged from my ex. The skills have helped me address potentially contentious subjects with more ease and less acrimony. Instead of feeling uncomfortable or resentful in conversations with my ex, I've felt sympathetic and relaxed. We've developed a cooperative, friendly relationship that has given our daughter opportunities she wouldn't have had if her father and I didn't get along as well.

The skills and concepts we share in this book are ones we've shared with families, couples, and individuals, as well as businesses, government organizations, and nonprofits. We're confident that our approach will reliably serve you, as it has us and many others over the years.

Part I will lay the groundwork for the communication skills we'll cover in part II. Then part III will look at common situations in which the skills can serve you, including parenting your kids, managing conflicts with your partner, and experiencing health challenges. We'll also share some important additional concepts to keep in mind as you communicate with people of different abilities, ages, cultures, gender identities, and sexual orientation. Finally, we'll discuss what role the skills can play in today's dynamic digital landscape.

This book may be the first communication book you've ever picked up. Or maybe you've read a lot about communication and want to take your skills further. Wherever you fall in the continuum, know that learning new communication skills is like learning anything new: with practice, it becomes easier and more natural. And for most of us, there's always room for improvement.

Part I
Foundations

Chapter 1

How Communication Goes Awry

When was the last time you had a thoroughly satisfying conversation? A conversation where you felt really in sync with the other person—where you thought they really *got* you. And perhaps they told you they felt the same. Most of us have had at least a few such conversations and know how wonderful they feel.

Most of us have also had some really difficult conversations. Maybe you tried to share your thoughts and feelings, but the other person didn't react the way you hoped. Maybe they didn't understand you, and no matter how you tried, you just couldn't clarify what you meant. Or maybe the conversation unexpectedly morphed into a conflict. Whatever the case, you were left wondering what went wrong.

Like many people, you might be tempted to think the other person was at fault. Perhaps you found yourself thinking things like, "He's impossible to talk to!", "They just don't get it", or "She's patronizing (or selfish, or pigheaded, or stupid)". On the other hand, you might have felt frustrated with yourself. "Why can't I get it together?" you may have thought, or, "Why can't I ever think of the right thing to say?"

Let us reassure you that smooth, enjoyable conversations can be as common as difficult, unsatisfying ones. Figuring out what makes the difference between the two has been a compelling focus in our work for the past thirty-five years.

Conversations can go awry for a variety of reasons, but we've identified several communication habits that are almost guaranteed to invite problems. These disruptors are so common they usually seem normal—just part of how nearly everyone talks with each other. You probably wouldn't even notice them unless they're pointed out. But as we describe them, odds are you'll recognize many of them. You just may not have realized how much they're affecting the quality of your conversations.

Unbalanced Talking and Listening

It's easy to assume that communication is about talking, but that's only half the equation. The other half is listening.

Listening lets you gather information about what the other person is thinking and feeling. It also allows them to express themselves and know they've been understood. If you talk more than you listen, you can miss important information, and your response might be irrelevant and unsatisfying to the other person. When you talk too little or not at all, they might not hear important details, including whether or not you've accurately understood them.

Discerning when to listen and when to talk, and finding an appropriate balance between the two, are essential skills for satisfying communication. We'll discuss both in more detail in chapter 4.

Inattentive Listening

To listen, you just need to be quiet when someone talks, right? Not necessarily. You might think you're listening when actually some or all of your attention is elsewhere. The other person can probably tell, too. Whether you realize it or not, you're likely giving an array of nonverbal signals that tell them, "I'm only partially here with you." Sensing your lack of attention, your conversation partner might well feel dissatisfied.

Inattentive listening can occur for a variety of reasons. You could be thinking about what you're going to say next and looking for an opportunity to talk. You could be distracted by something going on around you. You might be tired, worried, or excited by something happening in your life beyond the conversation. Or you might just feel bored. While you can't prevent some distractions, there are two common ones you can often avoid.

"I've Heard It Before" Syndrome

Sometimes you think you already know what the other person is going to say—especially if you know them well. If you have a history together, it's easy to assume you already know what they're talking about. Then you might be tempted to tune out, or you might respond too soon, perhaps before they even finish talking. In both cases, your response might not be helpful or appropriate.

Instead of jumping ahead, take time to make sure you accurately understand what you're hearing. Listen with an open mind to what the other person is saying. They might just surprise you with new information or a new point of view they haven't shared before.

Inadvertent Entanglements

When someone shares a problem they're having, you might automatically make it your own. We call this impulse an *inadvertent entanglement*. When you're inadvertently entangled, you might feel an urgent need to fix or solve the other person's problem. Your mind may swing into action, getting caught up in suggestions or advice you could offer. You might also feel a strong emotional reaction.

Wanting to help is admirable and potentially useful, but automatically thinking you *must* solve or fix someone's problem—and ruminating about how—can lessen your ability to listen carefully and think clearly. It also can be stressful. Getting inadvertently entangled can become a habit; in other words, you begin taking on other people's problems again and again without even thinking about it. With skillful communication, you can help others with their problems without becoming entangled.

Entanglements most often occur when someone is sharing a problem, but they can also come up in conversations involving blame, disagreements, decisions, strong opinions, and judgments. Taking issue with what the other person is saying, you immediately start thinking of a response and stop fully listening.

In chapters 4 and 5, we'll give you skills that can help you avoid "I've heard it before" syndrome, inadvertent entanglements, and the potential fallout from both. While fully engaged listening isn't required for many everyday conversations, it's crucial for consequential ones. Plus, in an age of endless distractions, giving someone your full attention is often a welcome gift. The skills in both chapters will improve your ability to listen attentively.

Lack of Clarity (and Not Knowing How to Find It)

Sometimes it's hard to put your thoughts and feelings into words. Helping someone else do so can be equally challenging. If clarity remains elusive, both you and the other person can begin to feel impatient and frustrated. At the same time, the odds of misunderstanding usually increase.

You also might not have a clear purpose in mind when you initiate a conversation. Or you might start with one purpose only to discover that what you're looking for is, in fact, something else. For example, when you're upset, you might call your sister for help. But when she starts offering suggestions, you start feeling more upset, not less. Afterward, you realize what you really wanted was for her to just listen and sympathize with you.

The good news is, the very act of communicating can be a means of clarifying your thoughts, feelings, and what you're looking for from the conversation. Intention and meaning can emerge and sharpen during the natural back-and-forth flow of a conversation. Chapter 2 explains more about this topic, and chapters 4 and 5 will give you skills for fostering clarity, understanding, and connection. Later in part II, we show you how to craft messages that others are more likely to understand and accept with less pushback. These skills are especially helpful for important conversations, but as you practice them, you'll see how they can improve your everyday interactions too.

Personal Characterizations

Characterizations are overgeneralized statements (positive or negative) about someone. Hardly anyone reacts well to being blamed or insulted or having their behavior characterized in an unflattering way. Labeling, name-calling, stereotyping, categorizing someone negatively—all of these typically damage the goodwill that fosters amicable communication.

Most of us have the urge to defend ourselves against personal characterizations we perceive as negative: maybe we shut down, argue that the other person is wrong, or lob insults at them in return. When goodwill gives way to defensiveness, communication usually breaks down. While the negative impact of personal characterizations may seem obvious, it's very easy to lapse into characterizing others in the heat of the moment.

Sometimes even characterizations meant to be positive aren't taken that way. You might, for instance, characterize someone's idea as "simple" and mean it as a compliment. Yet to the other person, *simple* implies their idea is stupid. Tone, context, personal interpretation, and power dynamics between people play important roles in how demeaning a characterization is regarded.

Underlying most characterizations are beliefs, assumptions, and values, many of which you might not even know you have. In chapters 6 through 8, we'll explore these hidden influences on your conversations. We'll give you skills to help you communicate clearly, without slipping into characterizations.

Red-Flag Language

Language that implies blame, an accusation, an insult, or a characterization is what we call *red-flag language*. It nearly always triggers a defensive response, disrupting the flow of the conversation and sometimes prematurely ending it.

The words *always* and *never* are hallmarks of red-flag language: "You *never* listen." "You're *always* criticizing me."

Sometimes the *always* and *never* are implied—as in, "*Every time* I want to discuss this topic, you shut me down" or "You *just can't* take a joke, can you?"

Other examples of red-flag language are statements implying that your feelings are the direct result of the other person's words or behavior: "You *made me* angry" or "You *made me* look bad."

Labels that the other person would find insulting or unflattering also qualify as red-flag language. "You're such a snob," "You're so self-centered," "You're way too sensitive," "What a hypocrite you are!" and "You're narcissistic" are just a few examples.

Chapters 6 and 11 will give you skills to help you avoid using red-flag language and find more constructive ways to express yourself.

Premature, Unsolicited, and Clumsy Expressions of Judgment

Not all expressions of judgment are harmful, and sometimes sharing a judgment is appropriate and necessary, particularly if it can be expressed in a constructive way. But not all judgment is necessary, helpful, or welcome, either. Chapters 6, 11, and 12 will discuss ways you can offer judgment helpfully and constructively.

Mistaking Opinions for Facts

Too often people convey their opinions as if those opinions were facts.[1] Sometimes they realize they're doing so, but more often they don't. As two people argue over these disguised opinions, they often become polarized, thinking one of them must be right and the other must be wrong. Then the communication between them is more likely to stall.

The habit of treating opinions as facts has become rampant in our society. Many of us aren't taught how to distinguish the two, nor do we learn the critical thinking skills to identify our errors. Sliding your opinion into a conversation as a fact can give you an air of confidence and authority. However, without bona fide facts, it's hard to make reliable decisions and agreements. You might end up making poor choices or evaluations based on inaccurate information.

One antidote to this disruptor is to label your opinions as such by prefacing them with phrases such as, "I think," "I believe," "I assume," "In my opinion," and "It seems to me." In chapters 6, 8, and 11, we'll provide more ways to avoid misrepresenting opinions as facts and explain how distinguishing the two will improve your conversations with others.

Overlooking Nonverbal Communication

Words are only one part of communication. Your body language, the tone and pitch of your voice, your facial expressions, and your gestures and other movements all speak as loudly as your words. Ignore or miss these nonverbal signals in others, and you're apt to miss or misunderstand what they're saying.

Nonverbal communication is an in-depth topic that we can't address fully in the scope of this book. We'll touch on it briefly in the appendix and give you some excellent resources to consult for further information.

Choosing an Inadequate Communication Medium

Many interpersonal communication mediums are available to us these days—texting and instant messaging, video chat or videoconference, email, phone, and face-to-face interaction. Using the medium best suited to your message increases your odds of having a satisfying conversation. Chapter 19 discusses how to assess which communication modes are best suited for particular communication goals.

Poor Damage Control

Conversations sometimes end up in the ditch even if you and the other person have a good relationship and positive intentions. That's bad enough, but if you don't know how to tow them back onto the road, a communication mishap can escalate into serious problems requiring time and effort to repair. Fortunately, many of the skills we'll share in part II can help you recover a conversation that's broken down, as well as help you avoid problems in the first place.

Once you're aware of these disruptors, you'll probably start noticing them everywhere—in the news media stories, speeches from politicians and businesspeople, social media posts, meetings, and, perhaps most notably, in your own everyday conversations. You may be alarmed by how prevalent they are and how damaging they can be.

But don't be discouraged. Give yourself a pat on the back instead. You've just taken your first step in learning to communicate more skillfully: recognizing the most common communication disruptors and noticing how they affect people's interactions.

The information and practical skills at the heart of this book can help you move away from these disruptive, problematic communication habits. Using even a few of these skills can help keep your conversations from going awry, even when you're discussing difficult topics, navigating conflicts, or facing challenging situations. As your communication becomes more skillful, your interactions with others can become richer, more enjoyable, and less stressful. Under these conditions, your relationships are more likely to grow and thrive.

Chapter 2

How Skillful Communication Can Help You

Our intention is to help you communicate *more skillfully* than you currently do. If you've come to this book thinking, "I want to learn to communicate *well*" or "I want to be a *better* communicator," the idea of communicating "skillfully" might seem unexpected at first. But we think that describing communication in terms of skillfulness is more accurate and useful than thinking in terms of *good* or *bad*.

Skillfulness reflects the fact that our approach is built on specific, practical skills—ones we believe just about anyone can learn. Being able to communicate skillfully means someone knows how and when to call on these skills instead of just defaulting to habitual communication patterns that often disrupt conversations. You don't need to overhaul your entire communication style to communicate with more skill. You just need a wider repertoire of options—a bigger toolkit, if you will—and some idea of what skills are most useful in which circumstances.

Practicality and usefulness are what first attracted us to the communication skills we're sharing in this book. Both of us were fascinated with human behavior. Our education included psychology, anthropology, and organizational theory, as well as Western philosophical and Eastern spiritual traditions. But we wondered, how could we bridge the gap between what we'd learned in our studies and how we interacted with others in our everyday lives? Understanding the factors and forces that shape human behavior was one thing; actually changing our own behavior was quite another. When you're facing an irate partner, having an unexpected disagreement with your friend, navigating workplace politics, or trying to find some way—*any* way—to connect with your fractious kid, an academic understanding of human dynamics isn't as helpful as you might wish.

Interpersonal communication gave us the missing link. When we discovered how principles from social sciences and philosophical traditions could be applied to this specific aspect of human behavior, we knew we were finally putting theory into practice.

Underlying Principles of Skillful Communication

We don't want to overload you with all the theories, research, and concepts that play into our approach to communication. (That would be a book unto itself!) But there are five important principles we'd like you to know about. They're integral to our approach, and you'll see them running like threads through the skills in part II.

The Language Principle

The way you use language both reflects and influences your beliefs, assumptions, perceptions, and experiences. Changing what you say and how you say it can profoundly shift how you see yourself, others, and the world. It's a powerful way to condition your mind and shape new behavior.

Skillful use of language includes using wording that accounts for change and uncertainty. Circumstances naturally change over time. People also change, and they don't behave the same way 100 percent of the time. Although change is inevitable, our language can, at times, fail to sufficiently recognize that fact. *Provisional language* acknowledges the possibility of change and helps you adapt your communication to shifting circumstances. Provisional language also recognizes that the world is complex; there are many, many factors contributing to and influencing people and circumstances at any given time, as described in *the systems principle.*

The Systems Principle

Human beings typically perceive themselves both as individuals and as parts of larger systems, such as their environment, family, and country. For example, Dan is a member of the Clurman family, a Californian, and an American all at the same time. If you want to make sense of your behavior and experience, you need to recognize that there are a wide variety of systems influencing you. No one person or thing causes your experience; instead, many interdependent variables contribute to it. You operate within a larger context, and that context is multifaceted.

When you understand this systems principle, you're less apt to blame one person or one thing for what happens to you. It also becomes clear that you, as an individual, can *influence* other people's thinking and behavior, but you can't *control* them.

This principle is rooted in systems thinking, which runs counter to dualistic, either-or thinking. The latter typically reduces variables and possibilities to just two opposites—*this or that, right or wrong, good or bad, us or them.* Dualistic thinking is often polarizing; systems thinking allows for more nuance and inclusiveness.

The Critical-Thinking Principle

Critical thinking is a means of assessing your communication, judgments, decisions, and evidence. People often use critical thinking when they talk to their partners about important topics, such as whether to get married, have kids, change jobs, or buy a house. Distinguishing between facts and opinions and between thoughts and feelings are important critical-thinking tools in skillful communication. So too is the ability to scrutinize assumptions and recognize the influence of beliefs.

The Beliefs Principle

Beliefs shape your communication, perception, and experience of reality. They also shape how you treat other people, including what you say to them. Suppose you believe that telling little lies is harmless and justifiable at times. This belief can affect the accuracy of what you say to another person, which in turn may influence their actions and the relationship between you.

Most of your current communication habits are related to your beliefs, some of which you might not even be aware of. Observing your communication habits can bring those background beliefs to light. The reverse is also true: making small, judicious adjustments to your beliefs can have a profound effect on your interpersonal communication.

The Loop-Communication Principle

People are interdependent and mutually affect each other when they communicate. When you have a conversation with someone, the two of you create a shared understanding. The ongoing, back-and-forth loop you form influences the quality and direction of your conversation. When you understand that communication develops *between* people, your thinking will often naturally shift from "I'm talking *to* them" to "I am talking *with* them."

A couple of these principles will be clearly visible in specific skills. The principle of loop communication, for example, will be applied to the skills of talking and listening in chapter 4. Chapter 6 will directly address the implications of the beliefs principle and show you how to put provisional language to use. The other principles might seem less obvious, but now that you're aware of them, you'll probably be able to detect their influence, even if they aren't specifically called out in the skills chapters.

In "Recommended Resources" you'll find sources that provide more in-depth information on these principles, including which branches of the social sciences or schools of thought they come from.

Why Bother with Skillful Communication?

When we first started using our newly developed communication skills, it was like we'd discovered a new superpower. In the short term, we saw people respond to us differently. They seemed less reactive and defensive than when we slipped into some of our usual communication habits. And we felt the same way—we didn't feel like we had to tread carefully or stay on guard in our conversations as often. Plus, we were able to stay calmer, more open to what others said, and more in tune with the flow of conversations. As a result, our exchanges were usually less stressful for all involved.

Early on, as we practiced the skills with each other, we were able to verify what it was like to be part of a conversation where the other person was communicating skillfully. We were more likely to think that our thoughts and feelings had value in the conversation, and in response, we usually felt more willing to participate. We also typically felt more receptive to learning something new by considering the other's perspective. Overall, practicing the communication skills was a recipe for connection and trust, and our relationship flourished.

Somewhat to our surprise, we learned that we didn't have to like or agree with someone to communicate with them constructively. And as we grew more comfortable using the skills, we found we could still communicate skillfully even when others didn't.

But the real eye-openers happened over time. Gradually, we realized that more skillful communication changed how we thought, as well as how we acted around others. Specifically:

We focused more on understanding what someone said.
We wanted to grasp what the other person was saying—before disagreeing or expressing judgment about it.

Reciprocity and balance became second nature. Recognizing that a conversation is a give-and-take—ideally a balanced one—we made sure each person had a turn to talk and listen. It also became easier to tell when a conversation was becoming imbalanced and adjust our communication accordingly.

Tolerating different perspectives got easier. We grew more curious about others' beliefs, ideas, and points of view. We were more willing to listen to their perspectives and make room for them in the conversation, even when those perspectives differed from ours.

We assumed positive intentions more often. We began asking ourselves what the person's positive intentions might be instead of automatically assuming they only had negative intentions.

Depersonalizing became the norm. We found it more beneficial to focus on debating or disagreeing with someone's ideas, rather than characterizing or attacking the person themselves.

It became easier to establish, build, and maintain trust with others. As we put our skills to use, we noticed others seemed to share more with us. We found that being more receptive to what others had to say over time allowed us to build rapport and mutual trust with them.

We assessed the usefulness and accuracy of what we wanted to say, particularly in conversations that had consequences.

Practicing restraint became easier. We realized that we didn't have to say everything we thought and felt. Our thoughts and feelings might be important or helpful to us, but saying them didn't necessarily serve a conversation. At times, saying nothing at all could be valuable.

We recognized that our communication might have consequences beyond the immediate conversation. And those consequences could affect our relationships or community, for better or for worse. So we aimed to keep potential consequences in mind when speaking with others.

By reshaping how we interacted with others, our communication skills changed our relationships, our lives, and ourselves. Like many who have learned these skills, we found it easier to get along with others. Arguments and discord came up less often. Challenging conversations seldom escalated into damaging verbal wars. And when conflicts did come up, they were a lot less scary and emotionally fraught when we addressed them with a larger toolkit. We spent less time cleaning up misunderstandings and hurt feelings. We were able to articulate our goals and values more clearly and easily in conversations, and we could help others do the same. Even the way we handled personal setbacks and challenges, like health issues, changed. Many problems became more manageable as the way we thought and talked about them shifted. Some of the changes were changes we'd hoped for; others were wonderful surprises. Virtually all were positive.

What Skillful Communication Is Not

Skillful communication doesn't mean using "good manners." It doesn't mean just being nice, polite, or agreeable. It doesn't mean being "politically correct." It doesn't mean staying calm, quiet, and measured at all times. And it doesn't mean being disingenuous or saying only things you think another person wants to hear.

Skillful communication also isn't just about saying the right thing at the right time. It doesn't focus on speaking "correctly" or using what some people consider "good" or "correct" grammar. It isn't about being "articulate," either.

Skillful communication simply means applying practical skills to your conversations. And those skills, as we teach them, are designed to foster clarity, mutual understanding, and satisfying interactions between people.

The Limitations of Skillful Communication

Clearly, we're strong advocates of skillful communication. Our own experiences and those of our students and clients have repeatedly shown us how helpful it can be. But we recognize there are some circumstances when skillful communication isn't easy or even possible.

First, it's often challenging to communicate skillfully when you're upset. The good news is, the more you practice the skills, the easier it will be to use them even when you're facing strong emotions—your own or those of others. (In chapters 4 and 5, we'll give you specific guidance for communicating skillfully when emotions run high.)

Sometimes people find it difficult to maintain skillful communication when the other person isn't communicating skillfully. Exchanges can still be constructive when one person is communicating more skillfully than the other. And skillful communication by one person often inspires the other to communicate more skillfully too. But if skillful communication remains one sided for a long period of time, the imbalance can become frustrating. It's equally frustrating when one person expects or demands skillful communication from the other but doesn't at least try to practice it themselves. It's pretty easy (and fairly common) for people to accuse others of not listening or to get upset when someone dismisses their point of view out of hand. Sometimes those same people ignore others' perspectives and make little effort to understand them.

Skillful communication is not a panacea. It can bridge many divides and help solve many problems, but not all of them. At times another person's views run counter to your personal values or to beliefs you've deemed immutable. In those cases, you might decide it's not worth trying to have a conversation with them. Or perhaps trying to communicate with someone—skillfully or otherwise—would mean compromising your physical, emotional, or mental health or safety. A person identifying as gay, for instance, may decide it's unsafe to even attempt a conversation with cousins who loudly and frequently proclaim homosexuality to be "amoral" and "an abomination." Just because you're able to communicate skillfully doesn't mean you're obligated to have a conversation.

Finally, all the skills we teach naturally orient you toward harmony with others. We think it would be tough to use the skills to manipulate others or gain an advantage at their expense. As you continue reading, we encourage you to think about your reasons for wanting to change how you communicate. Skillful communication can enhance your ability to interact with and influence others, but it's up to you to determine whether you're using your newfound superpower responsibly.

The Most Valuable Assessment Is Your Own

The more we work with individuals, couples, and small groups, in both personal and professional settings, the more we see how the dynamics between people can improve based on how they communicate. Over the years, our clients and students have told us that they experience the same helpful, positive shifts we did as they communicated with more skill. So while you might think focusing just on communication isn't that big a deal, be prepared for the effects to quickly ripple out into various areas of your life.

As you begin using the skills in part II, keep an eye on those ripples. They're a good way to gauge how skillful communication is working for you. When you use a skill, how do others respond? How does it affect your conversations? What changes do you notice—in yourself, in others, in the dynamics between you and others? How helpful are these changes? Ultimately, *you are the best person to determine how beneficial these skills are for you.*

Chapter 3

Set Yourself Up
for Learning

The idea of changing how you communicate may seem daunting at first. After all, you're scrutinizing something you've done habitually, without much thought, for a long time. But learning new ways of talking, listening, and thinking is much like learning to ride a bike, play a musical instrument, or speak a new language: the more familiar you get with the skills, the more natural they'll become, and the more confident you'll feel using them.

Before you dive into part II, we want to talk a little bit about learning in general, so you know what to expect as you start road-testing the skills. Then we'll introduce you to metacognition, a bonus skill you'll naturally use along the way. Finally, we have some tips and reminders that our students and clients have found handy and we think you'll find helpful too.

The Four Stages of Learning
Skillful Communication

Most professionals in psychology, organizational training, and education recognize that learning occurs in four stages. Understanding these stages can help you track your progress and feel a sense of accomplishment as you practice your new communication skills. Plus, if you know up front what challenges people typically face as they learn, the learning process might feel less awkward.

Stage 1: Unconscious Incompetence. In this stage, you don't know that you don't know. If you think the ways you're communicating now are working for you and others, you probably won't feel motivated to make any changes. But many people confuse knowing *about* communication with knowing *how* to actually communicate skillfully. This confusion often leads people to get stuck in the first stage of learning. They can overestimate how competent they actually are.[1]

Stage 2: Conscious Incompetence. If you've picked up this book, you're likely in stage 2: you know that you don't know something about communication. In this stage, you're also trying out new behaviors, and you're not used to them yet. With our communication skills, you might be using words and phrases you don't typically use and thinking in ways you're not accustomed to yet. You might feel awkward at first. It's helpful to remember that your usual communication patterns seem natural or spontaneous because you've been using them for so long. If you want to expand your communication toolkit, you need to temporarily forgo some comfortable but unhelpful habits in favor of cultivating new, more intentional ones. Don't worry—the new patterns soon begin to feel more familiar.

Also at this stage, you might feel self-critical, thinking that you're not picking up a new skill fast enough. If you do, take heart—many people feel the same at this stage. As you continue practicing your new skills, you'll grow more comfortable and confident with them. And you'll gradually transition into the next stage.

Stage 3: Conscious Competence. In this stage, you're practicing what you know. You're increasingly aware of what you're doing while you're doing it. During conversations with others, you're more apt to notice how you're communicating and, when needed, shift what you're doing to better suit the circumstances. You're increasingly comfortable with the new ways of expressing yourself and responding to others. In preparing for important, consequential conversations, you can quickly identify which skills might come in handy.

Stage 4: Unconscious Competence. Now you can automatically use what you know. Expressing yourself with certain words and phrases no longer feels awkward. Instead, these words flow into your conversations easily and spontaneously. They're now comfortable and familiar. They just sound and feel "right." Listening, focusing your attention on what the other person is saying, and sensing when to talk now come naturally.

The keys to reaching stage 4 are time and practice. It's not unusual for our students to spend quite a bit of time in stages 2 and 3 as they're practicing some skills. If you do, that's okay! Just keep at it. Be patient with yourself as you're learning and experimenting with the skills. You may not become fluent in a skill overnight, but your progress won't stop unless you do.

Metacognition: Thinking About Your Thinking

Your ability to learn new communication skills relies on metacognition, the ability to be aware of or analyze your learning or thinking processes.[2] Put more simply, metacognition is thinking about your thinking.[3] It includes two key components:

- Noticing and tracking your thoughts; observing the content of your thoughts in a relatively neutral way.

- Actively thinking about your thoughts; assessing the validity and usefulness of your thoughts using critical thinking.

Observing your thoughts requires some detachment, as if you were stepping out of your thoughts and simply watching them. You still have those thoughts, but you're not completely swept up in them. If you feel a response—pleasant or unpleasant, welcome or unwelcome—to your thoughts, you notice those responses too. And if you find yourself judging your thoughts, you simply note those reactions as well. Witnessing your thoughts from a neutral, almost third-party perspective reduces the odds of becoming entangled in them. It doesn't eliminate distressing thoughts, but it can help you avoid impulsively acting on them.

This first aspect of metacognition is akin to the Buddhist concept of mindfulness. But metacognition goes one step further: it asks you to engage with the content of your thoughts. Using critical thinking, you can assess how accurate and useful your thoughts are, if shifting them would be helpful, and what the optimal shifts in thinking might be.

Metacognition is crucial to skillful communication. It enables you to spot unhelpful communication habits. It's your means of recognizing previously unseen factors that may be influencing your communication. From there, you can apply the critical-thinking principle: you can assess which communication habits serve you and your relationships, and you can decide how to change those that don't.

Metacognition is a skill you're already using every day, such as when you're making decisions or solving problems. In addition, as you learn to communicate more skillfully, you naturally build your metacognition muscles at the same time—which in turn further enhances your ability to communicate skillfully.[4]

A Few Last Tips

As you begin learning, here are some last helpful things to keep in mind:

- You don't need to master a communication skill or use it "perfectly" every time to reap its benefits.

- You don't need to absorb and apply all the skills all at once. When in doubt, choose one and practice it until you feel comfortable and competent with it, then try another.

- As you use a skill (or elements of it) more frequently, it will likely feel a little easier and more natural. Practicing the skills bit by bit will help you build competence gradually and steadily.

- Not all conversations require careful, skillful communication. It's most useful for conversations that are challenging or important or where clarity and mutual understanding are crucial.

- An experimental mindset can be helpful: "Let's see what happens if I try this skill."

- Keeping a growth mindset—a belief that there's almost always something new to learn—can also be helpful.[5]

- Again, if something you're doing in conversations already works well, stick with it. But when you get stuck or have problems, you'll probably want to shift to more skillful communication.

Most likely, you won't need to seek out opportunities to practice your new communication skills. They'll come up naturally as you interact with your friends, coworkers, and loved ones. Just be ready to reach into your new, expanded communication toolkit and try a skill when it feels appropriate.

Part II
Skills

Chapter 4

Talking and Listening

Two Sides of a Conversation

Thanks to today's technology, conversations occur across a variety of channels. Real-time conversations can happen in person, over the phone, or via videoconference. Text messages, social media, and email allow you to have short or extended exchanges over time. But no matter what medium you're using, all exchanges have two sides: talking and listening. And skillful communication requires fluency in both.

Talking and Listening Are Equally Important

Talking and listening serve different purposes: talking is a means of giving information, while listening is a means of receiving information.

If neither party in a conversation can listen, not much of an exchange can happen. You won't have a conversation—just parallel monologues. Just talking, no matter how sincere and empathic you are, is not enough when mutual understanding is important. If you talk without listening, you won't know how the other person is reacting to your message. Say you give someone precise directions for doing a task. Without listening to their response, you won't know whether or not they have any objections or questions.

On the other hand, if you mostly listen in conversations, others won't know what you think, feel, and want. This is especially true when you have a problem. If you don't tell the other person enough about it, they're less likely to respond in a way you find appropriate and supportive. Even sharing just the basics of your problem can alert them to details of your predicament and what might be helpful for you.

Knowing when to talk and when to listen can often make the difference between a constructive discussion and a troubled one. So discerning which is suitable for a given situation is an essential communication skill.

Discerning Whether to Talk or Listen

Recognizing what you want to achieve in a conversation is key to deciding how much you should talk or listen. You won't habitually default to talking or listening when you consider what you're trying to do. At any point, instead of automatically talking or listening, you can ask yourself, "What am I trying to accomplish right now?"

Talking is appropriate when you want to:

Give information. "The next group practice will be at Karol's house this Tuesday at 4 p.m."

Influence someone. "I think unless Jasmine is nominated for the school board, parents won't have a strong advocate."

Clarify. "I didn't mean that Jasmine is the *only* candidate who can advocate for us—just that she's the strongest."

Solve a problem. "Just press the red button at the bottom of the unit, and it will start working again."

Listening is appropriate when you want to:

Take in information. The other person has information you're seeking, and you want to receive it.

Understand someone. In addition to taking in their basic information, you can learn what someone feels, how they think, what their point of view is, and what's important to them, among other things.

Build rapport. You can demonstrate interest in the other person and a willingness to consider what they're saying, both of which help build rapport. And if you don't listen to them, what are the chances they'll listen to you?

Help someone calm down. When someone is upset, it's often best to postpone lectures, advice, reassurance, and even encouragement. First just listen as they express how they think and feel. Being heard and understood frequently helps people feel calmer. (You can then offer ideas, suggestions, and supportive words afterward, if appropriate.)

When you consider whether to talk or to listen in a given moment, you can profoundly affect the outcome of your conversation.

Listening in Specific Circumstances

There are three common situations when people often have a hard time listening: when they're feeling a strong emotional reaction, when they're eager to give the other person advice or information, and when they've asked a question but the other person doesn't respond as quickly as expected. These aren't the only times people have difficulty listening, but they are ones our students and clients most frequently ask about.

Listening When You're Feeling a Strong Emotional Reaction

Unsettling emotions such as embarrassment, disgust, frustration, fear, anger, sadness, and defensiveness are among the numerous reactions that can interfere with your listening ability.

Emotional reactivity is especially common when the other person is talking about you, such as when you think they're criticizing you. It's natural to want to immediately defend yourself but doing so isn't necessarily the most skillful way to respond. Skillful listening includes noticing when emotions are coloring your perceptions. It also includes assessing how well you can listen when you're feeling emotionally reactive.

If strong emotions are inhibiting your ability to listen for whatever reason, consider taking a break from the conversation before you say something you might regret later. You can gently interrupt the other person and ask to pause. You can say something like:

- "I'm feeling very irritated right now, and I can't really focus on what you're saying."
- "I'd like to continue listening to you, but I'm not feeling calm enough right now. Can we take a break?"
- "Could you please pause a moment? My head is spinning. I need to calm down a little bit so I can continue listening to you."

Many people will wait for you to collect yourself if it means you'll be more able to hear them out.

Next, you can step away from the other person and calm yourself. Here are some tips for calming down and regaining your equanimity.

Connect with your breath, particularly the exhalation. Release and relax with your exhalation. As you breathe, you can also bring your attention to your feet in contact with the floor or your pelvis in contact with the chair.

Identify what you're thinking and feeling. Notice, with as little judgment as possible, the parade of thoughts and feelings you're experiencing: "I think she's wrong." "I think I'm accommodating too much," "I feel frustrated." "I feel resentful," "I feel doubtful," "I feel my stomach tightening."

If identifying your thoughts and feelings proves challenging, try shifting to a third-person perspective to describe what you're experiencing: "He's getting anxious now," "She's sticking up for herself," "They're feeling defensive." Taking this perspective, as if you were a sports commentator giving a play-by-play, can provide some distance for observing yourself.

Notice how your thinking may be affecting your emotions. Your thoughts are just thoughts—not necessarily an accurate representation of how things are, especially when you're upset. Recognizing this can give you the opportunity to shift your thinking.

Shift the language of your thoughts to shift your feelings. If you notice an especially sharp emotion in response to a particular thought, see if you can change the language of your thought to something that evokes a less strong emotion.

Take these thoughts, for example: "I can't believe she just said _____! She still doesn't see the big picture." How does the emotion change if the language were changed to, "She said _____. I just don't share her point of view. I wish I could get her to see the big picture the way I see it"? (For more on shifting your thoughts with language, check out chapter 6.)

Notice if you're characterizing the other person. When you're upset, it's easy to focus on how bad you think the other person is acting. But doing that usually intensifies your emotional state. Instead of labeling them or their behavior, focus on what's going on with you.

Notice whether you're attributing negative motives to the other person or yourself. Thinking the other person is intentionally aiming to hurt you won't help you feel calm (and it might not be true). Neither will berating yourself for what you're thinking or feeling.

Recognize that there's no single cause to explain human behavior. Remember the systems principle: every person is operating in a multifaceted context. That means there could be many reasons the person is saying what they're saying. It also means your reaction is likely fueled by not one but many different factors. Are there explanations for your own behavior or the other person's that can help you feel less upset and more calm? (We'll talk more about this idea in chapter 8.)

Notice whether you're taking the other person's words or behavior personally. Taking it personally means you believe it's only about you. That thought probably won't help you calm down. To shift to a less personalized point of view, consider that what they're saying is filtered through their own perspective, beliefs, attitudes, and feelings.

Remind yourself that emotions aren't permanent. Even though you're upset now, remember that you have felt calm in the past and will feel calm again.

Remember that you are part of our common humanity. We all suffer at times. Put your hand on your heart and feel compassion for yourself—and the other person, if you wish.[1]

After taking a few minutes to use some or all of the above techniques, you might feel calm enough to resume the conversation. Or you might not—and that's okay. Sometimes discontinuing a conversation is preferable to continuing it and risking saying something divisive or that you'll regret later. If it seems appropriate, you can offer to reschedule the conversation for another time.

One thing that can help you maintain equanimity in a challenging conversation is remembering what listening can do for you. Setting your intention to understand the other person, or simply to take in what they're saying, can relieve the pressure of having to come up with an immediate response. Listening to understand is the basis for *reflective listening,* a handy and important skill to have in your communication toolbox. Chapter 5 will introduce you to reflective listening and explain how it can be useful in challenging exchanges.

Chapter 8 will give you more guidance for responding skillfully when someone says they're unhappy with something you did or said, a common situation that often triggers defensiveness.

Calming yourself and maintaining your emotional equanimity can be challenging but doing so usually becomes easier with practice.

Listening Before Giving Advice or Information

When someone has a problem, you might be tempted to share ideas or suggestions. It's often hard to keep from jumping in before the other person has stopped talking, even if they haven't asked for help. Offering advice or information might work in some cases, but not in others.

Let's say your friend can't find her keys. If you know for sure where they are, you can say, "I see them on the kitchen counter." In this case, you're simply sharing information you know to be accurate. Things get dicey when you don't know where the keys are, but still wanting to be helpful, you offer unsolicited advice: "You should put your keys in the same place every time you come home. That's what I do, and I hardly ever lose my keys." While you might think this suggestion is helpful, your friend might not.

Other times, you might think you're simply sharing information, but the other person perceives it as unwanted advice. Imagine that your friend's husband is undergoing treatment for cancer. Your friend is wondering whether diet changes or supplements could help him. You immediately share the name of a naturopath who specializes in working with cancer patients. In your mind, you're just giving your friend a piece of information; you assume he and his husband will contact the naturopath only if they want to. But your friend thinks you're telling him to call. Already feeling overwhelmed, he doesn't appreciate one more person telling him what they think he should do.

The pitfalls of sharing information or giving advice grow even more pronounced if the other person's problem is a complicated one—especially an emotionally complex one. Imagine a close friend says she's wondering whether or not to have a child at this point in her life. Or your brother says he and his wife are trying to decide whether to continue caring for their developmentally disabled teenage son at home or find a professional care facility for him. It's often unrealistic to think that you can solve a complex problem, or help others solve it, just by giving them a piece of information or some well-meaning advice. So what can you do instead?

First, you can allow the other person to fully describe the problem. Listening lets you more completely understand its complexity, as well as how the other person thinks and feels about it. Then any advice or information you share will likely be more on target. Second, you can ask the other person if they want your advice or information. Then, depending on their answer, you can give it or not.

The same approach applies when talking with a child. Many parents make suggestions without first listening to their child's perspective. One signal that you've shared your advice too soon is your child rolling their eyes in exasperation. Like your friends, your child is more likely to be open to your suggestions if you've first listened in order to understand their problem. And your ideas will more likely be relevant to them.

This approach can also be useful in business settings. Let's say a software engineer encounters a problem in the program he's coding. When he talks to his manager, she begins making suggestions before he's even done talking. But she hasn't sufficiently understood the problem he's wrestling with, and her advice isn't useful. He leaves the conversation without a solution. On the other hand, perhaps she holds off giving advice and instead listens closely. As the engineer describes the problem, she learns that he hasn't yet understood a basic procedure the team uses. She realizes she needs to run through the details of the procedure. Now the engineer leaves the conversation with information that's truly helpful.

Listening After Asking a Question

Asking a question implies that you're ready to receive an answer—to take in information. However, after asking it, you might forget to actually listen and instead just keep talking.

Suppose you ask your friend where she'd like to eat dinner. Before she can answer, you describe your favorite place in detail. As you're talking, your friend silently assumes that you're not really interested in hearing her preferences. If you'd initially paused to listen to her answer, she'd have known you are, in fact, interested in what she wants.

The same applies when you have a problem and have asked a friend for advice, or when you've asked what she thinks about something you've said. As she begins talking, you may have the urge to immediately respond to what she's saying. But remember, you can't fully receive and give information at the same time. If you've asked a question, listening to her answer before responding will help keep the conversation and rapport flowing between you.

Loop Communication: Balancing Talking and Listening for Mutually Satisfying Conversations

In an exciting tennis volley, players take turns hitting the ball back and forth. In the same way, in a satisfying conversation, the participants take turns talking and listening. When they do so in a balanced way, their conversation can develop the same dynamic, back-and-forth rhythm that a good tennis volley has. We call this balanced, back-and-forth exchange *loop communication.*

As you probably recall from chapter 2, the loop-communication principle says:

- People are interdependent and mutually affect each other when they communicate.

- When you have a conversation with someone, the two of you create a shared understanding.

- The ongoing loop between the two of you influences the quality and path of your conversation.

When you practice the skill of loop communication, you notice how the other person takes in what you're saying. You adjust what you say according to how they understand and respond to your message, both verbally and nonverbally.

Suppose you're discussing your work with a friend, and you notice that he yawns and breaks eye contact. To bring him more into the loop, you might pause to let him speak. He'll probably find the conversation more interesting when he can participate in it. Conversely, if the loop communication breaks down and he becomes less involved, he may not want to continue listening.

Paying attention to how you continually affect each other—staying in the loop—keeps both of you actively engaged in a two-way conversation and builds mutual understanding.

Disrupting the Loop: How Flooding
Inhibits Conversations

One-way communication is when you speak without noticing how your listener is responding or whether they want to respond. It's the opposite of loop communication, which is by nature a two-way exchange. A common type of one-way communication is flooding—talking in pages rather than in paragraphs. When flooding, you talk at length without any breaks.[2]

Several things can happen when you flood: Your listener will probably feel impatient and may drift off as you're talking, perhaps even dropping out of the conversation entirely. They also may miss crucial parts of your message as you give them more information than they can take in at once. They don't get the opportunity to confirm what they understand, or to tell you what they don't understand or what they disagree with. Paradoxically, the more you flood, the less likely you are to be understood.

Chunking: Keeping Your Listener in the Loop

A better alternative to flooding is chunking your message. Chunking is speaking in short paragraphs instead of pages. You limit the amount you say at one time and pause often so your listener can reply. Chunking what you say promotes a back-and-forth dialogue and supports loop communication. Most listeners are more attentive to speakers who chunk their messages.

Suppose you ask a friend, "What's new in your life?" He launches into a long account of going on a date. He provides many, many details about where they ate, what they ate, whom they bumped into at the restaurant, and what they talked about. At first you try to find an opening in his monologue so you can respond to what he's said. But eventually you just space out.

On the other hand, suppose your friend chunks his reply. He answers your question by saying that he was excited to go out on a date recently. Then he pauses. Feeling curious, you say something in response: Maybe you express interest. Maybe you say you're happy for him. Maybe you ask a question. Maybe you simply encourage him to tell you more. He gives you a little more detail, which keeps you interested and prompts you to continue to respond. With this loop communication, not only are you able to stay engaged with what he's saying, but you're also more likely to enjoy hearing about his date.

In one-to-one conversations, you can stop another person's flood of information and prompt them to chunk their message by tactfully interrupting them, saying something such as:

- "I'd like to say something about what you've said so far."

- "I want to make sure I understand you. Did you mean . . . ?" (Then summarize what you've heard.)

- "Before you go on, I have something to say."

- "Excuse me for interrupting . . ."

Flooding in Group Conversations

Flooding can be a liability not only in one-on-one conversations, but also in group settings. It doesn't matter whether the setting is formal, like a business meeting, or informal, like a dinner party with friends. People are more likely to lose interest and stop participating in the group conversation when one person talks nonstop. And as people participate less, loop communication within the group breaks down.

Tactfully interrupting someone's flooding will let others in the group resume contributing and loop communication to redevelop. If you're leading or helping facilitate a group discussion in a formal setting, you might gently interrupt a speaker's monologue by saying something like:

- "If I could interrupt you for a moment, let's hear from Chelsea."

- "Excuse me for interrupting. Miguel hasn't had a chance to speak yet."

- "That's a good point. I hope we can get back to that. Right now, I'd like to hear from Amina."

- "I think your point makes sense. Let's see what others want to say."

If the setting is more casual or social, anyone in the group could jump in to tactfully stop the flooding. You might say something like:

- "Wow, that's a lot to consider! I'd like to hear what others think about it."

- "I didn't realize you have strong feelings about _____. I'm curious to hear if other people also have strong feelings about it."

- "I have some thoughts based on what you've said so far. Mind if I jump in?"

After you interrupt the speaker, it's important to quickly shift your attention to other people in the group. If you continue to make eye contact with the speaker, you might inadvertently encourage them to keep speaking.

It might seem rude to interrupt someone who's flooding, but you're actually doing them a favor. People tend to get annoyed and turned off when one person monopolizes the group conversation. When you can head off flooding and instead encourage people in your group to chunk their messages, others in the group will feel more interested, more receptive, and less annoyed with people who are dominating the conversation.

Summary: Loop Communication

The next time you're having an important conversation:

- Chunk what you say.

- Periodically pause and notice the other person's verbal and nonverbal reactions to what you're saying.

- If it looks like they want to talk, temporarily stop talking and switch to listening.

- When you think they're finished speaking, resume talking. Adjust what you say to take their responses into account.>

"You Just Don't Get It!": When Mutual Understanding Breaks Down

Every so often a client or student asks us, "Whose fault is it when one person doesn't understand what the other says? Is the speaker failing to get their message across? Or is the listener the problem?" Mudita has often encountered a similar question when counseling couples. One partner typically says to the other, "You just don't understand!" And the other partner responds, "Well, that's not my fault. You're not being clear!" Then they look at Mudita, expecting her to tell them which one is right.

From our perspective, neither the speaker nor the listener is solely "at fault" in such situations. It's usually up to the speaker to present their message in a way the listener can take in. And the listener has several options for clarifying the speaker's message. But it's rarely useful to point fingers or label one person or the other as the problem.

Instead, we see it this way: when one person doesn't understand another, something is interfering with the development of mutual understanding. That "something" is often one of the common communication disruptors discussed in chapter 1. It could be a breakdown in loop communication. It also could be any number of outside factors that are part of the greater context, such as cultural and social influences or power dynamics (see chapter 18). Very often, more than one thing is involved.

Whatever the case, the impasse is a signal for the speaker, the listener, or both to ask themselves, "Is what I'm doing in this conversation right now working for me and, hopefully, the other person?"

Also look at how you're regarding the impasse and consider how useful your stance is. Suppose you're the speaker, and you think the other person doesn't understand you in the way you want to be understood. Does it help you to think, "They just don't get it" or to say, "I shouldn't have to explain myself"? Or do you think the other person might receive your message more easily if you said something like, "I don't think I've gotten my point across yet" and then restated your message in a different way?

Clarifying Your Message

As mentioned above, we believe that mutual understanding largely relies on speakers expressing themselves in a way their listeners are likely to understand. What can you do when you know your listener doesn't understand your message the way you intend?

Rather than getting annoyed and blaming them, try to figure out what's limiting their ability to understand you. Then find another way to say what you want, so they can take it in more easily.

One problem might be in your delivery. You might be sharing too much information at once or not pausing often enough to give her a chance to respond. Remember, more is less; you don't have to say everything at one time. Giving your listener opportunities to respond allows them to ask questions or confirm their understanding of what you've said. It also gives you the chance to see where their understanding might not match what you're saying. You can then clarify your meaning as needed.

Perhaps you're already chunking your information and the two of you are actively engaged in loop communication, but your listener still doesn't understand you. Then the inhibiting factor might well be your content—*what* you're saying. Chapter 6, "Absolute and Relative Beliefs"; chapter 11, "I-Language"; chapter 12, "The Complete Message," and chapter 18, "Diversity and Social Context," will give you guidance for improving your content.

If you've made every effort to clarify your message, but they still don't understand you, don't assume their lack of understanding stems from a lack of love, interest, motivation, or something else. The systems principle is still at play; there could be many other factors affecting their ability to understand you. Maybe they're tired. Maybe they have a lot on their mind. Maybe something in the setting is distracting them. Maybe they simply have a different view. There is only so much influence you can have. Nevertheless, you're still responsible for expressing yourself in a way that your listener is more likely to take in.

As part II continues, we'll share more skills to help you convey your messages clearly. We'll also show you how to up the odds of understanding someone when you're in the listener's seat. And we'll explain how to discern when hidden factors, such as beliefs and assumptions, might be coloring your expectations in a conversation.

Practice
Balancing Talking and Listening

In this two-week exercise, you'll take stock of how much talking and listening you do in conversations with others. Then you can play with bringing a balance of both to your exchanges.

1. For one week, as you have conversations with others, notice whether you sometimes (or habitually) overuse talking or listening. At the end of the week, reflect on the following questions:

   * If you noticed an imbalance, was it talking or listening that you're overusing?

   * How did your overuse of talking or listening affect the information exchange between you and the other person?

   For example, if you talked excessively, the other person might not have shared much information. Or if you mainly listened, he might not have gotten enough feedback from you.

- How did the imbalance affect your overall participation in the conversation and your satisfaction afterward? And how do you think the other person's participation and satisfaction were affected?

2. After a week of observation, you can aim to create more balance in your conversations. When you notice that you're talking or listening disproportionately in a conversation, pause, ask yourself what you want to accomplish, and then choose whether more talking or listening would best serve your goal.

3. Afterward, reflect on how your choices affected the quality of your conversation. What shifted in the conversation when you consciously chose to talk instead of listen, or vice versa?

Practice
Evaluating the Effects of Balance and Loop Communication in Your Conversations

This multiphase exercise takes balanced talking and listening one step further by connecting it to loop communication. It's also an opportunity to flex your metacognition muscles. In the first three phases, you'll observe your talking and listening habits and assess how they affect the development of loop communication. Then the last phase invites you to try out the skills you learned in this chapter.

How much time you spend on each phase is up to you. A couple days to one week is optimal for most people. The more conversations you have throughout your average day, the more opportunities you have to observe your talking and listening habits. If it's helpful, use a notebook to record your observations as you go.

Phase 1: Balance Assessment. This phase is the same as the first step in the previous practice exercise. For this first phase, as you have conversations with others, notice whether you sometimes (or habitually) overuse talking or listening. At the end of the time period, reflect on the following questions:

- If you noticed an imbalance, was it talking or listening that you're overusing?

- How did your overuse of talking or listening affect the loop communication between you and the other person?

- For example, if you talked excessively, the other person might not have shared much information. Or if you mainly listened, the other person might not have gotten enough feedback from you.

- How did the imbalance affect your overall participation during the conversation and how satisfied you felt about it afterward? How do you think the other person's participation and satisfaction were affected?

Phase 2: Listening Assessment. Now take some time to focus just on your listening. Notice when you find it difficult to listen to another person. (Don't be too concerned about judgments that arise as you do this practice.) During these conversations or shortly after, ask yourself, what was difficult about listening in this situation? Think about:

- Were you itching to share information or advice?

- Did you ask a question that triggered more thoughts or questions that you just couldn't hold back?

- Were you experiencing a strong emotional reaction?

- Was the other person sharing a lot of information at once, without pausing or giving you (or others) an opportunity to respond?

- Were there any other factors interfering with your ability to listen in that moment?

No need to try to adjust your listening right now; the point is simply to take note of situations where you find listening difficult. What, if anything, do all these situations have in common?

Phase 3: Talking Assessment. For this phase, shift your focus to how you talk. For the next few days, observe your conversations. Note, hopefully with minimal judgment, how often you:

- Pause to allow the other person to respond to what you're saying.

- Notice the other person's nonverbal responses to what you're saying.

- Adjust what you're saying in light of the other person's responses.

- Continue talking without pause.

- Interrupt the other person to share your thoughts, opinions, or information.

- Remain silent even when given an opportunity to talk.

At the end of this time period, ask yourself:

- When was it easy to notice the other person's responses and adjust how you were talking in light of them? When was it difficult?

- Overall, how was the loop communication between you and the other person affected by how you talked and listened?

Phase 4: Balance in Action. Now you can experiment with bringing more balance to your conversations. When you notice that you're talking or listening disproportionately in a conversation, pause and ask yourself what you want to accomplish. Then decide whether more talking or listening would best serve your intensions.

Afterward, reflect on how the changes you made affected the quality of your conversation. Consider:

- What shifted in a conversation when you decided to talk instead of listen, or vice versa?

- How was the loop communication between you and the other person affected when you adjusted your balance of talking and listening?

- How satisfied did you feel after your conversations in this phase compared to the conversations in the previous phases? How satisfied do you think the other people in the conversations felt? If your conversation partners shared any thoughts, feelings, or observations with you, be sure to note them.

Chapter 5

Reflective Listening

The Gift of Understanding

Perhaps the biggest misconception about listening is that it's only a passive activity. Someone talks to you and you do nothing but take in what they say. But different types of conversations actually require different types of listening, some of which are active and participatory.

In this chapter, we'll quickly survey different types of listening and when each might be appropriate. Then we will dive deep into one especially important type, known as *reflective listening,* exploring how it can help you communicate skillfully and connect with others.

Different Forms of Listening

It pays to know what different forms listening can take, so you can see how to use (or how you may already be using) them in different circumstances.

With *passive listening,* you stay silent and just take in what someone says, without making any comments. Sometimes passive listening is exactly what's required for a situation—like when you're listening to a professor give a lecture or to a friend who's excited about something and needs no encouragement to fill in the details.

One step beyond passive listening is *door-opener listening,* where you invite the other person to continue talking by giving them encouraging comments, such as, "I see," "I'd like to hear more," or "Please go on." These door-openers tell the other person that you're interested in what they're saying. For example, when your friend says, "I just got a job offer from a new company," a natural door-opener might be, "That's great!" or "Sounds promising." Door-openers don't probe for details; instead, they allow the other person to decide how much and what to share. Door-opener listening is good for any situation where someone is sharing or reporting on something—such as a friend telling you about a new app, a colleague offering an idea in a meeting, or a fellow parent telling you what happened in a school meeting—and you want them to know they have your interest and attention.

Beyond door-opener listening is *reflective listening,* when you listen to the other person and then reflect to them, in your own words, what you heard. Here, your listening needs to be mindful, active, and fully engaged, so you can demonstrate your understanding and receive their clarifications as needed. Reflective listening usually isn't needed in casual conversations, where having a less-than-precise understanding of what the other person said doesn't matter. But in many situations, it can be invaluable.

Reflective Listening: The Basics

Reflective listening has four basic components:

- You temporarily put aside your own reactions.
- You mindfully focus on what the other person says.
- You listen to understand, rather than to agree, disagree, or otherwise respond.
- You determine whether you've understood them by reflecting back to them the essence of what you've heard, so they can confirm or amend it as needed.

It might sound straightforward, but in practice, reflective listening takes some finesse.

First, putting aside your own reactions, even temporarily, is often a lot easier said than done. Most people get caught up in their reaction to what they're hearing or how they want to respond. So your first challenge is keeping yourself from immediately offering your own ideas, opinions, thoughts, and feelings. It means resisting the urge to defend, analyze, interpret, advise, question, reassure, or make jokes. Temporarily putting your own responses on hold may be challenging but doing so keeps the spotlight on the other person. Then you can more fully hear and comprehend what they want you to understand.

The second component encourages you to stay attentive to what the other person is saying.

The third component emphasizes understanding the other person. Whether you agree or disagree is not your focus while using reflective listening. Many people jump to their response before taking time to sufficiently understand what the other person has said. Reflective listening asks you to understand first and share later. You typically *will* have the opportunity to respond, and at that time, you can express your thoughts and feelings, agreement or disagreement, if you decide it's appropriate. But while you're engaged in reflective listening, your intention is just to understand what the other person says.

How you share your understanding is the fourth component: you *reflect* what you heard the other person say. It's easy to say, "I understand," but unless you actually demonstrate your understanding with reflective listening, neither of you knows whether you really do. Reflecting doesn't mean repeating their words verbatim. Although such parroting can occasionally be helpful (and shows you have a good memory), it might indicate that you've only heard their words—not grasped their meaning. In contrast, reflecting using your own words more clearly shows that you've *understood* what you heard.

Your initial reflection may not be 100 percent accurate. That's not unusual. If it isn't, the other person can, and usually will, correct you. They can also modify, refine, or add to their message. It's important to continue reflecting their ongoing additions and corrections, so they know you're still listening and understanding them. Typically, it will take at least two or more reflections before they think you've sufficiently understood them. Eventually they'll signal that you have.

Here's an example showing the components in action. Taylor and Maggie often ride their bikes together in the morning. On their most recent ride, they discussed how much fun it would be to do an overnight bike trip together. Before they meet again, Maggie hears from a co-worker that Taylor had recently taken an overnight bike trip with a group of friends. Maggie is taken aback and confronts Taylor the next time they get together.

"I was surprised that you took an overnight bike trip without me," she says. "We had talked about doing it together."

"I know. I meant to tell you about that," Taylor replies.

"I'm really upset that I had to hear about your trip from someone else," Maggie continues.

Rather than immediately starting to explain or defend her actions, Taylor puts her feelings aside for the moment. She uses reflective listening to make sure she understands what Maggie is upset about: "It would have been a lot easier for you if you'd heard about the trip from me."

"That's right," Maggie says. "You wouldn't feel okay if I did this to you."

Taylor continues to reflect: "If the tables were turned, you'd have told me before the trip happened."

"That's not what I mean," Maggie says. "I just think friends should be honest and not hide things from each other."

Taylor reflects Maggie's correction: "You don't want me to keep secrets, especially since we're friends."

"Exactly!" Maggie says.

When Maggie pauses, Taylor responds. "I thought about telling you earlier, but was worried how you'd feel. I see now that not telling you sooner was a mistake. I'd like to tell you why I didn't invite you."

"Okay. So what happened?" Maggie asks.

"I was invited by a friend at work to fill in for someone who had dropped out of the trip. They wanted to keep the group small. I didn't think I could invite you to come along," Taylor says.

"I still wish you'd told me, but I get it." Maggie says.

"I wish I had too," Taylor says. "I'd like to find a date to take an overnight bike trip together soon. Are you up for that?"

Tips for Improving Your Reflections

It sometimes takes people a little while to get the hang of reflecting. In addition to paraphrasing instead of parroting, here's how you can keep your reflections constructive.

Don't mix in your own message. Be careful not to include your own response when you're reflecting. Inserting your thoughts, suggestions, or reactions will be confusing. Focus on understanding their message—both the verbal and nonverbal components.

Be patient. People often have to sift through many thoughts before selecting what they say. Most people discover what they want to say as they're saying it.

But don't wait too long to reflect. The other person, in their urgency to communicate, may fail to pause and instead keep talking at length. While you do want to give them time to figure out what they mean to say, letting them go too long may give you more information than you can reflect at once. If they start to say more than you can remember, gently interrupt and reflect what you've understood so far. (For examples on how to interrupt tactfully, see chapter 4.) As they continue to add more information, you should continue to reflect, so they feel understood and you know that your understanding is accurate.

Keep up with what the other person is saying. Each new reflection should include the thoughts and feelings that they've just added. If you repeat details you've previously reflected, you'll lag behind them and inadvertently keep the conversation from moving forward.

Keep your reflections concise. Typically the other person's message includes extraneous information that you don't need to reflect.

If you try to reflect every detail, your reflection might become longer than what they've said. So reflect only the information that seems essential. If your reflection is missing information they think is important, they can add to or repeat it.

Pause after you reflect. Pausing gives the other person the opportunity to make additions and corrections.

Don't argue. When the other person corrects your reflections, it might be tempting to argue or defend your paraphrasing. But don't. Simply change your reflection to incorporate the corrections.

Don't use jargon. Avoid phrases such as, "I hear you saying that . . ." This kind of jargon can sound formulaic and might put off the other person. It also creates an impression that you're doing something artificial rather than thoughtful. If you need an introductory phrase, try something like, "You believe that . . . ," "Perhaps you think that . . . ," "You feel . . . ," or "Maybe you'd like . . ."

Avoid psychoanalyzing. Most people don't appreciate your thoughts on *why* they're saying what they're saying. Suppose your partner tells you they want more support from their friends. Reflecting with, "You want more supportive friends because your mother didn't support you," would be *your* spin, not theirs.

Match the other person's tone of voice. For example, when someone is speaking in a somber voice tone, reflect their words in a somewhat low-key voice tone, rather than a fast, upbeat one. You don't want too much discrepancy between their tone of voice and your own. Even if you're accurately reflecting what they said, the other person may not find your reflection credible or helpful if your tone doesn't sufficiently match theirs.

The Value of Reflective Listening

Reflective listening is ideal for important and consequential conversations, where accurately understanding the other person is essential. It also can be helpful in situations where the other person is upset or is struggling with a problem. And it can help you maintain loop communication in challenging situations, such as when you disagree with the other person, when you feel a strong emotional reaction to what they're saying, or when you want to avoid becoming entangled with their problem.

In many professional or less-personal contexts, there are times when you need to be sure you've accurately understood details the other person has shared, such as when a doctor is telling you how to take a new medication. There are also times when you and the other person both need to confirm that you share the same understanding, such as when you've negotiated an agreement with a business associate or when you and a partner need to resolve a conflict between the two of you.

But reflective listening really shines in more personal contexts, where conversations can be emotionally charged. They might also involve the exchange of sensitive information, have important consequences for both you and the other person, or be vital to your ongoing relationship in some other way. Using reflective listening is a way of supporting someone, as well as cultivating goodwill, respect, and connection between the two of you. How?

It can help both you and the other person clarify their meaning. What someone says and what they mean can be two different things. Reflective listening creates and supports loop communication, the back-and-forth exchange that invites the other person to expand on and clarify what they're saying, which in turn fosters a shared understanding.

It allows you to understand the other person in the way she wants to be understood. Most people want you to understand what's important to them. In many personal conversations, their satisfaction will rely heavily on your ability to not just hear their words, but also understand them in the way *they* want to be understood. In reflective listening, the other person is the ultimate authority on what they're trying to convey, and you demonstrate that you understand in the way that's accurate *for them.*

It invites the other person to express themselves in a way that's satisfying to them. Allowing room for someone to say what's important to them is especially helpful when they're upset and confused. What greater gift can you give someone you care about?

It can help others find solutions to problems. When someone is sharing a problem, reflective listening can give them the opportunity to discover potential solutions for themselves. You often don't even need to offer advice or ideas. Not only can reflective listening help you understand the other person, but it can also help them better understand themselves.

It gives you a way to show empathy. "Empathy and listening go hand in hand," says Brigette Hyacinth, author of *The Future of Leadership*. "You can't show empathy if you do not listen."[1] Understanding the other person's thoughts and feelings is a precondition for empathy. As a bonus, people are usually more willing to listen to you after you've listened to them first.

It can help you stay calm in challenging situations. Reflective listening asks you to temporarily put aside your thoughts and reactions. Doing so can be a relief and help you to feel calmer, even in emotionally charged situations.

Let's take a closer look at some of the advantages reflective listening offers.

Creating Connection

Your teenager comes home from school. You ask how his day was.

"Terrible," he says. "School sucks."

Concerned, you want to know more. But how do you respond without him shutting down?

Reflective listening is extremely helpful in situations like this, where the other person is upset or angry. Demonstrating understanding and expressing empathy can foster connection between the two of you. Your son is also more likely to volunteer additional information if you allow him to decide what to say, instead of trying to steer the conversation in a particular direction by immediately asking a lot of questions. Plus, you'll probably find it easier to remain calm if you focus on listening and understanding.

You begin by restating what he said in your own words: "You had a really tough day." You offer this reflection in a sympathetic tone. And then you pause, giving him time and space to choose what to say next.

Dropping his voice, he says, "I got a D on my biology paper."

Again you reflect, in a soft tone of voice, saying, "That must be disappointing."

"Yeah, I put a lot of work into that paper," he says.

Now you can shift from reflecting and ask if there's something you can do to help.

He says, "Maybe you could look at my next biology paper before I hand it in?"

Other teenagers might not be as responsive as the one in this example. However, by using reflective listening and letting them guide the conversation, you're more likely to connect with them than if you pepper them with questions or immediately start giving them advice.

Helping Others Discover New Perspectives

Reflective listening can be more than just a tool to help you understand someone. Using your own words when reflecting can give them a slightly different take on what they're saying. In that way, reflective listening can help them better understand themselves, clarify their situation, and perhaps solve their problems.

Suppose Sandra is having a conversation with her friend, Yuki, about her young son's problems at school. Here's how the conversation might unfold as Yuki reflects what Sandra says.

Sandra: I've got a meeting tomorrow with Jay's kindergarten teacher. She said he's disrupting the class and can't easily join in group activities. I've been working on this issue with him for the

	past two months, but he hasn't made a lot of progress. I'm really worried about him.
Yuki:	So you'd like to help him get along better.
Sandra:	Exactly! I just don't know what else I can do.
Yuki:	(nodding) You're looking for a way to support him.
Sandra:	Yes, that's right. Maybe he's old enough now to have more play dates and overnights with other kids. He's usually more relaxed outside of school.
Yuki:	(shifting from reflecting and saying what she thinks) I think setting up more play dates and overnights is a great idea. My daughter loved them when she was Jay's age.

In her first two reflections, Yuki subtly rephrased Sandra's original two statements in a way that invited her to focus less on where she was stuck and more on potential new options. "You'd like to," "You're looking for a way," and "You want" are all handy opening phrases for saying what you think the other person might want, even though they're focused on what they *don't* want. Rephrasing the person's statement in positive language is often useful, but not required. Just restating the other person's thoughts in your own words can encourage them to see new perspectives and solutions.

Once the other person knows you've understood them, they might be receptive to your observations or suggestions, as Sandra was to Yuki's. If you've first taken time to understand their problem, any ideas and advice you choose to offer will be more on target. And you can probably spot the added bonus of using reflective listening this way: it allows you to help, but without the pressure of trying to solve someone else's problems.

When to Shift from Reflective Listening to Speaking

Thoughts and feelings often percolate in your mind when you're listening to and reflecting what another person has said. At some point, you'll probably want, or even feel compelled, to respond to what you've heard.

Before you shift to making your own points, it's best to wait until the other person indicates you've at least partially understood them. If you take time to understand them first, they're less likely to think you're changing the topic or trying to keep them from finishing what they're saying. And if your response is based on what they've said, it's more likely to be relevant and useful to them.

When someone is confused, upset, or emotionally triggered, it's especially important to judiciously time your shift from listening to responding. If their emotions are interfering with their ability to listen, you'll probably feel frustrated, and you won't get your message across. You might also mistakenly put all kinds of interpretations on the fact that they're unable to listen, such as, "They're blocking me," "He's not interested in what I say," or "She doesn't care." On the other hand, if you wait until they feel calmer, they're more likely to be receptive to what you say.

It's not always easy to tell when a person has felt understood and is ready to listen. Reflective listening actually helps you in this regard. It requires you to pay attention to not only what the other person is saying, but also how they're saying it. You're more likely to pick up on subtle nonverbal signals, such as voice tone, body language, facial expressions, sighs, pauses, or gestures. The other person might also give more overt clues, like saying, "Exactly!" or "That's right." Mindfully, actively engaged listening is the key to sensing when they're ready to listen to you.

Advanced Reflective Listening

Now that you understand the basics of reflective listening, we'll address some additional facets of this skill, including questions our students and clients frequently ask.

Finding the Implicit Meaning

As explained earlier, reflective listening involves reflecting not only what's said, but also what's unsaid or perhaps has yet to be said—the implicit meaning suggested in the other person's communication. Ongoing reflections can bring to light nuances and additional elements of their message. Meaning can emerge, take shape, and grow during the loop communication that reflective listening provides.

Suppose your partner says, "You don't support me enough." If you just parroted back, "You think I don't support you enough," you wouldn't know specifically what "support" means.

Instead, your initial reflection could involve an educated guess about what your partner means by "support." Perhaps you know that who makes dinner is a continuing point of contention between the two of you. So you might begin with, "Perhaps you'd like more help preparing dinner." You're not reading your partner's mind; instead, you're inferring what they might mean based on past discussions.

If you've guessed the implicit meaning correctly, your partner can confirm that: "Yeah, I would really appreciate your help getting dinner on the table." If your reflection isn't accurate, they can clarify: "No, this isn't about dinner. I wish you would ask me how my day was when I get home." Then you can reflect this new information: "So dinner isn't the issue. You'd like me to listen to how your day went at work. That's the support you're looking for."

Using reflective listening to discern the implicit meaning does come with a risk: you might insert your own assumptions or judgments into your reflections. Suppose when your partner said, "You don't support me enough," your reflection was, "You think I don't care enough to support you." The phrase "You think I don't care" is your assumption or your own personal judgment. It's not based on what you just heard. Your partner didn't say anything about you not caring or offer any hints about it.

Reflecting what's implicit is an advanced skill that takes practice. You need to be careful to distinguish between your interpretations and what the other person actually means. Plus, your reflection of an unspoken message might be inaccurate. It's essential to stay open to and reflect any additional corrections.

The Limitations of Asking Questions

If your goal is to understand someone, you might think asking questions is the best way to do that. After all, isn't asking questions a good way to get more information, as well as demonstrate your interest?

While asking questions can indeed elicit useful information, produce insights, and solve problems, it also carries some risks. Questions are often more about what information *you* think is valuable. They might indeed show the other person you're interested, but be only tangentially related to what she wants to talk about. So instead of helping you better understand her, the questions might actually get in the way. Or worse, your questions might hijack the conversation, distracting the other person and taking her in a direction she doesn't intend.

An analogy we use in our training is that the person speaking is like a driver of a car, and the person listening is the passenger sitting beside her. Both are looking out at the same landscape, but the speaker is the one guiding the car. When you, the listener/passenger, begin asking questions, it's as though you're trying to take the steering wheel away from the speaker/driver and direct the car (the conversation) in a direction you think is valuable.

Asking questions can also quickly turn into an interrogation. Some people feel put on the spot or think you have a hidden agenda when you ask questions.

Reflective listening allows the other person to steer the conversation and keeps it from veering into incidental or irrelevant details, which can slow down or block you from understanding her. It keeps the spotlight on her and tends to trigger less defensiveness, the way questions sometimes do.

Understanding Without Agreeing

Understanding isn't necessarily the same as agreement. As you become more skilled at reflective listening, others might think you're agreeing with them when, in fact, you are only grasping what they're saying. There are two ways to avoid this mix-up.

First, when reflecting, use phrases that indicate you're reflecting the *other person's* ideas—not your own. For example:

- "*You think* you'd be better off enrolling in school sooner rather than later."

- "*You believe* climate change won't affect us for many years."

- "*It seems to you* that your manager doesn't come prepared for most meetings."

Reflecting the thoughts of someone you disagree with is usually easier when you use phrases like these.

Second, when it's your turn to talk, make sure to clarify that you have a different perspective.

Sophie and Anna work for the same company, but in different departments. One day, as they're meeting about a project, Sophie unexpectedly brings up a coworker from her department.

"Between you and me, I can't believe Jean got promoted," she says.

Anna is taken aback. She'd recently collaborated with Jean on a different project. She'd enjoyed working with her and been impressed with her work.

Puzzled, she reflects what Sophie said: "Maybe you don't think Jean deserved to be promoted to project leader."

"Oh, I don't think she's a bad worker," Sophie clarifies. "But she hardly ever speaks up in meetings. She doesn't offer any ideas. Frankly, I don't think she knows enough yet to lead a project team on her own."

Anna reflects, "So you think she does her job well enough, but she's not ready to lead a project team on her own."

"Right. But it's not just her knowledge I wonder about," Sophie says. "A good project leader needs to be able to manage a meeting discussion. They need to be assertive to keep the discussion on track, or the team will just end up wasting time. I can't see someone as timid as Jean being good at that. She's going to be in over her head, don't you think?"

Anna may not agree with Sophie, but reflective listening has given her enough information to understand Sophie's point of view. The beauty of reflective listening is that it allows you to acknowledge the other person without having to agree or disagree with them. But many people, like Sophie, don't just look for understanding; they want you to agree with them too. At the very least, most people want to know how you're affected by what they've said.

As it happens, Anna feels a bit protective of Jean, whom she likes. She also sees similarities between Jean and herself—particularly in how they operate in team meetings.

"You know, I don't think Jean will have the problems you expect," she says to Sophie. "I've seen her be quiet in meetings, as you have. But when I've talked with her one on one, she's actually had a lot of ideas and made some good points I hadn't thought of. I also think that given her own experience in meetings, she'll be able to draw out other people who usually don't say much. I can see team discussions actually becoming more balanced with Jean in charge."

Anna and Sophie may disagree about Jean, but their different opinions don't result in a full-blown conflict that they need to resolve. When disagreeing does lead to conflicts, reflective listening can play a valuable role in skillfully resolving them, as we'll show you in chapter 14. In chapters 11 and 12, we'll give you skills that can help you share your perspective in a way that's less likely to trigger defensiveness or pushback from the other person. But even with skillful communication, strong feelings often come up when two people disagree. When that happens, the guidance in the next section can come in handy.

If You Feel Emotionally Triggered

Temporarily suspending your reactions and impulse to respond doesn't mean you won't ever feel strong emotion when using reflective listening. The key is noticing when an emotional reaction is interfering with your ability to listen and reflect. Making this discernment and knowing what to do when strong emotions are affecting you are advanced reflective listening skills.

Imagine you've been trying to set up a dinner date with a friend. He's asked to reschedule several times, saying he's overwhelmed at work. The next time you talk with him, he again asks to postpone your dinner. You listen to him talk about his stressful work situation for a little while. You know reflective listening could be a supportive response, but you also feel frustrated that he wants to change your plans yet again and annoyed that he can't seem to stop talking about his job pressures. What can you do in this situation?

We'd suggest skipping the reflections for now. Instead, gently but firmly interrupt him. Tell him concisely what you think and feel, and say that it's affecting your ability to listen. "I'm feeling annoyed right now, and I'm having trouble listening," you might say.

From there, if your friend can shift to listening, you can tell him what's upsetting you: you've gone out of your way to reschedule your dinner dates, and you're frustrated that he's cancelling again. Sharing your thoughts and feelings, and hopefully having him understand them, will probably help you feel calmer. Then you can invite him to speak again when you're able to shift back to reflective listening.

Another option is to say what you're feeling and ask to pause the conversation: "I'm feeling frustrated right now. I'd like to take a minute to calm down so I can keep listening." Then you can take a few moments to resettle yourself (perhaps using some of the tips offered in "Listening When You're Feeling a Strong Emotional Reaction" in chapter 4). You can resume the conversation when you think you can stay calm enough to listen and take in a different perspective.

If you find that both you and your friend are too emotionally reactive to listen to each other, you can suggest stopping your conversation and resuming at another time. Rescheduling can prevent you from saying things you'll regret and have to clean up later. You can say, for example, "You know, I'm feeling pretty worked up right now. I'm afraid I can't listen very well. Can we hit pause for now and try talking again tomorrow night?"

Reflective Listening Can Increase Your Tolerance

Over time, as you practice reflective listening, you may notice that it becomes easier to take in views you don't agree with. Putting your initial reactions on hold as you repeatedly listen allows your listening to become less cluttered with snap judgments. Disarm your snap judgments, and people are usually more inclined to share their views with you. You still may or may not agree with what they say, but at least you're becoming more receptive to diverse points of view.

Summary: Unskillful and Skillful Reflective Listening

Here are some key ways to tell how skillful your reflective listening is. With less skillful reflective listening:

- You reflect only what's obvious and overlook what's implicit in the other person's message. Subsequently, your reflective listening doesn't elicit much new information from them.

- You parrot the other person's exact words when reflecting.

- You keep repeating what you've previously reflected, rather than reflecting the other person's new thoughts and feelings as she adds them. Consequently, your reflections lag behind what she's saying.

- Rather than acknowledging and reflecting the other person's corrections, you argue that what you reflected is correct.

- Your reflections are longer than what the other person said and include nonessential details.

- You use jargon like, "What I'm hearing you say is . . . ."

- You switch from reflective listening to sharing your own ideas, thoughts, and responses before the other person indicates you've sufficiently understood her and before she's verbally or nonverbally signaled that she's ready to listen.

With more skillful reflective listening:

- You listen to understand and temporarily put your ideas, opinions, and judgments on hold.

- You paraphrase, or use your own words, to confirm that you accurately understand what the other person said.

- You reflect some of the implicit thoughts and feelings in the other person's message.

- You keep your reflections concise and omit extraneous details.

- You reflect at strategic intervals so that you don't lose track of what the other person is saying. If she starts to say more than you can follow, you gently interrupt and reflect what you've understood so far.

- You take in the other person's corrections if your reflections are inaccurate. Then you reflect her corrections to show that you've understood them.

- You begin reflections with phrases such as, "You think (or *believe*, or *assume*, or *realize*) that . . . ," or "You feel . . . ," or "You'd like . . . ."

- You keep your reactions out of your reflections. If you decide to share them, you wait until the other person signals you've sufficiently understood her and she's ready to stop speaking and start listening.

Practice
Reflective Listening

In this exercise, you'll practice reflective listening in a simple situation that has little emotional charge. As your competence grows, you'll be more able to use reflective listening in more emotionally charged conversations.

1. Pick a situation where you'd like to more fully understand what someone is saying. You don't have to tell them you're using reflective listening. On the other hand, if it helps you to feel less awkward, tell them you're practicing a new listening skill.

2. As they talk, keep the spotlight on them as you reflect what they're saying. Temporarily put aside your own

thoughts, emotions, ideas, judgments, and other responses.

3. Keep your reflections concise. They should be less wordy than what the other person has said.

4. Pause after each reflection to make room for their additions and corrections.

5. Notice when the other person verbally or nonverbally signals that they're ready to hear what you have to say. Then share how their message has affected you, as well as anything else you want to say.

6. Afterward, on your own, consider:

- How did reflective listening affect both your conversation and how well you understood the other person?

- Given what you've learned from this practice, in what other conversations would you use reflective listening?

Chapter 6

Absolute and Relative Beliefs

Undercurrents of Communication

Like many people, you might not notice how much your beliefs shape what you perceive, how you act, and what you feel. For example, when you're young, you might believe that hard work will always be rewarded. You don't notice this belief when the events in your life suggest that it's true, such as when you get that raise you think you've earned by working hard. On the other hand, if you work hard but don't receive a raise, you might realize your underlying belief doesn't always match what happens in real life. And that discovery might be jarring.

Even if you're not aware of all your beliefs, they still shape your life and your outlook. They also strongly influence how you talk and listen to others. In doing so, they can impact how much conflict you experience with others. It isn't necessarily the beliefs themselves that trigger conflict and communication problems; rather, it's the stance you take regarding those beliefs. Looking at the language of your beliefs is a key to discerning your stance. Knowing how to strategically adjust that language, when appropriate, is a helpful skill to have in your communication toolbox.

Absolute Beliefs Versus Relative Beliefs

An *absolute belief* is an idea that you consider to be true without exception. By contrast, a *relative belief* is an idea that you realize could be affected by changing circumstances. Relative beliefs include more than one way to view an issue. "Lying is wrong under any circumstances" is an example of an absolute belief. "Lying is wrong under *most* circumstances" is a relative belief. The latter acknowledges that there are situations in which lying could be justified, such as when it would protect someone from physical harm.

Absolute beliefs sometimes act as blinders, allowing you to see only what fits with your thinking while blocking out what doesn't. Let's say Mrs. Johnson believes teenagers today are rude and selfish. Holding that absolute belief, she focuses on the rowdy kids she sees in her neighborhood. She doesn't even notice the kids who help the elderly cross streets or smile and say, "Hi" when they pass her.[1]

Absolute beliefs also can limit the range of your emotional responses in certain situations. Suppose your daughter-in-law doesn't send you a thank-you card for a gift you've given her. If you believe people should always send thank-you cards for gifts, you'll likely feel upset. Getting past that feeling will be tough if you stick to your absolute belief. You'll be locked into thinking that you're right, she's wrong, and feeling upset is justifiable.

A relative belief would be, "A thank-you card is welcome, but it isn't necessary for every gift." You would have preferred to receive a thank-you card from your daughter-in-law, but it's not crucial. So while you may feel slightly disappointed, you likely wouldn't feel very upset. Holding a relative belief instead of an absolute belief often allows for more emotional flexibility on your part.

Here's how to tell the difference between the two types of beliefs.

Absolute Beliefs	Relative Beliefs
You think there is only one way to view a situation: "I should receive a thank-you card when I send someone a gift."	You think there are many ways to view a situation: "I'd like to receive a thank-you card when I send a gift, but not everyone follows that custom."
You think someone or something is either right or wrong or good or bad: "If I don't score above 90 percent on this test, I'm a failure."	You think a belief fits within a range of other possibly valid beliefs: "I really want to score above 90 percent on this test. But if I don't, I'll still have given it my best shot. Plus, my other test scores will give me a high enough GPA."
You think in terms of what *should* or *must* happen: "My son must go to law school, or he won't be a success."	You think in terms of what you'd *prefer* to happen: "Although I'd prefer my son go to law school, he might find success in a different career."
As an observer, you think you're independent from what you observe, and you believe your observations are objective: "My granddaughter is the most intelligent and well-behaved toddler in her school."	As an observer, you understand you're interdependent with what you observe, and you believe your observations are subjective: "I think my granddaughter is the most intelligent and well-behaved toddler in her school. Of course, I'm her grandmother."

We're not saying that you should never hold absolute beliefs. They can be especially important when they reflect core values that guide your life—values that shape your morality and ethics and are crucial for maintaining your integrity. For instance, you might believe that making fun of a disabled person is unacceptable—period. Or you might believe no adult should ever, under any circumstances, physically punish a young child. Even though these beliefs show you're not sympathetic to everyone, they might indicate that you especially value kindness toward the disabled and children. You're more likely to stick to your absolute beliefs when a core value underlies them. The key question is, which absolute beliefs help you, and which ones hinder you, especially in your interactions with others?

It might be tempting to think that absolute beliefs are a sign of strength or that relative beliefs are a sign of weakness. Not necessarily. Relative beliefs recognize the systems principle. By acknowledging that the world and human beings are complex, changeable, and unpredictable, they can foster more flexible thinking, which can be advantageous in many circumstances.

How Absolute and Relative Beliefs
Impact Your Conversations

The extent to which you take your beliefs to be absolutely or relatively true can affect your conversations with others. If you hold the absolute belief that people are kind and trustworthy, you're more likely to be open and self-disclosing when you talk and receptive when you listen. But if you think people are kind and trustworthy *depending on the situation*—a relative belief—then you'd likely assess a particular situation before deciding how open or guarded you want to be.

Absolute beliefs often constrain a discussion. When the person you're talking with disagrees with you, an absolute belief can lead you to overstate your claim and antagonize them. For example, while discussing a political issue with a friend, you might say, "People are either part of the problem or part of the solution"—an absolute belief. Hearing this, your friend might think they don't fit either of those two categories. Consequently, they might feel less inclined to listen further.

A relative expression of the same idea could keep your friend more engaged: "*I think most* people are either part of the problem or part of the solution." The small addition of "I think" creates a relative belief that's now stated as an opinion rather than a fact. Distinguishing between opinions and facts frequently prevents the annoyance and confusion that can arise when opinions masquerade as facts. In addition, saying "most people" acknowledges that some people might not fit into your two categories. These changes can open up your conversation by leaving room for your friend's opinion.

Absolute beliefs can also limit how you resolve conflicts. Suppose you and your partner are arguing. As your temper flares, he cuts you off and abruptly turns on the television. Your bottom-line belief is that if he really cared about you, he'd continue the discussion even when you're upset. Therefore, you think his response can only be the result of a lack of caring. And you feel even angrier.

On the other hand, you might believe that even though people love each other, sometimes they can't stay in a conversation when they're too emotional. This relative belief would allow you to consider other plausible, less dire explanations for your partner's response. Perhaps he turned on the television to help himself cool down. Or maybe he felt frustrated by the argument and didn't know what else to do. In light of these additional options, you're more likely to stay calmer and be ready to continue your discussion at some point soon.

Recognizing how you're holding a belief and how that stance might affect the dynamics of a conversation is a valuable communication skill. Relative beliefs aren't necessarily better than absolute beliefs. But when you think and speak from a relative perspective, you can gain more practical options for having a constructive conversation.

The Link Between Absolute Beliefs, Either-or Thinking, and Polarization

"How did we become so polarized?" "Our country seems more polarized than ever."

As we were writing this book, the term *polarized* was virtually ubiquitous. Every week we heard it crop up in news stories, social media posts, everyday conversation, and elsewhere. It usually referred to people and social groups with differing beliefs. And it usually meant they were divided into two opposites that couldn't be reconciled.

Polarization is an outgrowth of dualistic, either-or thinking, which reduces ideas into two contrasting and usually opposing options: someone/something is either A or B. It can't be both A and B. And there is no C, D, or any other possibility.

Boiling concepts down to their most basic opposites can sometimes be handy, making the concepts easier to understand. In fact, such oppositions are part of the nature of language. Concepts are often mutually defined by their opposites: you can't have *hot* without *cold*, for example. Dualistic, either-or thinking pretends that these concepts truly are separate. For the sake of simplicity and understandability, it ignores the ways in which they're actually interconnected and interdependent.

But problems can arise when you hang on to that division too absolutely, thinking that A and B *must be* the *only* two options. Dualistic thinking eliminates all the gray area between the opposites. In doing so, it eliminates the nuances, contingencies, connections, and possibilities that live in that gray area. As a result, dualistic thinking is nearly always narrower, more limiting, and less flexible than systems thinking. The latter, the systems principle reminds us, recognizes that people and circumstances are influenced by many interconnected variables. It acknowledges the myriad options that can exist between the two polarities. From a systems perspective, you see how your idea of *hot* influences your idea of *cold* and vice versa.

Dualistic, either-or thinking frequently creeps into beliefs, often reinforcing an absolute perspective. "You're either with us or against us" is a classic absolute belief rooted in this kind of thinking. "If you don't believe X, then you believe Y" is another. In both cases, the possibilities have been reduced to only two polar (and often polarizing) opposites. Absolute beliefs, either-or thinking, and polarization usually go hand in hand, each one supporting the other. And polarization can lead to conversational dead ends.

Holding and expressing beliefs in a relative way counteracts polarization by reminding you that a wealth of possibilities and variables can exist between two opposites. Depending on the subject, acknowledging additional possibilities can sometimes be difficult or feel uncomfortable. But doing so is important if your communication goals include speaking more accurately, connecting with others, and avoiding unconstructive arguments. If you're talking with someone whose beliefs seem completely opposite of yours, thinking about your own beliefs in a relative way creates the potential for finding common ground, as well as supporting loop communication.

The Liability of Being Right

"There are two sides to every question:
my side and the wrong side."

—attributed to Oscar Levant

If you find being right irresistible, you're not alone. Being right is appealing. It *seems* to confirm your superior intelligence and knowledge. But needing to show that you're absolutely right can alienate others and damage your relationships.

First, this attitude often diminishes your curiosity about differing views. Why bother listening to someone who's wrong? Second, it can keep others from wanting to listen to you or learn from you. If your "right" point of view leaves no room for their points of view, why would they want to engage in conversation with you?

A relative perspective is more likely to allow other perspectives into a conversation. In doing so, it offers opportunities to connect with others.

Provisional Words and Phrases: The Language of Relative Beliefs

"The unexpected is bound to happen, while
the anticipated may never come."

—Nisargadatta Maharaj, *The Wisdom of Sri Nisagadatta Maharaj*[2]

The difference between absolute and relative beliefs can be seen in the language of each. Shifting the language you use to express your beliefs can help you have more constructive conversations.

Absolute beliefs frequently include the words *always* and *never*. These words presume that people behave the same way 100 percent of the time, that the world is unchanging, and that you know what will happen tomorrow. *Provisional language*, on the other hand, recognizes that people and circumstances change over time. It also acknowledges that the future is unknown.

Some provisional alternatives to *always* are *sometimes, often, frequently, more often than I'd like*. Provisional alternatives to *never* include *almost never, practically never, rarely, very infrequently, less often than I'd like, I can't remember a time when*.

Other provisional language includes *perhaps, possibly, may, might*, and *maybe*. These words acknowledge that what's happening might change. In addition, phrases such as "It seems to me," "In my opinion," and "I believe" show that your perceptions aren't facts. They're influenced by your personal beliefs, biases, habits, social context, and history. They acknowledge that *who* you are impacts *what* you perceive and *how* you communicate.

"Parents are more focused on their phones than their kids" can be restated provisionally as, "*Some* parents are more focused on their phones than their kids." "I'm always cleaning the kitchen" can be restated provisionally as, "I'm cleaning the kitchen more often than I want to." These wording changes might seem insignificant, but they can help reduce the friction that can come with using nonprovisional language.

Provisional language allows for exceptions, creates more accurate statements, and usually triggers less pushback than nonprovisional language. For instance, saying to your friend, "You're always late" doesn't acknowledge any exceptions. Your nonprovisional *always* makes the statement a blanket accusation. Instead of listening to you, your friend might look for an exception to your *always*: "Wait a minute! I'm not late *all* the time—just every once in a while." You're less likely to get caught in arguments about "what really happened" when you speak provisionally: "I remember *several* times that I've waited for you when we had plans to meet." Your friend might still disagree but probably will be more likely to hear you out.

Keep in mind that not all absolute beliefs include the word *always* or *never*. Sometimes those words are implied. Mrs. Johnson's absolute belief about teenagers, for example, contains an unspoken *always*: "Teenagers today are (always) rude and selfish." Sweeping generalizations are also examples: "People are only out for themselves." "Given the chance, people will do the right thing." "People don't change." In each of these cases, the implication is that the statement applies to all people, without exception.

Should is another word frequently found in absolute beliefs. Many *should* statements are nonprovisional or come across as so: "People should send thank-you cards after receiving a gift." "Hard work should be rewarded." "Teenagers should be polite." An absolute belief about how people or things should be is a *prescriptive assumption*, a specific type of unquestioned belief (see chapter 7).

Some absolute beliefs that include the word *should* are based on core values. If you firmly believe "I should be honest," it might not be appropriate to shift your language to express a relative belief. Other *should* statements reflect prescriptive norms: "I should be productive." In these cases, restating it in provisional language can allow for more flexibility: "I try to be productive as much as I can." With this wording, you're still aspiring to be productive, but you're less likely to feel guilty or overly self-critical if you're not productive 100 percent of the time.

Some people object to provisional language, claiming it sounds too tentative. They believe that starting a statement with "I think," for example, weakens it, especially in business settings. They prefer nonprovisional language, believing it conveys more certainty and authority. However, as noted, provisional language is usually more accurate and lets you clearly distinguish opinions from facts, both of which can support your credibility. Conversely, nonprovisional language tends towards overstatement and often blurs the line between facts and opinions, which can reduce your credibility.

You can still express judgments and strong ideas without treating opinions as if they're facts or a universal perspective. "This plan will never work" is stated in nonprovisional language; "I can't think of a way this plan will work" is the same thought stated in provisional language. "Our team's the most exciting one in this league" is a nonprovisional statement, whereas "Our team's the most exciting one I've seen in this league" is a provisional version of the same thought.

Shifting Your Beliefs About Others: Using Provisional Language to Revise Characterizations

How you think about or characterize others—both individuals and groups—is part of your myriad beliefs. Typically, characterizations are held and expressed in an absolute way.

Characterizations frequently presume—implicitly or explicitly—that the other person's qualities are inherent and fixed. As such, they often limit your ability to see her from different perspectives. They narrow the lens through which you view her, making it less likely you'll see ways in which she doesn't match your characterization. If you characterize your daughter-in-law as selfish when she doesn't send you a thank-you note, you might think her phone call on your birthday is motivated by guilt instead of genuine goodwill. If you characterize your granddaughter as the most well-behaved toddler in her school, period, you might have a hard time believing it when her teacher says she's bullying another child.

When applied to groups, characterizations ignore the group members who don't fit neatly in the box you've put the whole group into. Many group stereotypes are rooted in absolute beliefs and characterizations. (We'll address stereotyping in more detail in chapter 18.)

Characterizations can also color your expectations. Research on confirmation biases shows that you're more inclined to notice when people act the way you expect them to and to overlook, dismiss, or ignore behavior that doesn't support your characterization.[3] Thus, your expectations of people can become self-fulfilling prophecies.

Provisional language helps you shift from characterizations to relative beliefs. It can keep your perceptions of others from becoming too calcified or generalized. If Mrs. Johnson were in one of our communication groups, for example, we might suggest she tweak the language she uses to talk about teenagers. If she were to spend more time thinking provisionally, "*Not all* teenagers are rude and selfish," or "*Some of* the teenagers *in my neighborhood* are rude and selfish," how might her perspective of the kids she encounters change?

It's important to note that just qualifying a characterization with "I think" doesn't necessarily make a statement provisional. Saying "*I think* teenagers are rude and selfish" would show that Mrs. Johnson knows the statement is her own opinion, not a fact. But "teenagers are rude and selfish" is still nonprovisional, implying that the characterization applies to all teenagers.

Also keep in mind that expressing your opinions in provisional language doesn't guarantee others will welcome hearing them. Sure, "I think you're sometimes boring" is a provisional statement and "You're boring" isn't. But your partner, friend, or date probably won't respond kindly to either.

Shifting Beliefs About Yourself: Putting Provisional Language to Work for You

"Do I contradict myself? / Very well then I contradict myself, / (I am large, I contain multitudes.)"

—Walt Whitman, "Song of Myself" (1892 version), *Leaves of Grass*

Your beliefs and the language you use to express them don't just influence your conversations and relationships with others. They can also affect how you see yourself.

If you think, "I'm a shy person," the implication is that you're always going to be shy. This absolute belief can restrict your choices. Suppose you want to go to a party where you don't know many people, but you automatically assume that, being a shy person, you'll be uncomfortable. If you decide not to go for that reason, you might stay home and feel lonely. Moreover, staying home would confirm your belief that you're a shy person. Now your absolute belief—"I'm a shy person"—has become a self-fulfilling prophecy that, unfortunately, might lead you to a self-limiting future.

Adding some provisional language would make this belief relative. You might say, for example, "I feel shy more often than I'd like" or "I *often* feel shy *in large groups*." The implication is that you feel shy sometimes, but not 100 percent of the time or on every occasion. You might even recall social gatherings where you felt shy and uncomfortable for part of the evening, but relaxed and engaged at other times. In light of this relative belief, you might feel more inclined to go to the gathering.

When you can shift your beliefs about yourself from absolute to relative, you can often see yourself in a new light. And all it takes is a few provisional words. (Chapter 10 will discuss in more detail the effect of your self-talk on your communication with others.)

Practice
Identifying and Adjusting Absolute Beliefs

This exercise invites you to identify and shift how you hold certain beliefs. We've included examples to illustrate each step.

1. Make a list of six to ten things you believe to be true. These can be beliefs about other people, the world, or yourself. Don't think too hard; just jot down what comes to mind—big or small, significant or insignificant.

   Examples:

   My neighbor's dog is always barking at people who walk by.

   No one in my office uses all of their annual vacation time.

   Our country is going to hell!

   My boss is impossible to please.

2. Look at the beliefs you've written down. Mark which ones are absolute beliefs and which ones are relative. If you're not sure, ask:

   - Does this belief statement contain the words *always* or *never* (or otherwise imply that the belief is always or never true)?

   - Does it allow for possible exceptions?

   - Does it include any provisional words or phrases?

3. Take each of the absolute beliefs and restate it, incorporating provisional words and phrases as you do.

   Examples:

   My neighbor's dog <u>often barks</u> at people who walk by.

<u>As far as I know, hardly</u> anyone in my office uses all of their annual vacation time.

<u>In my opinion</u>, our country is going to hell!

<u>Right now I can't think</u> of a way to please my boss.

4. Read your list of restated beliefs. How do the provisional words or phrases you added affect how you think or feel about each statement?

Chapter 7

Assumptions

Check Your Thinking

Assumptions are beliefs you haven't fully scrutinized and usually take for granted. For example, you might assume that if you're friendly, others will treat you well.

Everyone makes assumptions—it's part of being human. Without assumptions, human life would be unbearably tedious. Before you could make a move, you'd have to stop and figure out what you thought about each and every situation you encountered. Assumptions can often be pretty reliable guides, but sometimes they're inaccurate. When you have to make an important decision, work through troublesome feelings, or resolve a disagreement, acting on inaccurate assumptions can get you into trouble.

Whether accurate or not, assumptions form a foundation for what you expect and how you live. Yet many people are typically unaware of their assumptions, let alone how much those assumptions shape how they relate to others. Recognizing your assumptions and those of others can help reduce problems in your conversations.

Where Do Assumptions Come from?

Your assumptions can come from practically anything that's influenced you, including schools, books, entertainment, news media, social media, religion, and spiritual traditions. Family is a significant source. Your family often teaches you what's acceptable or unacceptable to do when, where, and with whom. If the subject of money was strictly verboten in your family as you grew up, for example, you might assume it's rude to have conversations about money in any form, including with your partner. Even your conversations with a financial advisor, whose job is to talk about money, may feel uncomfortable or invasive. Most people absorb their family's assumptions without question and carry those assumptions into adulthood.

Your social circle also strongly influences your assumptions. Some friends think nothing of asking one another about their sex lives, for example. In other circles, a person would be considered rude if they asked such questions, and if they persisted, others would likely avoid them.

Some of your more common assumptions arise from the culture in which you live. Every culture has numerous unstated assumptions about money, status, manners, aging, success, health, time, death, race, other cultures, and communication, among other things. On my (Mudita's) first trip to Bali, for example, I was served meals in someone's home. I assumed that finishing the food was a sign of my enjoyment and appreciation. Too many pounds later, I learned it's customary for guests to leave a little food on their plate to show they've had enough. When I'd eaten everything on my plate, my Balinese hosts had probably assumed they hadn't given me enough food and piled more on.

Even when two people share the same culture, they may still have different assumptions. You and a friend may have grown up in the same city, followed the same religion, and attended school together for your whole educational life. Still, a problem has arisen between you: you have a habit of being late, and your friend doesn't like it. This habit seems innocuous enough to you, but your friend is insulted by your regular tardiness. When you finally talk about it, you both discover some assumptions shaping your feelings. You'd assumed that she'd accepted your tardiness, like most of your friends had. In fact, she felt troubled by it, assuming that you valued your own time more than you valued hers.

Many assumptions are rooted in your personal experience and your interactions with others—both everyday interactions and out-of-the-ordinary ones. In addition, people typically form assumptions based on what fits with their existing beliefs, values, and prior assumptions.

The Challenge of Discerning and Questioning Your Assumptions

Detecting your assumptions can be tricky. They're practically invisible. Typically, they are so much a part of your thinking that they go unnoticed. Like fish that can't see the water they're swimming in, you often can't detect your assumptions—until you encounter people operating under different ones. If you're surrounded by people who share the same assumptions, it's easy to think of your own as self-evident truths instead of unquestioned ideas.

Identifying your assumptions is only half the battle. Assumptions are powerful, but they don't always hold up as true, accurate, or useful when they're brought to light. As you grow and change, even once valid assumptions can become outdated, problematic, and flat-out wrong. Critical thinking allows you to question and assess the assumptions that underlie your ideas, values, and actions.

Yet even when you recognize your assumptions, you may be reluctant to probe them too deeply. Questioning assumptions can disrupt ideas that you've firmly held as common sense or objective truth. When those assumptions have guided your life—and often those of your family members, friends, and community—thinking about them critically can be threatening to your sense of who you are.

You also risk uncovering uncomfortable truths about yourself and then having to decide what to do with that new information. Let's say you have a personal policy of never saying yes to friends who ask for a loan. You usually explain your position by saying, "Friendships are too valuable to risk losing over money." But when challenged to examine it more closely, you might discover a less noble underlying assumption: people who ask friends for loans don't know how to manage their money, and giving them a loan is a poor risk. Uncovering that assumption might well be unsettling if you think of yourself as a kind, helpful friend. You also might not realize how much it limits your generosity with friends.

Rather than go through the often-uncomfortable process of jettisoning cherished, convenient assumptions, many people cling to what is familiar, even when it no longer serves their best interests. Identifying, evaluating, and updating your assumptions can sometimes be emotionally and intellectually difficult. However, acting on and communicating from outdated, unhelpful, or inaccurate assumptions can create far more problems. Fortunately, with practice, discerning and examining your assumptions becomes easier.

And there's more good news: Just as you don't have to eliminate all of your absolute beliefs to communicate more skillfully, you don't have to eliminate all of your assumptions. (Actually, that would be impossible. You couldn't operate without any assumptions at all.) Just pay close attention to the ones that might be at play during your important conversations. Also be willing to question your assumptions; test their validity by checking them against current information, when possible; and revise them if they're inaccurate or not useful.

Three Types of Assumptions

Not all assumptions are alike. When you're identifying your assumptions, it's useful to know that there are three major types:

Prescriptive assumptions describe how things *should* be: "people *should* be on time." People use prescriptive assumptions to express how they want events to unfold and people to behave.

Paradigmatic assumptions describe the nature of things: "being on time is a sign of respect." People use paradigmatic assumptions to explain how they think life and the world work.

If prescriptive and paradigmatic assumptions remain unquestioned and inflexible, they can become absolute beliefs (see chapter 6). Like absolute beliefs, these assumptions aren't inherently bad. But it pays to be alert to the impact they may have on your communication.

Causal assumptions describe how things happen or can be changed. They usually predict what will occur using an "if . . . then" format: "If I'm a few minutes late, Bob will get upset." People use causal assumptions to forecast or explain how behavior and events can or cannot change.

Causal assumptions can become problematic if you believe they're the *only* explanations for how or why something occurs. (See chapter 8 for more.)

As you become more familiar with these three types of assumptions, you'll start to recognize which ones underlie your thoughts, feelings, and actions. Then you can assess their accuracy, validity, and usefulness.[1]

Assumptions in Conversation

Recognizing when assumptions are affecting a conversation, identifying what those underlying assumptions are, and then carefully testing out their validity and usefulness can bring clarity to a contentious discussion. Carlos and Ashley found this out when they were buying a car.

The couple had been married for a year. They had demanding, full-time jobs that paid similar salaries. They agreed that owning a house would provide stability for their future family and were saving for a down payment. They also agreed that they needed only one car.

But what kind of car? Carlos favored a new car, while Ashley believed a used one would be best. As each lobbied for what he or she wanted, their disagreement heated up. Finally, they realized they both had some fixed assumptions they hadn't evaluated.

One of Carlos's assumptions was that they deserved a new car because they worked hard. It was based on a belief he'd learned from his parents: hard work should be generously rewarded. It was a prescriptive assumption, reflecting his belief about how things should be. His second assumption was that home ownership provides stability for families. This paradigmatic assumption revealed how he thought the world worked. His last assumption was that buying a new car would save them money in the long run because it would need fewer repairs. This is a causal assumption, conveying a belief about how things happen.

Ashley had her own set of assumptions. Her prescriptive assumption was that couples should scrimp and save if they're serious about buying a house. She also had a paradigmatic assumption that buying and owning a house requires some sacrifices. Another paradigmatic assumption she held was that used cars cost less. Finally, she held a "this-because-of-that" causal assumption that said buying a new car would mean they'd need to delay buying a house.

After Carlos and Ashley identified their assumptions, they turned to objective information to help them with their decision. They researched how much more it would cost them to buy a new car, and they compared upkeep expenses for both new and used cars. With these new details, they realized that buying a used car would cost them less than a new car in the long run. Seeing that the money they'd save would help them buy a home sooner, Carlos agreed to buy a used car. Even so, he still wanted a more recent model. Ashley compromised by agreeing to a newer used model than she had initially wanted. Being willing to update some of their assumptions in light of new information enabled Carlos and Ashley to find a solution to their conflict.

Some assumptions, like Carlos's assumption that he and Ashley deserved a new car, can't be checked against objective information. When you can't factually verify the accuracy of an assumption, consider its usefulness. In this case, Carlos's assumption could be useful if it didn't interfere with their plan to buy a house. After discovering that it did, he revised it; he changed it from an absolute belief to a relative one: hard work often deserves to be rewarded, but not necessarily in this situation.

How to Detect and Assess Your Assumptions

Jackson, the editor-in-chief of a legal magazine, frequently received unsolicited advice from Noah, the chief financial officer, about how to edit articles. The last time Noah gave advice, Jackson told him, angrily and loudly, to back off and stick to accounting. Noah later complained to other members of the editorial staff that Jackson wasn't open to new ideas.

Jackson believed that Noah wasn't qualified to give editorial advice and had overstepped his role. He also resented being characterized as close-minded. Noah disliked Jackson's unwillingness to acknowledge his editorial ideas. He also thought that yelling at coworkers was unprofessional and disrespectful.

If you find yourself in a similar contentious situation, we suggest looking behind the scenes at the assumptions that might be influencing it.

First, identify your assumptions. Ask yourself, "What might I be assuming in this situation?" If possible, label each assumption as paradigmatic, prescriptive, or causal.

Taking a look at his side of the conversation, Jackson noticed that he'd assumed the following:

- People should stick to what they're hired for (prescriptive assumption).

- People shouldn't make suggestions outside their expertise (prescriptive assumption).

- When people stick to their area of expertise, the organization will run smoothly (causal assumption).

- Giving someone advice implies that you think they aren't doing a good job (paradigmatic assumption).

- The magazine's quality is a high priority (paradigmatic assumption).

- If he listened to Noah's advice, the magazine's quality would decline (causal assumption).

- He wouldn't have gotten upset if he didn't care about the quality of his work (causal assumption).

Noah, meanwhile, assumed that:

- He had valuable ideas that Jackson should be receptive to (prescriptive assumption).

- Companies thrive with free-flowing information (paradigmatic assumption).

- The magazine's quality is a high priority (paradigmatic assumption).

- If Jackson didn't listen to other people's ideas, the magazine's quality would decline (causal assumption).

Next, consider how your assumptions help or hinder your communication in the situation. When Jackson and Noah asked themselves this question, each felt alienated when he believed his assumptions were right. Both thought their professional relationship was strained by the incident. Both had trouble discussing other critical information related to the magazine. Not surprisingly, Jackson also realized that expressing his anger by yelling didn't help.

Once you've considered your assumptions, compare them to available information. Together, Jackson and Noah looked at the critical praise the magazine had received for its articles and editorial content (including an award from a state lawyers' association) and how well the magazine was doing financially (keeping within its budget and meeting its projected earnings). These facts indicated that Jackson had been doing a good job as editor, and Noah had been handling his financial duties well.

Finally, decide what action to take in light of what you learned. After recognizing his other assumptions, Jackson realized he had to freely exchange information with Noah. From a communication perspective, his anger was interfering with that exchange. He decided that a more useful communication strategy would be to listen calmly to Noah's ideas. Even though Jackson wasn't likely to use them, listening to Noah would demonstrate goodwill, which in turn would support their information exchanges.

For his part, Noah recognized that although his ideas about editorial content might be good, his attempts to influence Jackson to accept them were nearly futile. He decided to offer fewer editorial suggestions.

It was just as hard for Noah to restrain his editorial suggestions as it was for Jackson to restrain his anger. However, each of them recognized that it was worth changing his communication in order to reduce conflict between them.

Along the way, Jackson and Noah discovered that they shared a paradigmatic assumption: the magazine's quality was a high priority, and the quality was key to the magazine's success. Shared assumptions are like shared goals; they can provide a common ground on which to build a more positive interaction. Jackson might say to Noah, "I think we both agree that maintaining the magazine's quality and success are our shared goals. So far the public's praise and our financial data show that we're doing a good job. Our separate roles in the company have worked well. Let's stay with what's been working: I'll continue doing the editing, and you continue doing the numbers." Their conversations are less likely to turn contentious when both colleagues remember that, despite their disagreements, they're ultimately both on the side of the magazine.

Assumptions and Values

Most people have specific assumptions about how they and others should think, act, and feel. These prescriptive assumptions are often an expression of values—such as community, courage, fairness, freedom, generosity, honesty, loyalty, respect, and security. Values, says the *Cambridge Dictionary*, are "the principles that help you decide what's right or wrong, and how to act in various situations.[2] Like assumptions, values are shaped by a combination of family and cultural influences, spiritual or philosophical beliefs, and personal experience. The prevailing ethics of society, as well as the ethics of the communities someone identifies with, influence values too.

In our training, we've observed that people frequently prioritize their values, ranking some higher than others. Doing so allows them to make decisions when two values conflict. Let's say your personal financial security and supporting your local community are two important values for you. The next time you want to purchase a book, do you buy it at a discount from a large online retailer? Or do you choose to pay full price for it at a small, independently owned bookstore? Your decision will depend on which personal value you rank higher on the day you're ready to buy the book.

Although assumptions can be assessed for accuracy, values are harder to evaluate. Imagine five different people are each given a million dollars. The first person, who values education and knowledge, uses the money to pursue a doctoral degree. The second, highly valuing independence, starts their own business with the funds. The third travels around the world, in keeping with their value of adventure. Valuing security, the fourth puts the money into an investment account. The last person, motivated by stewardship and social responsibility, distributes their million between various charitable causes.

All five uses of money have merit. All five people are acting on specific values. But which values and uses have the most merit? Ultimately, we believe the answer is a personal decision.

In addition, different people often see the same value very differently. Consider fairness. Many people value it, but they rarely have the same definition of it. Disputes frequently arise when two people's assumptions about what's fair don't match. Too often, each person thinks their definition of "fair" is the right one. As you consider how beliefs, assumptions, and values—your own and those of others—are operating in a conversation, keep in mind that how they're defined is a significant factor.

Clashing values are at the heart of many disagreements. While you may be able to question assumptions that have grown out of a value, trying to convince someone else (or yourself) to change their values can be extremely challenging.

Suppose two parents have different assumptions about the value of religion in childhood education. One parent, who grew up in a particular religious faith and values its influence, assumes religious teachings are a crucial part of children's education. Learning faith-based values is important preparation for living wisely, they believe. This parent wants to send their children to a private, faith-based school. The other parent, an atheist, thinks religion in general is problematic. This parent believes religious teachings shouldn't be part of their children's formal education and a faith-based school would just be a waste of time and money.

In such cases, perhaps the best option is aiming to understand the other person's values and how they prioritize them. Then each parent can temper their expectations about what they could achieve in conversations. If maintaining goodwill and cooperation with the other person is important, as it is for these parents, focusing on shared values is also a good idea.

One way they can resolve their conflicting values and assumptions is by looking for more inclusive ones that provide a common ground. For example, both parents might value critical thinking. They both believe it will enable their children to consider the importance of religion and make thoughtful decisions as they mature. They might then agree that early education emphasizing critical thinking would be useful for their children.

Like beliefs, assumptions have a strong influence on communication. But you may not realize just how strong their influence is until they clash with the assumptions of others. In chapters 14 and 15, we'll discuss how assumptions frequently crop up during conflicts and how to address them when they do. Chapter 18 discusses how assumptions about the differences between people influence people's communication.

Practice
Detecting Your Assumptions and Evaluating Their Usefulness

With this exercise, you'll practice identifying assumptions and assessing how they impact your communication. We've included examples to illustrate each step.

1. Think of a stressful personal or professional situation that you wished you had handled better.

   Example: My friend discussed a problem she was having with her sister. When I tried to say something, she kept talking over me.

2. Ask yourself, "What did I assume during this situation?" If possible, label the assumptions as prescriptive, paradigmatic, and causal.

   Example: My friend wasn't interested in what I had to say (paradigmatic assumption). She should listen to me (prescriptive assumption). I could have helped her, if I'd actually had a chance to talk (causal assumption).

3. Ask yourself, "How did my assumptions effect my communication in this situation? Did they help or hinder it?"

Example: I felt resentful and less inclined to talk with her about her problems. I guess my assumptions probably hindered my ability to listen.

4. Gather information and compare your assumptions to it. If you can't assess the accuracy of your assumptions based on objective information, consider how useful your assumptions are.

   Example: She often talks a lot more than she listens when she's upset. However, she does listen more often when she's not upset. I don't listen a lot when I'm upset either.

5. Decide what action(s) you could take in light of what you learned. If you identify multiple options, you may want to list them individually. Then you can compare the options and weigh the pros and cons of each before making your decision.

   Example: Option 1: I could cut her some slack since she's usually interested in what I say. I could be more patient by remembering that I don't listen well when I'm upset either. Option 2: I could talk with her about my frustration at another time when she's not upset.

Chapter 8

Shifting the
Blame Mindset

Recognizing Multiple Influences

W hy?" is a fundamental question we ask throughout our lives. When we're young, we ask, why is the sky blue? Why is Jimmy mean to me? Why are beagles so cute? And later in life, we ask, why is John late so often? Why did I get cancer? Why do good people suffer? How you answer these "why" questions reveals your particular assumptions about cause and effect. And those assumptions often become lenses through which you explain people's behavior.

Sometimes your explanations are benign: John was late because of unexpected traffic delays. Other times, you might assume John was late because he's inconsiderate and doesn't care if he keeps you waiting.

Which explanation you embrace will shape how you feel about John. If you believe John was late because of traffic delays, you might feel annoyed or frustrated, but you probably wouldn't feel too angry. You'd understand he wasn't in control of the traffic. Now suppose you believe John was late because he's inconsiderate. You're more likely to feel angry if you think that his lack of concern for you is the cause of his tardiness. What's more, you might see John as the direct *cause* of your anger; in other words, you might blame him for making you feel angry.

The seduction of blame is almost irresistible. Practically everyone blames someone for something. But blaming others—viewing them as the single cause of your feelings or behavior—can have detrimental effects on your thinking and on your communication with them. Shifting out of a blame mindset can help.

Distinguishing Between Cause and Influence

When you blame John for your anger, you're taking one thing—John's tardiness—to be the only cause for your anger. This stance overlooks the fact that human behavior is complex. Many factors—including your mood, how much you slept, how hungry you are, not to mention your upbringing, culture, politics, and history—can all contribute to your anger. Ultimately, it's hard to accurately attribute your feelings or behavior to a single cause. Skillful communication includes using critical thinking to detect this problematic type of causal explanation in your communication.

However, it is true that what others say or do influences how you feel. The difference between *influencing* and *causing* may seem subtle, but it's significant. If you believe that John's tardiness is the only thing that caused your anger, then you might think his behavior *determines* how you feel. Next, you'll probably blame him for how you feel. But when you think in terms of influence, you recognize that it wasn't solely John's tardiness that evoked your anger. Perhaps you also felt tired from an off day at work, you had a fight with your spouse, or you skipped lunch. These negative events also contributed to your angry reaction. Consequently, you're less likely to blame John for how you feel. Although you still might have a problem with John's tardiness, he might be more open to listening to you if you can speak to him without blaming.

The Blame Mindset and Its Problems

Have you ever said to someone, "You made me feel . . ." or noticed yourself thinking, "He made me feel . . ."? Those phrases indicate that you're in a blame mindset, a point of view that sees another person's actions as the single cause of your feelings. When Jamie criticizes you, for example, you might initially think, "She *made* me feel bad." The phrase "made me" reinforces the idea that Jamie's criticism caused you to feel upset.

The word *because* can be another subtle indicator of a blame mindset, recognizing only a single factor as *the* reason for your feeling: "I'm upset because you forgot our anniversary."

"Hang on," you might be thinking. "What's wrong with that last statement? One partner forgetting an anniversary *is* the reason the other partner is upset. That seems like a pretty straightforward link between one person's action and the other person's feeling."

Even though other factors may not seem apparent at the time, they are there, and they do contribute to the feeling. Most likely the upset person has a prescriptive assumption that partners should remember anniversaries. Or maybe they believe that if partners really value each other, they wouldn't forget their anniversary. Some of the person's response does have to do with their partner's action, but not quite all of it. Their response is also related to their assumptions and doesn't center only on their partner.

Recognizing that multiple influences are at play doesn't mean your feeling isn't valid. It also doesn't mean it's your own fault that you're upset. (Blaming yourself is just a variation of the blame mindset.) Nor does it discount the other person's influence. This recognition simply reduces or removes some of the blame mindset, which in turn can defuse potential conflict and open new options for responding.

Blame usually triggers a defensive reaction in others, so that they're less inclined to listen to you. Being blamed isn't a big motivator for most people. Another problem is that blaming others can cut you off from hearing what they have to say, including the explanations for their behavior. When you can avoid blaming and no longer think of others as the sole cause of your problem, you often naturally become more inclined to consider their perspective.

Finally, blaming others can reduce how much influence you think you have in a situation. When you think John's late arrival *made you* upset, you've unintentionally started to assume he's determining your emotional state. It's easier to feel more helpless when you blame others for what you're feeling. Ironically, thinking that the other person is wrong and you're right can feel like an assertion of strength. But when you think their behavior must change in order for you to feel better, you've actually narrowed your options. Once you reduce thinking other people are the sole cause of your feelings, you may discover new options for handling upsetting situations.

Accountability Still Matters

Making a single-cause link between your feelings and another person's behavior can lead to problems. However, using causal explanations to assign accountability for people's behavior is sometimes appropriate. If you hand in a report late, your actions can have consequences for others. If you commit a crime, you can be found guilty. Being able to assess accountability is important for functioning responsibly and socially.

Blame and single-cause thinking typically focus on finding faults in others' behavior or character. Blame often involves shaming others, too, and tends to decrease trust. Accountability, on the other hand, clarifies people's responsibilities in specific situations. It also invites people to find solutions to complex problems.[1]

In situations not involving people, single-cause explanations are frequently valid. For example, a car engine didn't start because an essential part was broken.

Shifting Out of a Blame Mindset

Blaming is hard to stop, even when you know better. Like so many other habits, the blame mindset tends to perpetuate itself. But you can shift to thinking in terms of influence rather than blame. Here's how.

Change Your Language

When you catch yourself thinking or saying, "He *made* me upset when he told me I wasn't getting a raise," change it to, "I felt upset when he told me I wasn't getting a raise. I expected to get one." This change of language might seem minor, but remember the language principle: changing your habitual use of certain words and phrases can profoundly shift how you see yourself, others, and the world.

Acknowledge Your Subjectivity

Recognize that your explanations of people's behavior shape your feelings and that your explanations are subjective and apt to change. If you think that John was late because he's inconsiderate, you're likely to feel more upset. But if you remember that he's a new parent and caring for his baby, you're more likely to accept his being late. The same is true if you remember that many factors could have contributed to John's late arrival. Your first explanation casts John's behavior as a character flaw; looking at it this way, you're more likely to feel upset. But if you see John as a conscientious dad, or recognize he may have been late due to factors beyond his control, you're likely to feel sympathetic towards him.[2]

Think "Influence"

Don't forget that many factors influence your thoughts and feelings. Keeping this aspect of the systems principle in mind, you can consider what else besides John's tardiness is contributing to your current mood. Maybe you're still feeling upset over an argument you had with your son earlier. Or perhaps your boss kept you late at work, and you're tired. If you've read chapter 6, you might notice that you have an absolute belief—friends should always arrive on time—that is coloring your view of John's behavior.

One handy way to see whether other factors are at play is to think about how you've reacted to John's lateness in the past. You may remember that sometimes John's been late, and you haven't felt angry. That's a signal that other factors might be contributing to your anger now.

Less Blaming Means More Options for Responding

As noted, when you go beyond the narrow path of blaming John for your anger, you'll find more flexible, less stressful ways of responding to his tardiness.

One option is to discuss your expectations with him. You can tell him that when you invite guests to dinner, it's important to you that they arrive on time. Perhaps you've tried talking to John about why you value promptness, and he still arrives late. In that case, remember that not everyone can change their behavior—even when they want to. (Think of the times you've sincerely wanted to stop smoking, eat healthier, or exercise more but couldn't.)

Sometimes it's easier to change your expectations than the other person's behavior. Suppose John is frequently unable to arrive on time despite his best intentions. You might feel more comfortable and less stressed if you accept his tendency for now. If you can't do so, you could tell him that dinner starts thirty minutes prior to when it actually does. Then even if he's a half an hour late, he'll still arrive on time. As a last resort, you might decide not to invite him to dinner.

Let's look at another example of how reducing blame can give people more options for responding to one another—this time in an intimate relationship. Jill feels disconnected from her partner, Chris. She thinks Chris is making her unhappy by withholding physical affection. After some communication coaching, Jill realizes that her requests for physical contact often sound more like demands than invitations. Moreover, she realizes that she typically asks for physical contact when she feels insecure. But Chris, sensing Jill's insecurity, thinks she's being too needy and has a hard time feeling affection for Jill or giving her what she wants.

When Jill stops seeing Chris's behavior as the sole cause of her unhappiness, it's easier for her to see the other factors influencing her desire for physical affection and connection, such as her insecurity. With this new perspective, she's able to change the tone of her requests. She starts to get a warmer response from Chris. She also begins to ask for physical affection at times when Chris feels more relaxed and emotionally available. Then Chris finds it easier to respond more affectionately to Jill's new inviting tone. Their new-found connection is a natural outgrowth of Jill's shift out of her blame mindset.

Consider Your Influence on Others

Even if your behavior or words don't cause other people's feelings, you can still be sensitive to how they influence others' feelings.

Suppose you know that your friend is self-conscious about being bald, but you mention it in public anyway. Your friend feels embarrassed. While you weren't the sole cause of your friend's embarrassment, you were one of the factors influencing his feelings. You could hold yourself accountable for the part you played in your friend's embarrassment. That accountability would likely lead you to be more considerate in the future and not refer to your friend's baldness in public.

When Others Blame You

Blaming is so common it's likely you'll encounter at least a few friends or family members who routinely blame you (and others) for their feelings. Let's say your friend Susan says, "I felt so disappointed because you didn't call to wish me a happy birthday." What's a skillful way for you to respond?

First, take a deep breath and wait until your knee-jerk defensiveness subsides. By not getting too reactive, you'll be more clear-headed and able to hear her complaint. You'll also stay calmer when you remember that you didn't cause her disappointment, although forgetting her birthday likely contributed to her feeling.

If Susan is really upset, you can use reflective listening to show her you understand her disappointment. Demonstrating that you care how she feels and that you understand what she's saying may also help her calm down. (See chapter 5.)

Try not to get stuck on the idea that she shouldn't be upset. Thinking someone should feel differently rarely brings resolution. Also, don't try to educate her about the blame mindset or explain that your actions aren't the sole cause of her feelings. She might think you're negating how she feels or trying to show why you're "right" (and she, therefore, is wrong).

Next, consider how accountable you think you are for her feelings. You may need some time—be it a few minutes to a few days—to think about it. Delaying your response is fine, provided you let Susan know that you want to take time to think about what she said. If you do need to step away from the conversation, be sure to schedule another time to complete it. Committing to continuing the conversation will show Susan that her feelings and your relationship are important to you.

If you think you did contribute to (not cause) your friend's distress, you could acknowledge it and apologize. If you honestly don't think you've contributed to her distress—and you're not being defensive—tell her how you see it. Bear in mind that if she's still upset, she may not be able to listen to you. Then you might employ more reflective listening or propose discussing your different views at another time when you're both ready to hear each other out.

Practice
Shifting Out of a Blame Mindset

This exercise shows you how to shift out of a blame mindset to find a more satisfying perspective. We've included examples to demonstrate each step. Writing out your responses for each step can help you articulate and track your thoughts.

1. Think of a situation in which you blamed someone for something that upset you.

   Example 1: My daughter-in-law makes me feel unwelcome whenever I visit her and my son.

   Example 2: I feel angry because Brandon criticized the report I'd been working on for weeks. He makes me feel incompetent.

2. What assumption(s) did you make that convinced you that the other person caused your feelings?

   Example 1: My daughter-in-law should be more sensitive to how I feel when I visit. She probably doesn't like me. If she did, she'd be friendly and invite me to see her and my son more often. Maybe she's trying to come between my son and me.

   Example 2: I expected Brandon to recognize the hard work I put into that report, not pick it apart. I thought he liked and valued my work.

3. Identifying other thoughts and conditions related to how you feel can limit blame and lead to new perspectives. What other thoughts and conditions might have contributed to how you felt?

   Example 1: I've had less contact with my son since he got married. I'm worried that he and I won't be as close as we've been. I'd feel more secure if I saw more signs from my son and daughter-in-law that I'm welcome in their home.

   Example 2: I've noticed recently that other people in the company don't seem to put as much time and effort into their work as I do. I've been feeling angry when their work gets recognized and mine doesn't. I also haven't been sleeping well recently and have been feeling on edge.

4. In addition to what others say and do, your own subjective thoughts and actions shape your feelings. How could you rewrite your statement from step 1 so that you're not blaming the other person? And what actions could you take to shift your perception of the situation?

   Example 1 rewritten statement: My daughter-in-law isn't as outgoing and welcoming as I wish she were. I want to visit her and my son, but I often don't feel comfortable interacting with her.

   Actions: Maybe if I reach out to my son directly, I'll feel more connected to him. I can also adjust my expectations of my daughter-in-law and recognize that she's just not that effusive or easy for me to talk with.

   Example 2 rewritten statement: I'd already been feeling frustrated at work for some time. Hearing Brandon's critique only added to that feeling.

   Actions: First, I'll make a point of getting more sleep. I know I often get frustrated more easily when I'm not well rested. Second, I'll schedule a meeting with Brandon and ask for his assessment of my overall job performance. From there, I can evaluate whether I think this company can offer the acknowledgment and appreciation that helps me continue to feel motivated.

5. How might shifting out of a blame mindset affect your feelings or view of the other person?

   Example 1: If I adjust my expectations of my daughter-in-law, maybe I'll feel more understanding towards her. If I reach out to my son, I'll probably feel more connected to him.

   Example 2: When I see what else has been on my mind, I can tell it wasn't just Brandon's criticism that I was reacting to. There's also a bigger issue I need to address.

Chapter 9

Problem-Solving

Are We in This Together?

How you think about and discuss problems can enhance or compromise your connections with others. If you see yourself as entirely separate from other people, you might believe you can act independently and perhaps overlook how your actions affect them. In most relationships, finding mutually agreeable solutions will be more difficult if you ignore your interdependence and only think and act unilaterally. In contrast, if you feel too merged or joined with others, you might have difficulty acting autonomously. You might agree too quickly or have trouble saying no to people's requests. You also might end up taking on more of their problems than necessary.

The skills in this chapter can help you reduce potential friction with others, as well as help you see problems from a new angle.

Who Should Solve This Problem?
Plan A Versus Plan B

When you have a problem, especially involving another person, finding potential solutions often begins with how you define it—specifically, whose problem you think it is. It's quite common to think a problem belongs not only to you, but to the other person as well.

Mark feels bored and, though he doesn't like to admit it, lonely. He invites his friend Jeremy to hang out with him several times, but Jeremy repeatedly declines. Finally Mark texts him, "Dude, it's been forever since we've even had a drink together. Whatever you've got going on, can't you drop it for just one night?"

Implicit in Mark's question are two ideas. First, he's defined the problem and its solution to include both him and Jeremy. Next, he's deployed what we call Plan A: he tries to solve *his* problem by asking *Jeremy* to change his behavior.

Plan A: You Change

Thinking that another person (rather than you) should change their behavior to solve your problem is very common and often very appealing. How often have you heard someone say something like, "I'd feel less stressed if my manager stopped micromanaging me." or "If you'd recognize my contributions to this project more often, I'd feel more motivated"? In close relationships, someone might even cite love as a reason for their partner to change: "If you loved me, you'd spend more time with me." "If you loved me, you'd be nicer to my parents." "If you loved me, you'd take walks with me more often." These are all examples of Plan A: asking the other person to change so you can hopefully feel better.

Plan A isn't inherently negative or problematic. Sometimes it makes sense to include another person in the solution to your problem. In many cases, people will do what you request. In close relationships, for example, accommodating a partner or friend's wishes is sometimes a suitable, practical option, especially when it's done selectively. Plan A can also work in situations where people have the designated power to tell others what to do, such as in hierarchical organizations or in parent-child relationships.

Nevertheless, Plan A has limitations. Tensions may arise if you expect the other person to immediately and willingly change. Thinking they *should* change often triggers pushback and decreases their desire to help you. Problems also frequently come up if the other person says no to your Plan A, and you keep cajoling, nagging, or pushing them to do so. People are typically more willing to help when they aren't automatically treated as part of your problem or as its only potential solution. And even when they want to change, many people are unable to do so. Old habits are often hard to change.

Let's say Jeremy agrees to join Mark one night for a drink. During the evening, Mark suggests another Plan A: they could get together at the same time every week. Jeremy feels disinclined to spend that much time with Mark, but he has trouble saying no. So he agrees, unwittingly accepting his assigned place in Mark's problem and solution. (This is an example of an inadvertent entanglement, one of the common communication disruptors.) As the weeks go by, Mark feels less lonely and bored, but unfortunately, Jeremy begins feeling dissatisfied and resentful. Going along with Mark's first Plan A was okay for Jeremy, but this second, longer-term Plan A just doesn't work for him.

Plan B: I Change

Now let's suppose Jeremy says to Mark, "I'm afraid I'm just too busy these days to hang with you every week. But I get how being alone too much can be a drag. I'm up for helping you figure out how you can reach out to other people."

Jeremy has declined to be the only solution to Mark's ongoing problem. Even though he feels uneasy saying no, he also feels less pressure when he does. Less pressure, in turn, allows him to express empathy and willingness to help Mark.

What can Mark do now? He can accept Jeremy's decision and shift to what we call "Plan B: I change." Plan B asks, "How can I solve my problem without requiring the other person to change?" Mark can focus on what he can do to lessen his boredom and loneliness. After doing some brainstorming with Jeremy, perhaps he reaches out to other friends he hasn't seen recently, or maybe he joins a local hiking group. With Plan B, Mark doesn't have to solely depend on Jeremy, but he's still able to feel better.

When someone else can't or won't change to help you, staying attached to Plan A can be frustrating and futile. Changing your behavior is often easier than trying to change others' behavior. Plan B gives you additional options for getting what you want when your Plan A doesn't work.

Shifting from Plan A to Plan B means shifting your focus from an often unworkable option (trying to change another person's behavior) to other options. Instead of focusing on what you want them to do, you focus on what else *you* could do. To show you what we mean, let's go back to two of the Plan A examples from earlier in the chapter.

If you're thinking . . .	Ask yourself . . .
I'd feel less stressed if my manager stopped micromanaging me.	What can I do to feel less stressed, but without requiring my manager to change?
If you'd recognize my contributions to this project more often, I'd feel more motivated.	What can I do to boost my motivation when my colleague almost never recognizes my contributions to this project?

How to Say No and Still Express Empathy

Perhaps you think if you refuse to change your behavior to solve someone's problem, you're not being compassionate, kind, or empathetic. After all, saying no can sometimes seem harsh. However, you're more likely to stay calm and less emotionally triggered when you recognize that the other person is the one with the problem—not you. Empathy, kindness, and compassion are often easier to express when you don't take someone's problem personally. And you can still help them solve their problem without being part of the solution.

Jeremy recognized that Mark was the one who had the problem. He gently extricated himself from being its only solution ("I'm just too busy these days") while expressing empathy ("I get that being alone too much can be a drag"). He was also willing to help his friend:

"I'm up for helping you figure out how you can reach out to other people." In doing so, he implicitly suggested there could be alternative solutions to Mark's problem, subtly prompting Mark to shift to Plan B.

If you find yourself in a similar situation, here are some examples of what you might say to express kindness and a willingness to help, but also avoid inadvertently thinking you have to change to solve the other person's problem. You can adapt these phrases as needed to suit your particular circumstances and the person you're speaking with.

- "I'd like to help you solve the problem you're having. Unfortunately . . ."

- "I want to help, but I don't think I can. (*If it's useful, say what prevents you from helping.*) I'm up for discussing what else might work for you."

- "I do love you, and I understand that you're asking me to do _____. I know it means a lot to you. I'm sorry I can't do what you want. I'd have a hard time doing _____. Can we look for other ways to solve this problem?"

The Alternate Plan A: Shifting from Demands to Requests

Let's look at another example of Plan A in action. Suppose Tom gets upset when Darcy, his partner, doesn't wash the dishes after he's cooked dinner for them. He says, "You're just going to let the dishes sit in the sink all night? I just put a lot of effort into making dinner, and I want to just relax now. The least you could do is clean up."

In this case, Tom has the problem: he can't relax when there are dirty dishes in the sink, and he doesn't want to wash them himself. He has, understandably, defined the problem as one in which Darcy plays a role. He wants her to clean up, and to do so immediately, so he can unwind (Plan A). But she doesn't want to do exactly what he's requesting. "I like to take it easy right after I eat. I promise I'll clean up later," she says. Tom's Plan A, to get Darcy to change to in a specific way to solve his problem, doesn't work. And the more he pushes her to clean up immediately, the more unsympathetic she becomes.

By assuming Darcy should change her behavior to solve his problem, Tom came across as demanding. Darcy, like most people, might be more inclined to lend a hand if he'd requested her help, rather than demanding it. Requests usually invite more cooperation than demands and often foster goodwill.

Suppose Tom had said, "I have a hard time relaxing when the sink's filled with dirty dishes. Would you be willing to wash them sooner rather than later?" Although he's still employing Plan A, he's acknowledged that he's the one with the problem. And instead of assuming that Darcy shared the problem, he invited her to consider helping him. He shifted from demanding ("you should") to requesting ("would you be willing?").

Despite Tom's more inviting request, Darcy might still say no. Skillful communication can increase the probability of getting what you want, but it doesn't guarantee it. Don't assume you've communicated poorly simply because the outcome didn't match what you wanted. Remember: you can influence people, but you can't control them.

There are certainly some problems that one person can't solve on their own. And there are times, especially in close relationships, when one person thinks there's a shared problem but the other doesn't. In chapter 15, "Conflict Management for Couples," we'll talk about what you can do in these and similar situations.

Practice

Working with Plan A and Plan B

When addressing problems that involve others, people usually can come up with a Plan A, but can get stuck if others don't go along with it. This exercise is a step-by-step process for evaluating a Plan A and developing a potential Plan B that can be used if needed. We've included examples to illustrate each step.

You might find it helpful to write out your answers. With practice, you may begin going through these steps automatically in your mind when you're problem-solving.

1. Think of a situation in which you have a problem involving another person.

   Example 1: I want to quit my job and go back to school to get my master's degree. I'm not sure if my partner will support my plan, though.

   Example 2: My manager doesn't answer my emails or texts as quickly as I need her to. Sometimes she doesn't answer them at all. My projects get stalled as I wait for her to respond to my questions.

2. What's your Plan A? How would you like the other person to change their behavior? In addition, if Plan A works, how might you benefit?

   Example 1: I want my partner to support my plan enthusiastically. Then I'd feel more confident making this big leap from a secure job to a master's program.

   Example 2: I'll explain to my manager how my work is affected when she doesn't answer my questions within a couple days. I'll request that she respond to emails and texts within twenty-four hours. If she could do that, it would be easier for me to keep my projects on schedule, and I could do my job with less stress.

3. If you've already asked the other person to change, what response did you receive?

Example 1: My partner said she wants to support me. But she has concerns about my plan, especially how losing one of our incomes might affect us financially. She wants to discuss the financial details further. (This is an example of Plan A working.)

Example 2: My manager understood how her lack of responsiveness was interfering with my work. But she said that between the volume of emails she receives and her busy meeting schedule, she doesn't see a way to respond to my questions more quickly right now. Nor did she offer any alternative ways for me to get her input when I need it. (This is an example of Plan A failing.)

4a. If the person agreed to change to meet your request, what was your response? How did meeting your request affect the other person?

Example 1: I felt relieved and encouraged. I told my partner I was glad she wanted to support me. I assured her that I would look closely at our finances and come up with ideas for making our finances work in a way that's comfortable for both of us.

4b. If the person declined to change to meet your request, what was your response?

Example 2: I felt frustrated. I want my manager's input when I need to solve certain problems, and sending her emails and texts is usually the way she wants to communicate. But based on our conversation, I now know I can't always count on getting her help as promptly as I'd like.

5. If your Plan A failed, what's your Plan B? How could you solve your problem without the other person changing their behavior? How could you think differently? What different actions could you take? If Plan B works, how might you benefit?

Example 2: I'll need to figure out what to do when my manager can't answer my question soon enough. I could ask my manager who else I should consult when she can't respond promptly. Or I could just make the best decisions I can on my own. In case someone questions my judgment, I'll keep track of the emails in which I requested my manager's input, but she didn't reply.

Chapter 10

Self-Talk

Changing Unhelpful Thinking

Most of us talk to ourselves. We have what seems like an inner voice that comments on our lives throughout the day and into the night. This inner monologue usually arises without much choice. Often it reflects our unspoken beliefs, assumptions, and judgments.

Your self-talk doesn't just affect you; it also affects how you relate to others. Imagine your friend offers to help you move to your new apartment. Your inner voice might say, "She's so generous! I'm lucky to have such a helpful friend." You then express your delight and gratitude to her. On the other hand, if your inner voice says, "She's only offering so I'll help her move when her lease is up next month," you might become more guarded. Whether your reaction is grateful or cautious depends on what your self-talk says about your friend and the nature of your relationship with her. If you want to improve the way you communicate with others, it pays to look at how you talk to yourself.

Self-talk usually consists of habitual thoughts and patterns of thinking, not all of which are helpful. Examining your self-talk may reveal *cognitive distortions*, or persistent, inaccurate thought patterns that can limit your perspective. To help you counteract these cognitive distortions and detrimental self-talk, we'll introduce you to *reporting*. This communication skill is handy in many circumstances, but it's especially helpful when you're facing personal difficulties.

The Nature of Self-Talk

Typically, self-talk has the following characteristics:

- It can be helpful or unhelpful.
- It can seem plausible or reasonable even though it may be far-fetched.
- It has a life of its own. Your inner voice is like an independent entity on autopilot that talks to you.
- It happens spontaneously.
- It might still persist in spite of evidence that runs contrary to what it says.
- It doesn't necessarily arise from formal reasoning.[1]

Some of your self-talk is probably upsetting, yet you might believe it, especially if it's repetitive. Even self-talk about the unknown future—"I'll never be truly happy"—can seem true simply because you keep thinking it over and over.

Your self-talk strongly affects your moods. When you make a mistake, what do you usually tell yourself? Let's say you misplace your phone—something you do infrequently. Does your inner voice say something like, "Why do I keep doing this? I'm so disorganized!"? When this kind of disparaging, nonprovisional self-talk arises, you'll probably feel less understanding toward yourself. But if your inner voice says, "Oops! Not sure how I misplaced my phone. Next time I'll make sure to put it on the table by the door when I come home," or something similarly kind and helpful, you'll likely feel more forgiving towards yourself.

Too often, self-talk can build traps that keep you feeling stuck. Consider the following thoughts:

- "I didn't score well on the test. I'll never pass this course."
- "I was in a bad mood when I woke up. Today's going to be awful."

- "There's a traffic jam on the bridge. I'll never get any work done today."

In each case, your inner voice has turned a single event into a prediction about the future. But when you think about it, the predicted outcome won't necessarily follow from the event: Not scoring well on one test doesn't mean you'll never succeed. A bad mood in the morning doesn't mean that the rest of your day will be awful for sure. Running into a traffic jam doesn't mean you'll never get to work.

Identifying and scrutinizing your self-talk can seem daunting at first. But doing so gives you the opportunity to cultivate new self-talk that's more kind and understanding. When we got bogged down in the midst of writing this book, we realized that our self-talk had become inadvertently pessimistic: "If we write at this pace, we'll never finish this book." So we revised it to be more encouraging: "Getting bogged down is a natural part of writing a book. We've gotten stuck before, and we still moved on." Feeling more optimistic, we continued writing the book you're now holding.

As you become more skilled at noticing and, when necessary, changing your self-talk, you won't be as hoodwinked into believing your thoughts are true just because you think them.

Cognitive Distortions

Self-talk can sometimes create negative frames of reference called *cognitive distortions*. These thought distortions limit how you think, talk, and listen. Distortions are by definition exaggerated or irrational. If you take them to be true, you might unwittingly use them to your detriment. Uncovering and revising your cognitive distortions often leads to less stress and more useful self-talk.

Here are several common cognitive distortions and how you can address them.

Filtering involves magnifying negative aspects of a situation while ignoring the positive ones. For example, you receive nine positive evaluations on a project, but totally discount them as you focus on the one negative review.

Focusing excessively on the negative is quite natural and partly due to people's innate negativity bias. Psychologist Jonathan Haidt of New York University's Stern School of Business, says, "Over and over the mind reacts to bad things more quickly, strongly and persistently than to equivalent good things."[2] But you can curtail a habit of leaping to negative conclusions. When you recognize that you're overemphasizing the negative in a situation, you can substitute a thought with a more neutral or positive conclusion: "I would have liked 100 percent positive reviews, but 90 percent is good enough this time."

Personalizing is thinking that what people say or do is a reaction to you. When you wave to a friend across the street and she doesn't wave back, you may think she's ignoring you and feel upset. But your revised self-talk would consider other factors that could explain her behavior: "Perhaps she didn't see me wave. Maybe the sun was in her eyes. Or maybe she was preoccupied with her own thoughts."

Overgeneralizing is when you arrive at a conclusion based on a single incident or limited evidence. Even if something bad happened only once, you expect it to keep happening.

Suppose you weren't attracted to the first person you met through a dating app. You may prematurely conclude that you'll never meet a compatible partner through the app, and so you stop using it. You'll have made a global conclusion based on a single negative experience.

When you catch yourself overgeneralizing, consider other possibilities. Think of times when one negative experience led to a neutral or positive outcome. For example, "Two of my friends met their spouses online after several disappointing initial dates. Maybe I'll meet someone if I keep trying."

Catastrophizing is a specific form of overgeneralizing. When you catastrophize, you imagine only the worst possible conclusion and exclude all other possibilities. It's especially easy to do when you have a health challenge, as chapter 17 will explain.

Shoulds are fixed or ironclad rules that you believe people and life events ought to follow. But often a should is just your personal opinion and not a universally shared rule of behavior. When others don't follow your should, you're likely to feel indignant or angry. Suppose your should is, "People should reply to my texts within an hour." When they don't, you feel annoyed or offended. Just as troubling, you'll feel guilty when you don't follow your own shoulds, such as, "I should call my grandparents every Sunday."

Shoulds are a type of prescriptive assumption that's held as an absolute belief (see chapters 6 and 7). They can be disarmed the same way other absolute beliefs or assumptions can: by making them relative. A relative version of your should about texting could be, "I'd really prefer to get an immediate response to a text. However, not everyone feels as I do." This revised, provisional self-talk acknowledges that even though you feel strongly about your should, others still might not think the same way.

A fallacy of fairness occurs when you think you know what's fair no matter what others think. You believe your standard of fairness is the only legitimate one. When you believe life's events should be fair according to your standards, it might be harder for you to deal with things you don't like.

Let's say your friend's son got married, but you weren't invited to his wedding. Earlier in the year when your daughter got married, you'd persuaded her to invite your friend to her wedding. You believe it would have been fair for your friend to have reciprocated, and you feel disappointed that she didn't.

To counter the fallacy of fairness, remind yourself that different people have different standards of fairness. You can't be sure what guided your friend's decision. You could tell her you were hoping to go to her son's wedding and give her a chance to explain why you weren't invited. Perhaps she didn't think it was fair for you to feel obliged to go to another wedding so soon after your own daughter's. Or perhaps she was honoring her son's wishes for an intimate wedding of only close family and a few friends.

Emotional reasoning follows the logic, "I feel it, so it must be true." But too often what you "feel" is true doesn't sufficiently factor in other information.

If you felt awkward during a job interview, you might conclude you'd done poorly. But suppose you didn't succumb to emotional reasoning in this situation. Instead, you recognized that even though you felt awkward, you could still have made a favorable impression. Telling yourself this, you're now more likely to remember details you may have overlooked at first, such as the interviewer nodding and smiling as you discussed your previous work. You're also more likely to reserve judgment on your performance until you've heard back from the company.

These are some of the most common cognitive distortions we see in our coaching and teaching. Experts in the field of cognitive psychology have identified others.[3] As you start to notice cognitive distortions, you might be concerned about how prevalent they are in your thinking. But they're just like any other communication habit: noticing them is the first step to shifting to new, more constructive self-talk. A little patience will go a long way as you practice and become more adept at recognizing and amending cognitive distortions.

We've found that using provisional language is an effective way to shift most cognitive distortions, but not all of them can be easily revised. Some are pretty tenacious, and in these cases, adjusting the language of your thoughts can be difficult. Acceptance and Commitment Therapy (ACT) offers other tools for working with distortions. ACT's techniques include cultivating a different, perhaps friendlier relationship with distortions and diffusing the intense emotions that some thoughts trigger. For more information about ACT and its techniques, please see the books listed in "Recommended Resources."

Reporting: Putting a Skillful Spin on Your Experience

Unhelpful self-talk and cognitive distortions often assert themselves when you're struggling. Unfortunately, they can make a tough time even tougher. But there is an antidote. *Reporting* is a way of saying what's going on for you right now, in this moment, including how you think and feel about it. Used skillfully, it can be an alternative to detrimental self-talk.

Perhaps the best way to understand reporting is to compare it to complaining. There are distinct differences between the two.

First, reporting can include a range of information—positive, negative, and neutral. Complaining focuses primarily on the negative. Second, complaining tends to be repetitive, sharing the same details (usually negative ones) again and again. Reporting focuses on the details of your current experience, which may or may not be the same as previous experiences.

Third, reporting uses provisional language, which recognizes that circumstances can and do change. Complaining usually employs extreme, dramatic, absolute, or all-or-nothing language, such as *always* and *never*. That language usually reflects cognitive distortions. "This is the worst thing that could have happened to me! Nothing ever works out!" is a complaint. "I didn't see this coming. I feel so discouraged and caught off guard," conveys the same sentiment, but in more provisional language.

Finally, complaining is often laced with self-pity. Reporting, however, can include a wider range of emotions. "Why does this always happen to me?" is an example of a self-pitying statement. It's a narrow, nonprovisional lens through which to view your situation. It also suggests that you've been singled out—that no one else has gone through what you're going through. Compare that statement to this one: "I didn't expect this to happen. I'm having trouble dealing with it. I feel scared." This statement simply describes how unaccustomed you are to the situation and doesn't imply that you're the only one to experience difficulty. "Bad things always happen to me" is another example of a self-pitying statement. "Lately I've been having a tougher time than usual" is more provisional and doesn't overgeneralize. Repeatedly using self-pitying statements typically gives rise to feelings of depression and of being overwhelmed. In contrast, the feelings that arise when you use reporting are usually less intense and easier to manage.

A shift from complaining to reporting entails mindfully adjusting what you say and how you say it. The phrase "I'm noticing that" can help you get started. For example, "I'm noticing that my back's hurting in a new place. I wonder if it's getting worse. I feel scared." The phrase "I'm noticing that" might initially sound odd, but using it becomes more natural with practice.

Reporting does not necessarily mean replacing a statement or thought with something more positive. Nor does it mean denying or sugar-coating what you're really feeling or experiencing. Your reporting statements must be accurate and credible to you. It won't work to change a complaint to something that theoretically sounds true or nice but isn't realistic or believable to you.

Say you're struggling financially. You notice yourself thinking, "I can barely pay my bills every month, much less put any money into savings. There's no way I'll ever be able to get ahead." Trying to replace those thoughts with something like "I'm sure things will look up for me soon" or "I am getting wealthier every day" may not help. These statements may seem hopeful, but unless they feel authentic to you, they probably won't work. Sometimes reporting means acknowledging the difficulty of the situation, as well as your feelings about it, but in a way that's more relative and provisional than your original thoughts: "This month, like last month, I only have enough money to pay my bills. I wish I could save more. Right now, I don't know how to change the situation. I'm noticing that I feel very anxious and discouraged."

Reporting isn't just about cheering yourself up or cultivating a more optimistic mindset. It's also not intended to minimize real, serious problems. The main point of reporting is to convey what's happening for you right now, in the moment, using provisional language.

Reporting puts the language principle to work for you. Employed over time, it can revise the messages that your inner voice feeds you and even disable some cognitive distortions. And reporting has a bonus benefit: it's often easier to listen to than complaining. Other people are more likely to respond with empathy if you report what's happening with you, rather than complain about it. We'll explore the value of reporting further in chapter 17, "Health Challenges."

Practice
Revising Your Self-Talk and Cognitive Distortions

This exercise is an opportunity for you to identify and change some of your self-talk and cognitive distortions. We've provided examples to illustrate each step.

1. Briefly describe a situation that's distressing for you.

   Example: I've applied for three different jobs but haven't even gotten one interview.

2. Write down your thoughts and feelings in this situation without censoring them.

   Example: My résumé must be pretty thin compared to others'. These companies must think I'd be a bad hire. I feel so frustrated. What am I doing wrong? How can others be getting jobs, but no one wants to even interview me? No one will ever want to hire me.

3. Identify and list any cognitive distortions you find in your thinking.

   Examples

   Personalizing: My résumé must be pretty thin compared to others'. These companies must think I'd be a bad hire.

   Emotional reasoning: I feel so frustrated. What am I doing wrong?

Fallacy of fairness: How can others be getting jobs, but no one wants to even give me an interview?

Overgeneralizing: No one will ever want to hire me.

4. Write down how these cognitive distortions hinder you.

   Example: When I believe these distortions are true, I feel deflated, depressed, even hopeless.

5. How could you revise these distortions so that your thinking is more useful to you? Write down your revised thoughts.

   Note: It's important that your revised thoughts are realistic and credible to you, not just that they sound good.

   Examples

   Revised to counter personalizing: I actually don't know how my résumé compares to those of the other people who applied for the same positions. I also don't know what the companies thought of me after seeing my résumé and cover letter. There could be many reasons these companies didn't respond to my application, including reasons that have nothing to do with me or my résumé.

   Revised to counter emotional reasoning: Just because I feel frustrated doesn't necessarily mean my résumé is weak. But I'll check it just to make sure.

   Revised to counter a fallacy of fairness: It doesn't seem fair that some people are finding jobs and I haven't been interviewed yet. But sometimes that's the way it goes. I don't know what's going to happen next. It doesn't really help me to compare others' experiences to my own. Given the job market, many people probably aren't getting interviews.

Revised to counter overgeneralizing: Just because the companies I've applied to haven't responded doesn't mean other companies won't.

6. How have the feelings you listed in step 4 changed after you revised your cognitive distortions?

Example: Though I still feel frustrated, I also feel calmer and a little more hopeful about the future.

Practice
Complaining Versus Reporting

This exercise will help you detect the differences between complaining and reporting. Spotting these distinctions will help you become more adept at reporting. We've provided examples to illustrate each step.

1. Describe a situation you're struggling with (or have struggled with in the past). Write down your thoughts and feelings in this situation without limiting or censoring them.

Example 1: I can't believe I had to move back in with my parents. I'm a grown woman! What kind of person has to live with her parents at this age? A failure, that's what kind. And OMG, are Mom and Dad set in their ways! If I don't wash the dishes or take the laundry out of the dryer right away, they're on my case until I do it. And they want me to spend so much time with them, like when I used to stay with them for short visits. They don't care that I have other priorities, like my job or exercising or staying in touch with my friends. They don't seem to get that this is a different situation. I'm not a kid anymore, and I'm not a guest in their house either. We're going to be living together indefinitely. Moving in with them seemed like a good idea for all of us, but now I don't know if I can stand it for very long. But what choice do I have? I feel so stuck and helpless.

Example 2: I'm so overwhelmed right now. Between taking care of the kids and working, I have zero time for taking care of myself. Exercise—hah! What's that? I think I had a clean house once, but never again. And it's impossible to get a good night's sleep. I'm just dragging myself through my days, and there's no end in sight.

You know what really bugs me? Hearing other parents complaining about how their partners don't do enough work around the house or with the kids. At least they have partners! In my house, it's just me, trying to hold it all together. I've got no friends, no help, and no family members who can pitch in. And with what most things cost these days, I certainly don't have any extra money to hire someone to clean or watch the kids for even half a day. I'm just so tired.

2. Set your description aside for a little while—anywhere from one hour to one day would work well. Taking a break after step 1 will allow you to come back and complete steps 3 through 6 with a more neutral frame of mind.

3. Returning to your description, review what you wrote.

   • Are any details stated more than once? If so, cross out the repetitive information.

- Are there any details that seem more like complaining than reporting in your description? If so, cross them out.

Example 1: I can't believe I had to move back in with my parents. I'm a grown woman! ~~What kind of person has to live with her parents at this age? A failure, that's what kind.~~ And OMG, are Mom and Dad set in their ways! If I don't wash the dishes or take the laundry out of the dryer right away, they're on my case until I do it. And they want me to spend so much time with them, like when I used to stay with them for short visits. ~~They don't care that~~ I have other priorities, like my job or exercising or staying in touch with my friends. They don't seem to get that this is a different situation. I'm not a kid anymore, and I'm not a guest in their house either. We're going to be living together indefinitely. Moving in with them seemed like such a good idea for all of us, but now I don't know if I can stand it for very long. But what choice do I have? I feel so stuck and helpless.

Example 2: I'm so overwhelmed right now. Between taking care of the kids and working, I have zero time for taking care of myself. ~~Exercise—hah! What's that? I think I had a clean house once, but never again. And it's impossible to get a good night's sleep.~~ I'm just dragging myself through my days, and there's no end in sight.

You know what really bugs me? Hearing other parents complaining about how their partners don't do enough work around the house or with the kids. At least they have partners! In my house, it's just me, trying to hold it all together. ~~I've got no friends, no help, and no family members who can pitch in. And with what most~~

~~things cost these days,~~ I certainly don't have any extra money to hire someone to clean or watch the kids for even half a day. I'm just so tired.

4. Of the remaining information, how much seems positive, how much seems negative, and how much seems neutral to you? If the overall balance of your statements skews toward the negative, are there any positive or neutral details you could add? If not, that's fine. (No need to create new positive or neutral statements if they aren't authentic to your experience.) But if there are some other positive or neutral details you didn't originally include, jot them down.

Example 1: At least my parents are willing to let me live here. Not everyone has still-living parents, parents in a position to help their adult children, or parents they're on speaking terms with. And I appreciate that they want to spend time with me.

Example 2: (No positive or neutral statements to add.)

5. Does any of the language seem too absolute or extreme? If so, how could you restate the same thoughts in more provisional language? Adding provisional language won't necessarily change current conditions, but it can sometimes help you see things in a more workable light.

Example 1: ~~I can't believe~~ I had to move back in with my parents. ~~I'm a grown woman! What kind of person has to live with her parents at this age? A failure, that's what kind. And OMG, are~~ Mom and Dad <u>seem to be</u> set in their ways! <u>I've noticed that if</u> I don't wash the dishes or take the laundry out of the dryer right away, they're on my case until I do it. And they want me to spend ~~so much~~ more time with them than I have available. ~~, like when I used to stay with them for short visits. They don't care that~~ I have other priorities, like my job or exercising or staying in touch with my friends. I could let them know that. ~~They don't seem to get that this is a different situation. I'm not a kid anymore, and I'm not a guest in their house either.~~ It seems like we're going to be living together for a long time. ~~Moving in with them seemed like such a good idea for all of us, but now I don't know if I can stand it for very long.~~ But what choice do I have? I wish I could think of other options. I feel ~~so~~ stuck and helpless.

Example 2: I'm ~~so~~ overwhelmed right now. Between taking care of the kids and working, I haven't yet found enough time for taking care of myself. ~~Exercise—hah! What's that? I think I had a clean house once, but I can't remember what it looked like. And sleep seems like just a dream now.~~ Too often, I'm just dragging myself through my days, and ~~there's no end in sight~~ I don't know when things will change.

~~You know what really bugs me? Hearing other parents complaining about how their partners don't do enough work around the house or with the kids. At least they have partners! In my house, it's just me, trying to hold it all together. I've got no friends, no help, and no family members who can pitch in. And with what most things cost these days, I certainly don't have any extra money to hire someone to clean or watch the kids for even half a day.~~ I wish I could find people to help me. ~~I'm just so tired.~~ I don't feel much hope right now.

6. Now look at your whole revised description.

- How have the changes you've made above affected your perspective about the situation?

- If someone else were sharing these thoughts and feelings with you, would it seem like they were describing their experience, positive and negative, without self-pity? How has complaining been reduced with the changes?

Chapter 11

I-Language

Go Beyond Your Projections

Imagine you're not able to get in touch with a close friend. After texting them several times throughout the week you decide to call them. Which of the following options are you more inclined to use: "You're avoiding me" or "I've been having a hard time reaching you"?

Both options describe the same situation, but each does so in a different way. "I'm having a hard time reaching you" is an example of *I-language*. It expresses what you're experiencing. "You're avoiding me" is an example of *you-language*. It conveys what you think your friend is doing.

With I-language, you're talking about your own experience—how you think and feel. With you-language, you're saying what you imagine *others* might be thinking and feeling. You-language often projects your own assumptions about others onto them or characterizes their behavior in a certain way. When you-language implies there's a negative motivation behind their behavior, it can become the sibling of blame, or thinking that others are the cause of your thoughts, feelings, or behavior (see chapter 8). An unhelpful side effect is that you may mistakenly think your projections are facts.

Suppose your friend Joshua asks you to help him set up chairs for a meeting later that day. You say yes without thinking about it. When you show up to help, he has more tasks he wants your help with. You'd hoped to return some business calls before the meeting began, but you don't say no. Instead, you agree to do the additional work, but feel resentful. The next day you still feel resentful. As you tell another friend what happened, you say, "Joshua's so self-centered. It didn't even occur to him I might have other things to do before the meeting." Instead of focusing on how you're reacting to Joshua, you've projected a negative characterization onto him. That's classic you-language: describing what you think about the other person, rather than what you're experiencing.

Your situation would likely look different if you thought about how Joshua's behavior affected you. When describing the situation to your friend, you might say, "I often say yes to helping Joshua, and then I end up spending more time than I'd anticipated. I need to think more carefully and check my schedule before agreeing to help him again." Now your description is in I-language: you report what's happened and the effect it's had on you. In addition, you focus on what you could do to prevent the same thing from happening again in the future.

Here's a snapshot of the differences between you-language and I-language:

You-Language	I-Language
Reports your thoughts about the other person.	Reports your thoughts about your own experience.
Examples:	**Examples:**
You're pressuring me to get married too soon.	I don't want to get married right away.
My boss isn't giving me the support I need.	I haven't found a way to get the support I need from my boss.
You do a thorough job summarizing your research.	I can easily use your research for my project.

You-Language	I-Language
Characterizes or describes the other person or their behavior.	Describes what you're experiencing in response to another person.
Examples:	**Examples:**
It's so rude of you to change our dinner plans on the day we're meeting.	I really don't like changing our dinner plans when you ask to do so on the day we're meeting.
My contractor is ignoring the budget we initially agreed on. He insists on buying the most expensive insulating materials. He's unreliable.	My contractor wants to use more expensive insulating materials than we initially agreed on. I can't afford to spend more than I'd budgeted for. I don't know if I can continue to work with him if he insists on increasing the budget now that the project has started.
My daughter isn't trying hard enough to make friends at her new school.	My daughter says she hasn't been able to make friends at her new school. I had the same problem when I was her age. I'd like to figure out if there's a way I can help her make more friends.

How I-Language Is Useful

I-language initially may sound like a self-centered or narcissistic concept. After all, talking about yourself can seem selfish and unproductive. Most people have an easier time characterizing and talking about others. Instead of revealing your own thoughts and feelings, it's often more comfortable to project them onto others. But in fact, I-language enhances your interpersonal communication in several ways.

It's More Accurate Than You-Language

When you focus on your own experience, you'll be more accurate than when you project thoughts, feelings, or motivations onto others. After all, you are the one who directly perceives how things taste, feel, and smell, or what you hear and think. And it's unlikely you know for sure what another person's experience or motivation is.

It Can Help Reduce Misunderstandings

Sharing your experience in I-language typically helps others understand you better. In potentially tense situations, it lets them know where you stand. If you don't say specifically what you're thinking and feeling, others can make assumptions that might lead to serious misunderstandings, especially in difficult situations.

Suppose your sister says she'll host the New Year's Day family gathering, though it will take a lot of work. "You're giving me mixed messages," you respond. "You say you'll host it, but then you complain about the extra work you'll have to do. Just be straight with me." This you-language statement does tell your sister that you don't know what she really wants. However, when you tell her to be straight with you, she thinks you're being critical and don't understand how much work goes into the event.

Using I-language, you can be more precise: "When you said hosting would take a lot of work, I wasn't sure what you actually wanted and didn't know how to be supportive." You could also add, "I'm happy to help out with the tasks or even host the gathering at my house. I'd just like to get a better sense of what you really want." Your I-language helps you express more clearly what you're confused about and how you'd like to help.

It Typically Evokes Less Defensiveness and More Receptivity

Using I-language can influence how receptive others might be to what you say. It usually triggers less defensiveness than you-language, which can come across as blaming, patronizing, and judgmental. It also doesn't characterize others or their actions in a negative way—something most people dislike.

Suppose you it was your turn to take out the garbage, but you forgot. The next morning, your roommate says, "You're not following our cleanup agreement. You're just hoping I'd take the garbage out for you." How would you react to hearing this you-language message?

Now imagine how you'd react if your roommate used I-language: "Hey, I thought we'd agreed to each take the garbage out on specific days. I don't want to do more than my share." You still may not like what they're saying, but you'd probably feel less defensive and be more likely to consider it.

Here's another example: You're feeling frustrated as you try to make something clear to your partner. "You just don't get it!" you say. The implication: it's your partner's fault they don't seem to understand you. Hearing this you-language can dampen their desire to listen further; most people become defensive when they think they're being accused of a shortcoming. I-language would allow you to clarify that your intention is to be understood, rather than to blame your partner: "I think I still haven't gotten my point across." Your frustration is still evident, but your partner is probably more likely to stay open to you. (Chapters 12 and 13 will provide more guidance for crafting and framing messages that are less likely to trigger defensive, knee-jerk reactions in the other person.)

It's Empowering

I-language asks you to notice your thoughts and feelings. In doing so, it can also reveal the assumptions and beliefs you use to make sense of your life. In this way, I-language improves your ability to understand yourself.

Using I-language also helps you focus on what *you*, rather than other people, can do to improve a problematic situation. Then you can more easily see Plan B options, rather than only Plan A options, as explained in chapter 9. With this self-knowledge, you'll likely feel less helpless. You'll strengthen your ability to recognize what you can do to take care of yourself.

Consider this example from earlier in the chapter: "My daughter isn't trying hard enough to make friends at her new school." The focus of this you-language statement is what you think your daughter isn't doing right. There's no explicit reference to how the situation affects you. With this focus solely on your daughter, you're more likely to think your options are limited to Plan A solutions, such as telling her what to do differently. You could try Plan A solutions, but if they don't work, I-language will help you identify possible Plan B options.

Shifting to I-language clarifies how you're impacted by the situation: "My daughter says she hasn't been able to make any friends at her new school. I had the same problem when I was her age. I know how hard that can be. I'd like to figure out what I can do to help her make more friends." While this shift doesn't change the situation itself, it can change your perspective on it. And it can allow you to see options for your next steps. For example, you could share your experience with your daughter: "I switched to a new school when I was around your age, and it took me a while to make new friends." You can also let her know you're willing to help and offer her some options: "I'd like to help you, if I can. I could tell you some things that worked for me, if you like. Or maybe we could come up with some new ideas together." Using I-language in this way can give you more options for moving forward.

Finally, I-language typically evokes more benign feelings in yourself than you-language does. You-language that contains judgments or beliefs (especially absolute ones) about others is often accompanied by strong feelings. Strong feelings aren't inherently bad or inappropriate, but they may not be helpful in every situation.

Imagine you're giving a birthday party for your partner, and he's concerned that no one will come. To assuage him you say, "You worry too much! You've had the same anxiety at your past birthday parties, and plenty of people came. You should just relax." What emotions might you feel saying these words? Perhaps frustration? Maybe impatience? Now imagine using I-language to convey your thoughts: "I wish there were something I could say to help you relax. Based on the RSVPs, I think most people will come. I don't see a need to worry." How might your emotions change with this shift to I-language? You're more likely to feel concerned, supportive, and possibly relaxed.

Shifting to I-language can help you keep from getting too caught up in the emotions that often accompany you-language characterizations. With I-language, you might still feel many emotions, but they'll be based on your direct experience rather than your projections about other people. The emotional shifts I-language typically brings can often help you feel more resourceful, especially in challenging situations.

The Nuances of I-Language

Describing your thoughts in I-language might seem simple enough, yet almost everyone finds it tricky at first. To help you become more comfortable with it, let's look at some of its nuances, including some questions our students and clients frequently ask.

I-Thoughts: Going Beyond Feelings

Sometimes people think just saying how they feel gives listeners enough information to sufficiently understand them. But sharing just your feelings isn't necessarily enough. You also might need a clarifying thought stated in I-language—an I-thought.

Here's an example of just a feeling: "I feel overwhelmed at work!" Here's the same feeling paired with an I-thought: "I feel overwhelmed at work! I haven't found a way to get the support I need from my manager." Adding this thought clarifies what prompted your feeling. Although your feeling might initially grab the other person's attention, your I-thought gives them more context, enlarging their understanding of your situation.

I-thoughts often help you, the speaker, as well. Putting your feeling together with a thought can clarify what a situation means to you. It might also help you figure out what to do about it, if you're seeking solutions. Plus, I-thoughts can reveal underlying assumptions and beliefs you might not have been aware of. Finally, I-thoughts encourage metacognition: they illuminate how you're thinking about yourself, often adding new insights about who you think you are. All of these I-thought benefits are part of what makes I-language empowering, especially compared to you-language.

Mentioning Other People in I-Thoughts

People practicing I-language sometimes ask if they can mention another person in their I-thoughts. The answer is, yes, you can, but the *primary* focus should be on what *you* think, feel, or experience. That's what distinguishes I-thoughts from you-thoughts: With I-thoughts, the spotlight shines on you. With you-thoughts, it's on the other person.

To show you what we mean, let's go back to an earlier example. "My daughter's not trying hard enough to make friends at her new school" is definitely a you-thought; the focus is entirely on the daughter. "My daughter says she hasn't been able to make friends at her new school" could at first seem like a you-thought. In fact, it's a neutral statement about the daughter that provides context for the mother's I-thoughts that follow: "I had the same problem when I was her age. I'd like to figure out what I could do to help her make more friends." Even though the daughter is mentioned, the spotlight is on the mother.

In chapter 12, we'll share more about skillfully referring to others in your communication while still using I-language to your benefit.

Faux I-Language: "I Think That You . . ."

You and your friend had arranged to drive to a concert together, but he arrives at your house only ten minutes before the concert's scheduled to start. You're upset. When he asks you what's wrong, you say, "I think you're being rude coming so late."

This is an example of what we call faux I-language. Although you said, "I think," you're still projecting characterizations onto your friend ("you're being rude"). An I-language statement would be, "I feel really uncomfortable cutting it this close. I prefer to leave early and arrive at the concert relaxed." Both messages show you're distressed. But while "I think you're being rude" insults your friend, saying "I don't like cutting it this close" doesn't put your friend down or invite defensiveness. And you have a better chance of being heard.

We'll share more examples of faux I-language in chapter 11.

Positive Characterizations Are Still You-Language

You-language can include positive characterizations of the other person, as well as negative ones. "You do a thorough job summarizing your research" is a positive characterization of another person's work. "You're a tidy person" is a positive characterization of another person's habits. Both are also examples of you-language.

Like many of our students, you might be thinking, "How can positive characterizations be problematic? What's wrong with saying something nice about another person?"

First, as we've already noted, what you say about others may or may not accurately match their experience of themselves. In addition, positive characterizations don't reveal how you're affected by others; as such, they have limited utility. Using I-language to let them know specifically how their actions affected you can provide them with more valuable information.

Imagine that you're a manager giving one of your employees a performance review. "You follow all safety procedures in your work," you tell her. Then you might offer an I-language statement: "I feel confident about you working without my supervision." On the other hand, you might say, "I think you're conscientious." Although the latter is a you-language statement, it's still a positive characterization. Most people would feel happy receiving either statement. However, the you-thought is missing an important piece of information: that you trust your employee's work.

Using I-Language to Give Critical Feedback

Generally, people will accept positive feedback no matter how it's phrased. Not so with negative feedback. But people *are* more likely to accept negative feedback when it's skillfully expressed in I-language.

Suppose you need to give your employee some less-than-favorable feedback. You begin with an observation: "Last week, your team members asked you to participate in a problem-solving meeting. You said you had other high-priority projects to deal with first." Which next statement do you think would be better received: "You're not being a team player" or "Without your participation in the meeting, I'll still need to provide your information. I don't have time to do that"?

The first option is in you-language. Most people would bristle at hearing themselves characterized as not being a team player. The second statement, an I-language thought, says how their action affects you. Your employee still may not like this feedback, but now they know how their actions will affect you. Then they might make the meeting a higher priority.

I-language is one of the more advanced skills we teach. It requires not only a change in your interpersonal communication, but also a shift in the way you think. Most people have spent their whole lives thinking in you-language, and altering this habit isn't something that happens overnight. But here's where the language principle can work to your advantage: Language not only reveals, but also shapes how you think. Using I-language, therefore, is a powerful way to shape new patterns of thought. Over time, changing what you say and how you say it can profoundly change how you see yourself, others, and the world. In other words, using I-language can be revelatory! Being both attentive to your language and patient with yourself as you practice I-language will serve you well in the long run.

Practice
Using I-Language

This exercise will help you recognize you-language when it crops up in your conversations, so you can start thinking in I-language instead. We've included examples to illustrate each step.

1. Briefly describe a problem you're having with another person, such as a friend, family member, or someone you work with.

   Example 1: My partner frequently tailgates other cars.

   Example 2: One of my employees habitually shows up late for team meetings.

2. What would you usually say to the other person in this situation, especially when you're upset? Write down the first words that come to mind, without censoring or editing them.

   Example 1: I hate the way you get so close to other cars on the road. You sit on someone's bumper just because they're not driving as fast as you think they should. Your driving is going to get us killed one of these days!

   Example 2: You don't take our meetings seriously. You don't seem to realize that we can't get started until everyone is here. You're wasting everyone's time. Apparently, you think your time is more important than ours.

3. Review your answer to question 2. Note or underline any phrases or sentences that focus on the other person instead of you.

Example 1: I hate the way <u>you get so close to other cars on the road. You sit on someone's bumper just because they're not driving as fast as you think they should. Your driving is going to get us killed one of these days!</u>

Example 2: <u>You don't take our meetings seriously. You don't seem to realize that we can't get started until everyone is here. You're wasting everyone's time. Apparently, you think your time is more important than ours.</u>

4. Now describe the problem again, this time using only I-language to share your experience of the situation. (Remember that you can use the word *you* to refer to the other person as long as your words primarily focus on your own experience.)

Example 1: I don't feel safe getting so close to the backs of other cars while driving. I'm worried we'll hit the car in front of us if the driver stops suddenly. I'm afraid I'll be killed.

Example 2: I like starting meetings on time so that we're all on the same page. I don't think I'm using the meeting time efficiently when I backtrack to fill you in on what you've missed. From now on, I want you to arrive on time for our team meetings.

Chapter 12

The Complete Message

Details That Make a Difference

Let's say your new manager tells you she wants regularly updated project reports. You think that "regularly updated" means once a month—as usual. Later, she criticizes you for not updating the reports often enough. She didn't specify that "regular" means twice a month to her.

Insufficient information isn't always a big deal. But in conversations that have consequences—such as when you're negotiating agreements, handling conflicts, or sharing important feelings—you definitely want others to have enough information to understand what you mean. By "enough information," we mean the facts and details that might make a difference in how the other person understands you. Anthropologist Gregory Bateson defines this type of information as "a difference which makes a difference."[1]

When you know you'll be participating in an important or potentially challenging conversation, we suggest thinking about your message in advance. That way, you can make sure it includes sufficient and accurate information. You might even consider writing out your opening message beforehand. Then you'll be more likely to remember what you want the other person to know and even some phrases you might want to use. This preparation will not only help you communicate more clearly but may also boost your confidence and help you maintain your equanimity during the conversation.

If you don't think through your message beforehand, you might omit helpful details. Then the other person would have to guess or infer the missing information for themselves—something they may not do accurately. You're also at risk for flooding them with too much information. Afterward, you might wish you'd been clearer and regret that you weren't.

All these problems can be avoided with some thoughtful preparation. And that preparation can start with what we call a *four-part message*.

The Four-Part Message

Our format for a complete message will help you give others enough specific information to minimize the odds of misunderstanding. It can also help you get right to the point by weeding out unnecessary and potentially confusing details.

The four parts of a complete message are:

The referent—whom or what you're talking about (what the message refers to).

The thought—your thoughts, opinions, beliefs, or assumptions about the referent and how it affects you.

The feeling—your emotional response that accompanies your thought.

The intention—what you want (stated positively).

This format is straightforward, yet each part is more nuanced than you might first imagine. We're going to break down each one for you in turn, addressing the most common things our clients and students ask us about as they're practicing this skill. (And they've asked us a lot of questions over the years!) As we do, you can begin to appreciate each part's unique function. And you'll see how all four parts work together to create a succinct yet well-rounded message.

Part 1: The Referent

Most messages are about a situation, a person, a thought, or a feeling. Your referent specifies what you're talking about. Imagine you need to talk with your company's human resources representative about a new sick-leave policy. Your referent could be, "I see that the new insurance policy has changes that will affect how much coverage I'll have for my illness."

Referents don't need to be complete sentences. *When* clauses, for example, can be very useful ways to phrase a referent: "When I think about . . . ," "When I noticed . . . ," "When I heard you say . . .". A manager opening a potentially sensitive conversation with an employee might say, "When I heard you start talking about a new topic before Shawna had finished her presentation in today's meeting . . ." and then continue with the rest of the message. Even if it's an incomplete sentence, a referent concisely spells out what you're talking about, so the other person won't have to guess or wait to see what it is.

In general, others are more likely to stay open to what you say if your referent is phrased in I-language. Like provisional language, I-language allows you to think and communicate more accurately. Take this referent, for instance: "When you mentioned my divorce to our friends before I was ready to reveal it to them. . ." The I-language clarifies that this statement is *your* point of view or opinion. If instead you say, "When you *inappropriately* mentioned my divorce to our friends . . . ," the other person might bristle and debate the accuracy of what you said ("My comments weren't inappropriate!"). And they may be less inclined to listen to the rest of your message.

"As I recall" is a provisional I-language phrase that's especially useful when your message is about something that happened in the past. Acknowledging that a recollection is subjective and possibly inaccurate can often reduce pushback. Someone wanting to talk to her ex about attending their daughter's sporting events might state her referent as an observation: "I didn't see you at Jacqui's soccer match last Saturday. As I recall, we both agreed to meet there."

Part 2: The Thought

To paraphrase the Stoic philosopher Epictetus, people are affected not by events, but by the views they have of them.[2] It's difficult to talk about something if you don't know what you think about it. For example, if someone criticizes you, your thoughts about the criticism show what it means to you. Do you consider it a sign that you're deficient in some way? Or do you think it's an opportunity to learn something? The criticism itself doesn't have much meaning for you until you think about it in a particular way.

In a four-part message, the thought shows how you're making sense of a situation, person, thought, or feeling described in the referent. The thought lets both you and your listener clearly understand the meaning you give that referent. Without your thought, they have to guess how you might be making sense of it.

You might say to your manager, "I've noticed that my quarterly reports are shorter than those from other members of the team." While this referent tells her what your message is about (your quarterly reports), it doesn't tell her what you think about the situation or reasons you're making this observation. She might well think, "Yes, and . . . ?" But what if you added this thought: "I wonder if I need to include more detailed information in my reports." Then your manager would understand how you're interpreting your observation (the referent) and what its relevance is to you. Knowing what you think about the referent helps both of you have a fruitful conversation about it.

We recommend using both provisional language and I-language when phrasing your thoughts. Then they're more likely to be accurate and easier for the other person to hear. For instance:

Referent: I didn't see you at Jacqui's soccer match last Saturday. As I recall, we both agreed to meet there.

Thought: *For me*, supporting Jacqui is a high priority. *I don't know* what to make of your absence.

"I realize that I . . . ," "I think that I . . . ," "I assume that I . . . ," "I believe that I . . . ," "I wonder if I . . . ," and "I notice that I . . ." are all examples of I-language phrases that can begin thoughts. Here's another example:

Referent: When you mentioned my divorce to our friends before I was ready to reveal it to them . . .

Thought: *I realized* that I'm taking longer than I'd expected to go public with being divorced.

You might have more than one thought about your referent. Remember the earlier referent about a company's new sick-leave policy? Here are two thoughts that might go with it.

Referent: I see that the new insurance policy has changes that will affect how much coverage I'll have for my illness.

Thought 1: I wonder if I'll have enough insurance to cover my expenses.

Thought 2: I think I might have to dip into my savings.

Sometimes you can have a *forked* message, or a message with one referent and two differing thoughts about it. The construction "On the one hand" and "On the other hand" is useful for organizing forked messages. For example:

Referent: When I heard you start talking before Anthony had finished his presentation in today's meeting . . .

Thought 1: On the one hand, I think part of my job is making sure people can finish what they're saying before someone else jumps in.

Thought 2: On the other hand, I'm also interested in what you have to say.

You-Language in Referents and Thoughts

Occasionally a referent might say something you're thinking about another person. It may be phrased in you-language, but you can clearly indicate it's your own point of view with phrases like "I think that . . ." or "I assume that . . . ." In other words, you acknowledge that you're projecting a thought, feeling, or motivation onto the other person.

For instance: "When I come home from work and you don't ask me how my day was, *I think you might not care about how I'm doing.*" The italicized statement is in you-language; the speaker is projecting a thought onto the other person. Yet "I think" (I-language) and "you *might* not care" (you-language and provisional language) indicate that what the speaker is saying is their own opinion, not a fact.

Referents about another person need to have a follow-up I-thought. It would tell the listener what the overall referent means to the speaker. The previous referent ("When I come home from work and you don't ask me how my day was") already contains a thought phrased in you-language. But it's the follow-up thought, phrased in I-language, that tells the listener how the referent affects the speaker.

Referent: When I come home from work and you don't ask me about my day, *I think you might not care how I'm doing* (you-thought).

Thought: I start to question how important I am to you (I-thought).

Part 3: The Feeling

In a four-part message, your thought reveals the meaning you give to the referent; your feeling shows how you emotionally relate to this meaning. We define *feelings* as the emotional responses that accompany your thoughts. The two are closely linked: how you think about the referent shapes your feelings.

Here are feelings that go with the thoughts in previous examples:

Referent: When you mentioned my divorce to our friends before I was ready to reveal it to them . . .

Thought: I realized that I'm taking longer than I'd expected to go public with being divorced.

Feeling: I felt uncomfortable.

Referent: I didn't see you at Jacqui's soccer match last Saturday. As I recall, we both agreed to meet there.

Thought: For me, supporting Jacqui is a high priority. I don't know what to make of your absence.

Feeling: I feel upset.

The Importance of Feelings in a Message

Expressing both your thoughts and your feelings can create a more well-rounded, influential message. Sometimes in important conversations, we give feelings too much weight; other times, we don't give them enough. Not thinking about the potential consequences of an angry outburst at a business meeting is an example of overemphasizing a feeling. On the other hand, using only reason to try to persuade someone to do something, without conveying the emotional impact their actions would have on you, might not be as compelling to them.

Your company's human resources director may not think your message about the new sick-leave policy is that urgent if you include just thoughts. Adding how you feel at the thought of not getting all the time off you need clarifies your distress. Here's how the first three parts of that message might look:

Referent: I see that the new insurance policy has changes that will affect how much coverage I'll have for my illness.

Thought 1: I wonder if I'll have enough insurance to cover my expenses.

Thought 2: I think I might have to dip into my savings.

Feeling: I feel anxious.

In the same way, your thoughts alone might not persuade your partner to express interest when you get home from work. But knowing that you feel worried might touch them emotionally, so that they feel more empathy. Before talking with your partner, you might sketch out the first three parts of your message in this way:

Referent: When I come home from work and you don't ask me about my day, I think you might not care how I'm doing.

Thought: I start to question how important I am to you.

Feeling: I feel worried.

Including a feeling in your message is typically helpful. In some organizational settings, however, expressing feelings might not fit well with the culture. In that case, you could omit them.

Including More Than One Feeling

If one feeling is too limiting, your message may include two or more. Multiple feelings are especially common in messages with more than one thought, such as forked messages. For example:

Referent: When I heard you start talking before Shawna had finished her presentation in today's meeting . . .

Thought 1: On the one hand, I think part of my job is to make sure people can finish what they're saying before someone else jumps in.

Thought 2: On the other hand, I'm interested in what you have to say.

Feelings: I feel concerned and curious too.

Beware of Thoughts Masquerading as Feelings

In informal speech, the words *think* and *feel* are often used inter-changeably. The problem is, people too often mistake their thoughts for their feelings. For instance, when you say, "I *feel that* I should do better," you may think you're expressing a feeling. In fact, you're sharing a thought: "I *think* I should do better." Putting the word *that* after "I feel" makes what follows a thought, not a feeling.

Politicians' speeches are loaded with examples of thoughts mas-querading as feelings. They often say, "I feel that" followed by an opinion rather than an actual feeling. Feelings can often seem more compelling than thoughts, and saying "I feel that" can give the impression of greater authenticity and commitment. You are less likely to be swayed by these false emotional appeals when you under-stand that thoughts and feelings are equal but separate parts of a complete message.

You also mistake your thoughts for your feelings when you say, "I feel disrespected"—or *manipulated, misunderstood, rejected, unloved,* or *taken for granted.* These statements are what we call *dis-guised you-thoughts.* Instead of describing how *you* feel, they actually reveal your thoughts about the other person. They're really saying, "I think you don't respect me," "I think you're manipulative," "I think you're rejecting me," "I think you don't love me," "I think you're taking me for granted." They're additional examples of the faux I-language discussed in chapter 11.

It's not just negative projections that can masquerade as feelings. Statements such as "I feel accepted," "I feel valued," and "I feel cared for" might sound nice, but they're still you-thoughts trying to pose as feelings. They still contain your projections about the other person: "I think you accept me," "I think you value me," "I think you care for me."

The "List of Feelings" that follows can help you distinguish feel-ings from thoughts. These feeling words fit with I-language. You're more likely to get your message across if you use the feeling words on the list instead of disguised you-thoughts (especially negative ones). Plus, with an enlarged feeling vocabulary, you can convey how you feel with more nuance and specificity, instead of using vague phrases like "I feel good" or "I feel bad."

List of Feelings

Note: The relative intensity of the feeling words on this list is subjective. How intense a particular feeling is compared to others on the list can certainly vary from person to person.

Excitement	Pleasure	Distress	Grief
chipper	amiable	fretful	blue
amused	calm	impatient	sad
cheery	mellow	aggravated	disappointed
delighted	at ease	agitated	discouraged
gleeful	warm	abashed	gloomy
jolly	happy	annoyed	lonely
jovial	peaceful	discontented	glum
merry	touched	displeased	melancholic
excited	pleased	dissatisfied	sympathetic
enthusiastic	relaxed	disturbed	sorrowful
joyous	relieved	regretful	unhappy
jubilant	satisfied	irritated	dismal
thrilled	serene	rankled	deflated
elated	tender	dissonant	dejected
splendid	comfortable	frustrated	despondent
	glad	conflicted	forlorn
	amorous	pained	mournful
	marvelous	perturbed	desolate
	enthralled	riled up	despair
	turned on	shaken	
	ecstatic	anguished	
	exalted	overwhelmed	
	blissful	shattered	

Fear	Disgust	Resolution	Wonder
concerned	averse	assured	interested
on edge	repelled	certain	curious
uncertain	repulsed	sure	intrigued
insecure	ashamed	grateful	bemused
shy	disdainful	devoted	surprised
apprehensive	contemptuous	confident	puzzled
anxious	repugnance	determined	startled
nervous	revolted	encouraged	perplexed
worried	loathing	optimistic	bewildered
leery	nauseated	hardy	baffled
embarrassed	scornful	strong	confused
afraid	sickened	potent	boggled
frightened		resolved	enchanted
scared		inspired	amazed
alarmed		courageous	astounded
panicked		daring	astonished
horrified		fearless	awed
terrified			aghast
			appalled
			awestruck

You-thoughts disguised as feelings	disrespected, manipulated, controlled, misunderstood, ignored, blamed, not listened to, unheard, taken for granted, put down, rejected, insulted, shut out, abandoned, punished, excluded, betrayed, picked on, unloved, unvalued, judged, unsupported, unaccepted, unappreciated
	Although less likely to be problematic, the following are also you-thoughts disguised as feelings: respected, understood, heard, seen, valued, supported, accepted, taken care of, appreciated.

The Benefit of Distinguishing Thoughts from Feelings

The ability to identify your thoughts is an aspect of metacognition. It's also a key critical thinking skill. Sometimes it's hard to know what you're thinking, but if you know how you're feeling, you can often figure it out. Thoughts and feelings are interdependent, each affecting the other. Your thoughts suggest possible feelings, and your feelings point to possible thoughts. You can often infer one from the other.

Suppose you're leaving work with unfinished tasks on your to-do list. You feel dissatisfied. If you look at your thoughts, they might say, "I didn't manage my time as efficiently as I would have liked today." Or maybe, "If I didn't have to be in meetings all day, I'd have gotten more done." Or, "I have too much on my plate. I can't make much headway." Any of these thoughts might go with the feeling of dissatisfaction.

Distinguishing thoughts from feelings might seem like nitpicking, but when you blur this distinction, it's more difficult to recognize how your thoughts fuel your feelings. And if you want to shift your feelings, knowing how your thoughts affect them is crucial. After a first date you might think, "Wow, I talked about myself way too much! I should have listened to her more." You'll probably feel disappointed or discouraged at that thought. On the other hand, maybe you think, "Okay, I talked about myself quite a bit. But I'll text her and explain how nervous I was. Then I'll ask if I can make it up to her on our next date." With this thought, you'll probably feel more hopeful.

As we explored in chapter 10, shifting your thoughts can dramatically influence how you feel. And you'll probably have an easier time shifting your thoughts than changing your feelings. If you're in an unhappy mood and want to feel better, consider different ways to think about what's happening. Cognitive behavior therapy (CBT), an effective method for treating depression, uses this approach to address problematic feelings. (For more on CBT, please see "Recommended Resources.")

Part 4: The Intention

Knowing and expressing intentions is essential for resolving conflicts and living harmoniously with others. For example, as authors, our intention is to present ideas you can readily use to improve your communication with others. Notice that we didn't state our intention negatively: "We hope our ideas won't be too hard to use." By putting our intention in positive language, we shaped a clearer path towards one of our writing goals.

Negatively stated intentions say what you *don't want*. Positively stated intentions say what you *do want*. If you're like most people, you're probably more adept at saying what you don't want. As a result, you may sometimes find it tricky to say what you do want. Phrasing your intention in the negative typically makes it harder for others to know how to help you. Moreover, a positively stated intention sets a less adversarial, more productive atmosphere. Plus, it usually just feels better.

Suppose a dad says to his son, "Don't text during dinner." Compare this negatively phrased intention with a positively phrased one: "I'd like you to put your phone away while we're eating so we can all talk together." Or suppose you say to a colleague, "Don't send me the data at the last minute." This negatively stated intention doesn't say what you do want. A positively stated intention clarifies it: "I want to get the data at least twenty-four hours before the staff meeting." When you're specific about what you want, your listener doesn't have to guess.

Here's how the intentions for two previous examples might be phrased:

Referent: When I heard you start talking before Anthony had finished his presentation in today's meeting . . .

Thought 1: On the one hand, I think part of my job is to make sure people can finish what they're saying before someone else jumps in.

Thought 2: On the other hand, I'm interested in what you have to say.

Feeling: I feel concerned and curious too.

Intention: In the future, before you begin speaking, I'd like you to consider whether others have finished what they're saying. Once they're done, I'd like to hear your ideas.

Referent: I see that the new insurance policy has changes that will affect how much coverage I'll have for my illness.

Thought 1: I wonder if I'll have enough insurance to cover my expenses.

Thought 2: I think I might have to dip into my savings.

Feeling: I feel anxious.

Intention: I'd like to better understand the new insurance policy so I can budget for any additional costs.

Interpersonal and Inner Intentions

There are two types of intentions: *inner intentions* and *interpersonal intentions*. Inner intentions express what you want *for yourself.* Interpersonal intentions express what you want *in relation to others.*

If you think you're not studying enough, a positively stated inner intention might be, "I want to spend more time studying" or "I'd like to develop better study habits."

"I'd like you to put your phone away while we're eating so we can all talk together" is an *interpersonal* intention. Interpersonal intentions also fit as part 4 of the following examples.

Referent: When I come home from work and you don't ask me how my day was, I think you might not care how I'm doing.

Thought: I start to question how important I am to you.

Feeling: I feel worried.

Intention: I wish you'd give me a hug and ask me how my day was so that I know you care.

Referent: When you mentioned my divorce to our friends before I was ready to reveal it to them . . .

Thought: I realized that I'm taking longer than I'd expected to go public with being divorced.

Feeling: I felt uncomfortable.

Intention: I'd like information about my divorce to stay just between the two of us for now.

Referent: I didn't see you at Jacqui's soccer match last Saturday. As I recall, we both agreed to meet there.

Thought: For me, supporting Jacqui is a high priority. I don't know what to make of your absence.

Feeling: I feel upset.

Intention: I'm really hoping you can make it to her next match on Sunday. If not, I hope you'll text her before it starts to wish her good luck.

No matter how skillfully crafted your intention is, there's no guarantee you'll get what you want. You can't force someone to do or feel what you wish. The aim of clear communication is not to control others, but to promote mutual understanding and to influence them. Using this four-part message format when necessary usually gives the other person enough complete information to understand you. It can also increase the odds that they'll stay open to hearing what you say. (See chapter 8 for more about influence versus control. In chapter 14, we'll discuss how positively stated goals are useful in resolving conflicts.)

Using a Four-Part Message to Give Critical Feedback

Receiving critical feedback can be challenging for many people, even when that feedback is well intentioned or they've specifically asked for it. One reason is it often comes in the form of an incomplete message.

If you give someone incomplete yet positive feedback, your listener will typically fill in the missing pieces in benign ways. But if your feedback is incomplete and critical, your listener might make negative assumptions about the missing information. Using a complete message can prevent this problem:

- Your referent clarifies the specific action or behavior you're giving the person feedback on.

- The thought and feeling, stated in I-language, tell the other person how you were affected by their behavior.

- The positively stated intention lets them know what you want.

Imagine a client has emailed you with a time-sensitive question about their account. You need some information from a coworker in order to answer. You know she's been at work, but she hasn't responded to your texts and emails. Here's how you might craft your four-part message to her:

> It's been three days since I contacted you for financial information for our client. I can't respond to her request until I receive your data. I feel concerned. I'd like you to send me your data by 4 p.m. today. If you can't, I'd like to know immediately.

Now imagine that you and a friend have decided to pool your money to buy a wedding gift for another friend. You paid for the gift, and your friend agreed to reimburse you for their half. Two weeks after the wedding, however, you still haven't received your friend's share. Unhappy, you decide to bring up the situation:

> When we agreed to go in together on the gift, as I recall, you said you'd pay me back before we went to the wedding. It's a week after the wedding, and I still haven't received your payment. I don't think I'll be able to fully pay

my credit card bill without your share. I feel concerned and irritated. I'd like to know what happened to your payment and receive it by the end of this week.

Thinking through the four parts of your feedback message helps you couch your feedback in a way the other person is more likely to take in. But even when you use a well-composed four-part message, they still might respond defensively. Most people are sensitive to feedback that indicates they did something wrong. If you receive pushback, be prepared to shift to reflective listening. Doing so can help your listener feel calmer and become more receptive to your subsequent message. And their objections often reveal what's keeping them from taking in your feedback.

Discerning the Four Parts in Others' Messages

When you know the four parts of a complete message, you may start noticing when others include referents, thoughts, feelings, and intentions in their messages—and when they don't. With practice, you'll be able to detect the missing parts even when the other person hasn't done so. Sometimes, surprisingly, you might even understand what people are trying to say more fully than they do.

The four parts of a complete message are interrelated and can be inferred from each other. The thought often suggests the intention. One way to think about it is asking, "Given that the speaker is thinking X, what would they want?" Similarly, the intention often suggests the thought: "Given that they want X, what might they be thinking? The thought can also be a bridge between the referent and the feeling. Based on the person's referent, what might they be thinking in order to feel what they're feeling?

Suppose your sister comes to you and offers this referent: "I was looking forward to being a bridesmaid in your wedding this summer. But now that my job has been eliminated, I'm financially strapped." She then shares her thought and a feeling: "I don't know how I can pay for a bridesmaid's dress on top of my travel expenses. I feel embarrassed." Based on these three parts of her message, you could infer her unstated intentions: perhaps she wants to back out of being a bridesmaid and for you to feel okay with her decision.

Now imagine the same message, but this time your sister includes a referent, a feeling, and an intention: "I was looking forward to being a bridesmaid in your wedding this summer. But now that my job has been eliminated, I'm financially strapped. I feel disappointed. I'd like to back out of being a bridesmaid and hope you'll be okay with my decision." The only thing missing from this message is her thought. The referent "I'm financially strapped" suggests that money is a key element in her thinking. So you might guess that she thinks she can't easily afford both a bridesmaid dress and travel expenses.

If you think you've detected a missing part, you can use reflective listening to help the other person fill in the blanks. Doing so can help them clarify their message—for both themselves and for you. Second, as you track unstated, implicit parts of their message, you'll probably learn more about what's going on for them. Then you can more fully understand their perspective, even if they don't explicitly state it. Finally, helping them clarify what they're trying to say can lead to a greater sense of connection or even intimacy between the two of you. (See chapter 5 for more on using reflective listening to discern implicit details without inserting your own assumptions and judgments.)

Four-part messages aren't necessary for all interactions. Again, they're most useful for difficult or important conversations when you don't want people making inaccurate assumptions. In friendly, casual conversations, people often fill in your missing information in favorable or unproblematic ways. But in stressful conversations, people tend to assume that your missing information is more negative than it might be.

Along with I-language, using four-part messages is one of the more challenging skills that we teach. Please be patient with yourself as you mentally digest the nuances of the four parts and put this skill into practice. We're confident you'll appreciate its value once you get the hang of it.

Summary: Four-Part Messages

- A complete message includes four parts: a referent, a thought, a feeling, and an intention.

- A message that includes all four parts usually provides enough information to minimize potential misunderstandings.

- The referent tells your listener what the message is about.

- The thought tells your listener the meaning you give to the referent.

- Referents and thoughts in I-language and provisional language are typically easier for your listener to take in.

- The feeling tells your listener how you relate emotionally to the meaning expressed in the thought.

- The intention tells your listener what you want.

- State your intention positively, saying what you *do* want. Stating what you *don't* want is less likely to move the conversation forward.

- Your message might contain more than one thought, feeling, and intention.

Practice
Creating a Complete Message

This exercise walks you step by step through creating a four-part message. We've included an example to demonstrate each step.

1. Pick a potentially challenging conversation you'd like to prepare for. Don't select the *most* challenging conversation you expect to have—just one you think a little prep work could be useful for. (As you become more skillful at crafting four-part messages, you'll be able to prepare for increasingly difficult conversations.)

   Example: You're concerned about your aging father's living situation and want to talk with him about it.

2. Write down your **referent**, or what your message refers to. Make sure it's *specific* enough for the other person to know what you're referring to.

   Example referent: Lately, I've been thinking about how you live alone, at age eighty-five, and that you've fallen twice in the past two months.

3. Write down your initial thought(s)—your beliefs, assumptions, inferences, and interpretations based on the referent. Then give them a second look: are they stated in I-language? If not, revise the wording.

   Example thought: I realize that, with Jenny, the kids, and my job, I can't be there to help you as often as I'd like.

4. Write down your feeling(s)—the emotions that accompany your thought(s). Then look at what you wrote and assess:

   • Is this feeling directly related to your I-thought?

- Is this feeling a true feeling and not a you-thought disguised as an I-thought?

Revise your feeling statements as needed to ensure they're directly connected to your stated thought(s) and are in I-language.

Example feelings: I feel sad and worried.

5. Write down your intention(s)—what you want, stated in the positive.

Example intention(s): I want you to be safe and happy. I'd like to explore the possibility of you getting more care at home or in a retirement community.

Practice

Detecting Missing Parts of Someone's Message

In this exercise, you'll practice finding missing parts in other people's messages based on one or more of the other stated parts.

Below are three messages. In each, one of the four parts is missing. First see if you can identify which three parts are present. Then you can make an educated guess about how the missing part might be stated. Use the answer key at the end to find out if you correctly identified the missing part.

Message 1: A friend says, "I texted two times on Monday and didn't hear back from you. I feel worried. I hope things are okay between us."

1. To figure out which part is missing, write down which three parts *are* included. What is:

   - the referent?

   - the thought?

   - the feeling?

   - the intention?

2. How might this friend have stated the part of the message that's missing?

Message 2: A coworker is addressing a problem with a fellow team member. He says, "You texted me you'd be late for your shift right when it started. Even though my shift had ended, I stayed an extra hour to cover for you. Finding out at the last minute I'll be staying late doesn't work for me. I feel annoyed."

1. Which three parts *are* included in this message:

   - the referent?

   - the thought?

   - the feeling?

   - the intention?

2. What is the missing part, and how might the coworker have phrased it?

Message 3: A partner says, "When we're making decisions about Kwan's education and we have different views, I think I could consider your ideas more easily if I knew you were also considering mine. I want us to be open to each other's ideas when we're discussing his education."

1. Which three parts *are* included in this message:

   - the referent?

- the thought?
- the feeling?
- the intention?

2. What is the missing part, and how might this spouse have phrased it?

Answer Key

Message 1: This message is missing a thought. For example, "I didn't know what to make of not hearing from you. I thought I might have said something that upset you."

Message 2: This message is missing an intention. For example, "In the future, text me a few hours in advance if you're going to be late."

Message 3: This message is missing a feeling. For example, "I feel frustrated."

Chapter 13

Framing Your Message

Setting Up Your Conversation

If you're visiting the Louvre museum and see Leonardo da Vinci's iconic *Mona Lisa*, you'll notice that its frame highlights the painting. Similarly, a frame around your message highlights what you want to emphasize in a conversation and how you'd like your message to be received. The frame also provides a cognitive shortcut that helps you and others make sense of complex information. It orients both you and them by:

- announcing and narrowing down what you wish to talk about,
- helping both of you understand your message's overall purpose,
- preparing the other person for a potentially sensitive topic,
- establishing the tone and direction for the conversation.

For most messages, there are any number of frames you could use to preface them. Typically, the most useful frames are those that invite people to listen to and consider your message. Framing entails communicating about your communication, which is called metacommunication. When you talk about your communication, you're metacommunicating.[1]

Setting Up Your Message

A message conveys *what* you're talking about; a frame introduces *how* you'd like the other person to think about it. The frame is not part of the message itself; instead, it conveys your aim for the conversation. It sets the tone and prepares the other person for the message to come.

Let's say you need to talk with a friend about a birthday dinner party the two of you have been planning for a mutual friend. You might open the conversation with a frame such as this: "I'd like to talk with you about changing our cooking plan. I feel awkward asking for a change when I've already signed on to cook certain dishes." This frame lets your friend know immediately that you're not blithely asking him to cook more, that this isn't a frivolous request. It also tells him that you want to be consistent and live up to your agreements. Then you'd share your message: "I've realized that I agreed to cook more dishes than I think I can handle. I feel a little worried. I hope you can take on more of the cooking. I also want to make sure that you're okay with how much help I'm asking for."

When you're thinking about how to frame a message, it helps to consider how you hope the other person will receive it and what you want your message to achieve. In the previous example, you want to reduce the amount of food you have to cook while staying on good terms with your friend.

Here's another example: You started going out with your friend's ex-boyfriend not long after they ended their relationship. You want to tell her about it. Ideally, you want her to feel okay with you and to continue your close friendship. A good frame would help you ease into this delicate topic. You might try this one: "I want to talk with you about Jason. Even though this conversation could be difficult for us, I value our friendship a lot and want to be honest with you." This frame asks your friend to try to hear your message in a positive light and appreciate your honesty while also acknowledging that she might think or feel differently.

Then you'd share your message: "I started going out with Jason shortly after you broke up with him. I'm not sure how you might feel about this. I notice I've been stalling about bringing it up. I feel anxious. I'd like to know what you think. I hope you and I will still continue to have a close relationship." Now your intention for the conversation is clear. Without first hearing the frame, your friend wouldn't know that you'd thought a lot about how to share your news with her. She still might be unhappy that you're going out with her former boyfriend, but at least the frame has alerted her that delicate or potentially disturbing news is coming and that you care about her response.

Frames can be used for other reasons too. First, they can add clarity. If you want to prevent a colleague from misunderstanding your previous message, you might open with, "I'd like to clarify what I meant in our conversation this morning." They can also set up encouraging messages. To bolster your caregiver's morale, for instance, you might frame your message by saying, "I want to let you know how much I appreciate your help."

A good frame states your aims for the conversation in positive language. It says what you want, not what you don't want. "Now, I don't want you to get mad, but . . . ," "Okay, don't panic," and "Please don't get upset" are all examples of commonly used, but negatively phrased frames. Odds are, these frames will trigger a reaction that's opposite of what you're hoping for. Most people's mental and emotional alarm bells go off when they hear these phrases, no matter how nicely you say them. Here's an equivalent frame stated in positive terms: "I need to tell you something important, and I hope you can listen with an open mind and heart."

When you can skillfully use frames, others are more likely to understand your overall intention and stay open to what you're saying. However, the same disclaimer for four-part messages also applies to frames: You can't control how others receive your frame. You can only hope to influence them.

Self-Talk Influences How You Frame Your Message

The frames you use for your messages are often based on your self-talk. You might say to yourself before an important business conversation, "There's every chance this negotiation will turn into a knock-down, bare-knuckled fight." This type of self-talk might support an overly combative mindset that isn't helpful. Consider how your mindset might change if you revised your self-talk to say, "This could be a tough negotiation. But with a little bit of creativity and skillful listening, I think we can prevent it from becoming adversarial and come up with a deal that works for all of us. Shifting from combative to friendlier, more cooperation-oriented self-talk can set a different tone for your frame.

Suppose you think it's time to talk with your ten-year-old son about sex. Before approaching him, notice your self-talk. Are you thinking, "I don't know if I'm ready for 'the sex talk,' but I know it's a good opportunity to connect with Darryl and make sure he's getting useful information"? Or are you thinking something more like, "This might be the most awkward conversation between a parent and kid in the history of the known universe"?

Whatever your self-talk is, you can bet it will color the frame you come up with. Take note of your self-talk and assess how useful it might be. You can adjust your self-talk as you prepare for your conversation. For example:

- This conversation could become very awkward, but it could also be eye-opening. The world has changed a lot since I was a kid. I'm curious to see what Darryl has already learned and where he picked it up.

- I feel nervous talking about sex. However, I want Darryl to get sex information from me and feel comfortable asking me questions instead of going to other kids or the internet.

- I'm not sure I'm ready for this conversation. I hope I can find a way to honestly answer Darryl's questions. Even if the conversation gets awkward sometimes, I think it will be worthwhile for both of us.

After you've taken into account your self-talk, you can consider how to frame the conversation with Darryl. For example: "I don't know how much you already know about sex. But as your dad, I think it's my job to talk about it with you. I hope you're up for talking with me."

"Is This a Good Time to Talk?"

No matter how carefully you've planned your message or set it up with a frame, the timing might not be right for having a conversation. As part of your frame, you can ask whether it's a good time for the other person to talk with you.

If they say no, don't just wait for another opportunity. Ask to schedule a time that you can both talk, especially if it's an important conversation. The more significant the conversation or the bigger the potential consequences, the more important it is that the timing works for both of you.

Using Frames with Four-Part Messages

Frames can be very helpful when you're preparing for a conversation that could have consequences. Again, we recommend thinking ahead to ensure that your message contains complete information, as described in chapter 12. Then consider what kind of frame you might use to open the conversation.

Imagine that you're preparing for a conversation with your manager. Ahead of time, you think through the four parts of your message to ensure that it's complete yet doesn't contain superfluous details. You sketch out your message like this:

Referent: In our last meeting, you said you'd evaluate my performance based on last year's job description.

Thought: I think that my role in the organization has expanded significantly. Last year's job description seems too limited.

Feeling: I feel concerned.

Intention:I'm hoping my performance appraisal will take into account my expanded role.

What kind of a frame might suit this message? Perhaps you could say, "I'd like to discuss some changes that could affect my upcoming performance appraisal."

Here's another example. You and your cousin seem to argue every time you get together. You don't like this situation and want to change it. Before getting together with him again, you prepare a four-part message, making sure to use I-language for the thought and feeling:

Referent: Often when we talk about politics . . .

Thought: I get caught up in arguing with you and . . .

Feeling: feel frustrated.

Intention: I'd like to find a friendlier way to discuss politics with you.

You can also use I-language in your frame: "I'd like to discuss a pattern that I often fall into when we talk about politics." As you already know, using I-language is likely to trigger less defensiveness.

Let's look at one more example. You're a student who's three-quarters of the way through a college semester. You're concerned about your final grade in your psychology class, and you want to talk to the professor. Here's how your frame and subsequent message might look:

Frame: I'd like to discuss my final grade before the course ends and hope you'll consider my request.

Referent: As you might know, I'll need at least a 3.5 GPA to qualify for financial aid next semester. Based on my grades in this course so far, I might not qualify.

Thought: It's crucial for me to complete my degree. If I don't, I won't be able to go on for my MBA.

Feeling: I feel worried.

Intention: I'd like to do an extra-credit project to raise my grade, and I'm open to other options you suggest.

Frames in Mass Communication

Framing goes beyond one-to-one conversations. Frames are used in the media and politics to influence how people think about and discuss various topics. People who want to leverage their influence strategically choose frames that steer conversations in specific directions.

For example, the issue of abortion is framed differently by those who support and oppose it. People who think abortion should be legal typically believe a fetus isn't a person until it's living outside the womb, and it doesn't have the same rights as a person until after birth. But the woman carrying the fetus does have rights, and seen through this frame, preventing her from having a legal abortion is a violation of her rights. Those who oppose legalized abortion usually consider a fetus to be a person from the moment of conception. Seen through this frame, legalized abortion is a violation of the rights of the fetus/person. Your attraction to either of these frames will influence your perception of abortion and which laws you believe are appropriate.

Another example is conflict and the metaphors people use to frame it. Is a conflict framed as a war in which battle lines are drawn and casualties are a natural consequence? Or is it depicted as a situation where different parties come together to sit at a bargaining table and discuss their positions? The war metaphor gears people to be oppositional. The bargaining table metaphor orients people to work together to seek a common ground.[2]

Understanding how frames shape perception can help you think more critically about issues. It can also help you recognize how others think about issues, which can be useful if you want to influence them. If you can speak in terms of how *they* frame an issue, rather than trying to prematurely convince them to accept your framing, your influence will typically have more leverage.

Practice
Framing Your Message

In this exercise, you'll practice framing by applying this skill to a situation in your own life. We've provided examples to illustrate each step.

1. Think about an upcoming conversation that has consequences for you.

   Example 1: You want to ask your ex-spouse to change your shared child-care arrangement.

   Example 2: You want to ask your manager to increase your salary for the next year.

2. Consider how you want the other person to receive your message and what your overall objective is. You're not composing your frame yet—just capturing your starting-point thoughts. Jot down a concise statement, making sure to say what you want (instead of what you don't want).

   Example 1: I want my spouse to be open to my request to change our child-care arrangement.

   Example 2: I want my manager to listen to the reasons I think I deserve a raise.

3. Craft your four-part message, as explained in chapter 12. Again, you're not composing the frame yet; you'll create it in step 4.

Example 1:

Referent: My company requested I meet with a new team for the next three Mondays, on my usual child-care days. They want to me to join a new project that will increase my salary.

Thought: I realize that asking you to switch child-care days over the next three weeks disrupts our schedule. However, I think this is a rare opportunity that will help my career.

Feeling: I feel excited.

Intention: I want to check whether switching my child-care day from Monday to Tuesday for three weeks could work for you.

Example 2:

Referent: Over the past two years, all my projects have been completed under budget. I've also taken on two additional projects in the past six months.

Thought: I think the work I've done over the past two years has demonstrated my value and commitment to our company.

Feeling: I feel proud.

Intention: I'd like you to consider increasing my salary, starting in the next quarter.

4. Now create a frame to set up your message. Keep it short: just one or two sentences will do. Don't overload it with detail. Don't include information that's part of your complete message.

Frame for example 1: I appreciate how well our current child-care arrangement has been working for us. I'm hoping that you'd be open to a temporary change for the next three weeks. Is now a good time to talk?

Frame for example 2: I'd like to talk with you about my salary before our department's budget is set for the next year. I'm hoping we can discuss it sometime this week.

Chapter 14

Managing Conflict

Skills for Navigating Disagreements

Differences between people are inevitable. Given everyone's varying backgrounds, experience, personalities, and ways of looking at things, disagreements are bound to arise. At the same time, conflict often feels so uncomfortable that many people shy away from it. If you think conflict is wrong, bad, or dangerous, you might even avoid it entirely. Fortunately, you can learn how to handle conflict in a constructive way.

In a conflict that's been worked through constructively, both people believe their primary concerns have been heard and addressed, and they feel reasonably satisfied with the outcome. Very likely, they also believe the other person has understood them, and they feel more connected to each other (or at least not more alienated from one another). As a bonus, they may feel optimistic about their ability to work together to resolve conflicts between them in the future.

In this chapter, we'll share two key conflict communication skills: identifying your goals and choosing a conflict-management strategy. With these skills, you can increase the odds of resolving a conflict in a way that's acceptable and feels good to both you and the other person. We'll also show you how some of the skills from earlier chapters, like reflective listening and I-language, can help you have more constructive conflict conversations.

Identify Your Goals

During a conflict, it helps to understand what each person wants. If you can do that, you're more likely to find potential resolutions that work for both of you. If you know only what *you* want, you might focus on outcomes that work for you alone. Understanding both your own goals and those of the other person is also essential for maintaining trust and goodwill.

There are different types of goals, including content goals, relationship goals, and short- and long-term goals. Though there are other types, understanding these three is particularly useful for conflict conversations.

Content and Relationship Goals

Your first and clearest goal usually focuses on the tangible content of the conflict—what each of you explicitly wants. For example, Alisha and Jacob disagree about what to do with their house after they're divorced. Jacob wants to sell it so he can have money to buy a small condo, where their seven-year-old son, Alex, can live with him part time. Alisha wants to keep the house so Alex can continue living in their familiar neighborhood and attending his school, an excellent one where he has many friends. They also disagree about how to divide their shared financial assets.

Adding to Alisha and Jacob's difficulty, their relationship goals don't overlap. Relationship goals focus on the type of association people want to have with each other. Psychologists William W. Wilmot and Joyce L. Hocker, who are experts on interpersonal conflict, put it this way: "Relationship goals define how each party wants to be treated by the other and the amount of interdependence they desire."[1] Alisha wants to be more autonomous. She wants to make financial decisions without having to consult Jacob. She also wants to feel free to make plans with friends on her own. But Jacob wants to stay more interdependent. He wants them to work together when making financial decisions or plans to be with their friends. On the surface, these relationship goals may seem to have little to do with the house disagreement. But they do influence it, as you'll see.

Couples can share similar relationship goals yet argue over their differing content goals. Suppose you and your partner have different ideas about vacation destinations. You want to go to the mountains, but your partner wants to go to the coast. These are two different content goals. Fortunately, your relationship goals are the same: you both want to feel close and enjoy being together.[2]

It's easy to forget or lose sight of relationship goals. Sometimes people get so focused on their content goals that it doesn't even occur to them how their relationship might be affected by the conflict and how they approach it. But people who live and/or work together, even for short periods of time, are interdependent to varying degrees. So paying attention to the quality of your relationships is an important aspect of managing conflicts.

Occasionally, relationship goals might take a backseat to content goals. Sometimes maintaining an equitable relationship isn't a high priority for you or the other person. Perhaps you know your alliance is only temporary or your interaction is a one-time occurrence. Or maybe you don't consider your relationship goals to have the same immediacy and urgency as your content goals. Recognizing when your content goals are clearly more important to you than your relationship goals will inform your choice of a conflict-management strategy.

Short-Term and Long-Term Goals

Your content and relationship goals can be a combination of short- or long-term goals. It's very common for people to focus more on their immediate or short-term goals, to the exclusion of their long-term goals, especially during heated conflicts.

Imagine an argument has cropped up between you and your partner about how much time you spend with each other. You think your partner is a workaholic and spends too much time dealing with professional texts and emails outside their workday. Your short-term goal is to persuade your partner to watch a movie with you tonight. One of your long-term goals is to have more personal time together. Another is to prevent future arguments on the same topic. The conflict quickly escalates, as do your emotions. After just a few minutes, your partner throws up their hands and says, "Fine! Have it your way. Let's watch the movie." The good news is, you've accomplished your short-term goal: your partner has stopped working and will watch a movie with you. But have you resolved the conflict in a way that will likely keep it from recurring? Probably not. You haven't achieved your long-term goals or even addressed them in your communication.

We encourage you to keep in mind what you want in both the short term and long term, as well as what your content and relationship goals are. Doing so will help you determine which conflict-management strategy to apply to your disagreement.

Prioritizing Your Goals

How important to you are each of your content, relationship, and short- and long-term goals? And how important are each of the other person's goals to them? Prioritizing particular goals can help you both narrow down which ones to pursue. That information can then help you choose an appropriate conflict-management strategy.

Discerning the Other Person's Goals

Ideally, both people will be able to share their own goals clearly and directly and take in the other person's goals, without getting caught up in judgments. But several problems can come up as you're identifying what each of you wants.

First, it's not unusual to assign a negative motivation to the other person. For example, you might assume they're intentionally trying to keep you from getting what you want. Very often, those assumptions are expressed (aloud or in your own mind) in you-language, such as, "She's just trying to piss me off," "He can't stand to see me happy," or "You care more about your own needs than mine." Sure, sometimes people might be out to thwart you. But most of the time, they're simply pursuing their own goals without taking yours into account. Sometimes they're fully aware that they're disregarding your goals, but frequently they aren't. Don't automatically assume others are purposely trying to block you or that they're intentionally ignoring what you want.

It's also not unusual to characterize other people or their goals in negative ways—especially when you don't understand those goals or they don't match the goals you'd have in the same situation. Again, this kind of thinking often expresses itself in you-language: "He's just being stubborn and selfish." "How can she not see how inconsiderate she's being?" "That's crazy! What a hypocrite you are!"

It's especially easy to fall into these traps when you're upset. Taking time to calm yourself and recover your emotional equanimity is important in these situations. Doing so might be challenging at first, but it typically becomes easier with practice. (See chapter 4 for specific suggestions.) Once you're feeling less reactive or emotionally triggered, you can check whether you're using you-language and, if so, consciously shift to I-language, as described in chapter 11.

Very often, negative views of the other person's intentions or motivations stem from your assumptions about their goals. Especially in ongoing or long-term relationships, you might think you know exactly what their goals or motivations are when in reality you're way off base. If tensions are already heightened between the two of you, you're more likely to see their intentions through a negative filter.

Having a conversation to clarify your respective goals is better than making inaccurate assumptions (negative or positive). You can initiate a goals conversation and set an amicable tone with a frame that uses I-language and states your positive intention. Here are some possibilities:

- I've just started to see what this disagreement is about for me. But I'm not that clear about what *you* want. I'd like to know more about what's important to you.

- After thinking about our last conversation, I realized that I don't fully understand what you want. I'd like to fill in the pieces I'm missing.

- I realized I might have made some incorrect assumptions. I want to check whether they're accurate before we talk about possible resolutions.

- During our conversation, I thought I clearly understood what you wanted. But thinking about it now, I realize that I don't quite understand what you meant by _____.

- I realized I was getting so caught up in my own ideas and what I wanted that I didn't listen that much to what you were saying. I'd like to circle back and listen more fully now.

- The last time we talked, I was too upset to listen. I've calmed down and can listen now.

- What I really want is to resolve our disagreement in a way that feels good to both of us. But to do this, I still need to know more about what you want.

From here, you can use reflective listening to ensure you've accurately understood what the other person wants. *Don't forget this crucial step.* And don't assume you've understood what they want after hearing only one sentence. Just listening and then saying, "Okay, I got it," "I understand," or similar phrases, is rarely enough.

Reflective listening can also come in handy for other problems that frequently come up in goal-clarifying conversations. First, it's common for people to state their goal as what they *don't* want. In your reflection, you can restate their negative phrasing to reflect what you think they *do* want.

Goal Stating What the Person Doesn't Want	Reflection Restating What the Person Does Want
"I don't want to get stressed out dealing with your family."	"You want to feel more relaxed when we're around my family."
"I don't want to accept the cuts to my benefits that come with my new health insurance."	"You'd like to see if you have any options for keeping your current health insurance benefits."
"I don't want to get all riled up talking about _____."	"You'd like to find a way to stay calmer when talking about _____."

(Positively stated goals are akin to positively stated intentions. They both express what you want and suggest a direction forward. Please refer back to chapter 12, "The Complete Message," especially the section "Part 4: The Intention," for more on positive versus negative phrasing.)

Sometimes people are reluctant to share their goals. They may think that it will trigger an uncomfortable reaction from you or in themselves. "If I tell you what I want, you're just going to get mad," they might say. Or, "I don't want to tell you. It's too embarrassing." Or perhaps, "I'd tell you, but I just don't think you'd understand." They may also think sharing their goals will only escalate the conflict. So when you ask what they want, they might say something like, "I really don't want to argue with you," "I'm sick of fighting about this," or "I just want this conflict to go away."

Although it may seem like they're being evasive or unhelpful, they're implicitly telling you something about their priorities. Your reflections can zero in on and clarify—for both of you—what those priorities are, as well as show them you're willing to listen and understand them.

Other Person's Statement	Potential Reflections
"If I tell you what I want, you're just going to get mad."	"You'd like me to stay calm when you tell me what you want." "You're concerned that telling me what you want will create more conflict between us.
"I don't want to tell you. It's too embarrassing."	"You think you might feel uncomfortable telling me what you want." "You'd like to feel more at ease when you talk about this."
"I'd tell you, but I just don't think you'd understand."	"You want me to try to understand where you're coming from." "You'd like to know that I understand what you want."
"I really don't want to argue with you."	"You'd like to resolve this conflict peacefully." "You want to work this out constructively."
"I'm sick of fighting about this."	"Perhaps you're ready to move on." "You'd really like to be closer to finding a resolution that works for both of us."
"I just want this conflict to go away."	"You'd like to get past this conflict as soon as possible."

Remember that skillful reflective listening requires temporarily setting aside your own thoughts and reactions. Be careful not to let your assumptions and judgments sneak into your reflections. Staying open to the other person's corrections is also crucial. When you're reflecting, you're demonstrating how you've understood the other person. Then they can confirm, correct, or add to your understanding as needed.

Reflective listening might seem like a time-consuming way to clarify the other person's goals. Wouldn't it be easier and more straightforward to just ask? The problem is, when you ask people what they want, they might not be able to tell you. "I'm not sure" is a common answer. And being confronted with direct questions can be stressful for some people. Reflective listening is often less confrontational and a more inviting way to elicit information.

Emily and George are discussing how to stay fit during the coronavirus pandemic. Here's how George could use reflective listening to clarify Emily's implicit goal.

Emily: I know you've been looking forward to working out at the gym again. But I don't think working out indoors is safe yet.

George: The gym is following the Center for Disease Control's guidelines about masks and social distancing. They regularly sanitize the equipment. Plus we're both vaccinated.

Emily: Okay. But I'm worried about how well the vaccines will protect us from the variants.

George: (reflecting) So, even with our vaccinations, you're still worried about the variants.

Emily: Yes, at least until we know more. We still might have to be cautious depending on how well the vaccines hold up.

George: I agree that being cautious makes sense. I also think that following the CDC guidelines at the gym will keep us safe when we go back. I'm eager to get to the gym. And I want you to feel safe too.

Emily: (reflecting) So even though you're ready to get back to the gym, you're okay with exercising outdoors for now.

George: At least for now.

Emily and George have overlapping but slightly different content goals. They both want to stay safe and fit, but they differ on whether they feel safe working out at a gym. They both share the same unstated relationship goal: to maintain a harmonious relationship as they find a solution.[3]

Trying to guess another person's implicit goal is fine as long as you remain open to their corrections and ready to reflect those corrections back to them. And here's a helpful tip: when you're reflecting a person's implicit goal (guessing what the other person wants), use a tentative tone of voice so you don't come across as a know-it-all or assume you already know what they want.

Sometimes disagreements arise quickly and unexpectedly. In the heat of your reaction, you might not immediately know what you want. One way to figure it out is to consider what you don't want. For example, Emily initially knew that she didn't want to work out in the gym. After her conversation with George, she realized she still wanted to exercise; she'd just prefer to do so outdoors. Like many people, she first recognized what she *didn't* want before realizing what she *did* want.

Choose a Conflict-Management Strategy

There are several strategies you can use when addressing conflicts with others.[4] Which one you choose depends on:

- your content and relationship goals,
- how important each goal is to you,
- whether each goal is a short- or long-term one.

Collaborating

In collaborating, both your own goals and those of the other person are important to you. This strategy seeks solutions that don't feel like sacrifices to either person. It's a good fit when you and the other person have differing content goals, but both want to resolve the conflict constructively and maintain a collaborative relationship.

If you're good at finding collaborative solutions, you're probably good at thinking outside the box. Rather than fixating on a solution that works for you alone, you're able to recognize multiple possibilities that could work for both you and the other person.

Let's look again at the example of two partners disagreeing over vacation destinations. You want to visit the mountains; your partner wants to go somewhere near the ocean and spend time on a beach. The two of you might find a mountainous coastal region, such as the California coast, where you could spend time in the mountains and on the coast in a single trip. This collaboration satisfies both of your content goals, while at the same time honoring your shared relationship goal.

Compromising

When you can't find a solution with collaborating, compromising could be a viable strategy. As with collaborating, you regard your content goals and those of the other person as having equal weight. But with compromising, each of you gives up something in exchange for getting enough of what you want to feel satisfied.

In the vacation example, the two of you might decide to alternate going to the coast and the mountains. This solution is a compromise because each of you gives up your preferred destination every other time you take a vacation.

In a successful compromise, neither of you thinks you're giving up more than the other. You both believe your sacrifice is equal and recognize that you must give to get. Ideally, both of you are also *willingly* giving up or letting go of part of what you want.

In an unsatisfactory compromise, one or both of you thinks you're giving up more than the other. Either or both of you might also feel dissatisfied with the outcome because it doesn't give you enough of what you wanted. And if either of you gives up too much, there's a chance you'll feel resentful—now or later.

Accommodating

When you don't care that much about your content goal, accommodating what the other person wants can be a simple way to resolve your conflict. If where you and your partner go on vacation isn't that important to you, or it isn't as important as keeping the peace with your partner (your relationship goal), you might choose this strategy. You'd agree to what your partner wants—a vacation on the coast. Your accommodation would likely promote goodwill between the two of you—a benefit that ultimately means more to you than taking a vacation in the mountains.

On the other hand, if you truly care about where you go on your trip and accommodate your partner only to end the argument, you might feel dissatisfied. In the long run, if you care about your content goals and accommodate too often, you'll feel resentful about giving up too much. In that case, collaborating or compromising would likely be more satisfying.

The benefits of accommodating are often underrated and overlooked. You may think this strategy is a cop-out or that you should be more assertive and firm when trying to get what you want. That's when it's important to realize that you and your partner mutually affect each other's happiness in both the short and long term. Over time, continually getting what you want at the other person's expense often diminishes the trust and goodwill between you. For the accommodating to lead to a constructive resolution, it's essential that whoever lets go of their content goal is able to do so without feeling resentful. Otherwise, accommodating won't work well.

Competing

Pursuing the strategy of competing usually indicates that your content goals are a higher priority for you than your relationship goals. When you use this strategy, you usually don't care that much about relationship goals—especially not long-term ones. A lawyer might successfully use this strategy when arguing cases in court because she might not care that much about her relationships with the people testifying or with members of the opposing counsel. However, carrying it into her home could create problems with her family. In the short term, she might enjoy getting her way at home, but nobody likes being continually thwarted in conflict situations. When her family members are unhappy about repeatedly not getting what they want, their sense of connection with her (the "winner") might weaken over time.

Here's another example: Suppose your partner is unwilling to collaborate or compromise to resolve your vacation conflict and insists that you join them for a vacation on the coast. (Perhaps they even want to see you capitulate to demonstrate your love.) In the short run, you might resent that they weren't willing to find a solution that works for both of you. In the long run, if they continually use the strategy of competing, you'll probably begin to feel disheartened and less close to them. Consistently using this strategy in a close or highly interdependent relationship usually erodes goodwill over time.

Trying to collaborate with someone who's committed to competing typically doesn't work. While you might be open and self-disclosing, the other person might hide key information in order to benefit at your expense. Remember Alisha and Jacob, the divorcing couple? If either of them pursued this strategy while negotiating the division of their shared financial accounts, they might be tempted to conceal some of their personal assets. Then the forthright person might think the other is entitled to get more money than their actual fair share.

Given the drawbacks of competing, you might think that it's best to avoid this strategy. But there are situations where it's suitable. In competitive games like sports, for instance, players agree to rules that allow them to play fairly in a particular game, and they all understand they're operating under this strategy. The same is true in business, especially in a fairly regulated marketplace.

Competing resembles accommodating in that one person gets what they want and the other person doesn't. The difference is whether the latter person feels satisfied or not with the outcome, both in the short and long term.

Although you might prefer to find mutually satisfying resolutions by collaborating or compromising, it's not always possible. Consider a couple that disagrees over whether or not to have children. One partner absolutely does and the other absolutely does not. If they share a relationship goal of staying together for the long term, then one partner must give up their content goal. If one partner does so willingly and feels satisfied with her decision, she's successfully used accommodating.

It's important to note, however, that even if she's willing to give up her content goal, she may also have other feelings—like sadness, grief, or disappointment—in the face of what she's lost. We humans are complex beings and able to feel many feelings, including contradictory ones—sometimes seemingly at the same time. Moreover, feelings can change over time. In cases such as this one, accommodating may lead to the most constructive resolution possible, but that resolution brings up a constellation of feelings for one or both people, rather than just mutual satisfaction. Over time, the accommodating partner's feelings might resolve into contentment. Therefore, in the long term, accommodating can lead to a constructive outcome both partners wanted: preserving their mutually satisfying relationship.

If the partner giving up her content goal does so unwillingly and feels unsatisfied, accommodating didn't work. Instead, she's ended up on the losing side of competing. The same is true if sadness, disappointment, or even resentment continue to dominate her emotions over time.

Avoiding

Suppose you're sitting in the window seat on an airplane and begin chatting with the passenger in the aisle seat. You're having a pleasant enough conversation. Then suddenly, they express a viewpoint that's offensive to you.

You immediately decide you're just not up for discussing different views with this person—a short-term content goal. You'll probably never see this person again, so you hardly have a long-term relationship goal.

Yet you know you'll probably need to get past them to use the restroom at least once during the rest of the five-hour flight. So your short-term relationship goal is to maintain goodwill with your fellow passenger.

In this case, avoiding is a good strategy. It allows you to disengage from the conversation and steer clear of a potential conflict.

This strategy can also be useful in conflicts when you think you or the other person are too emotional to work things out immediately. It's usually tough to have constructive conversations when people are highly emotional. For example, if your manager is angry and berating your coworkers, waiting before talking with them might be prudent.

Another time avoiding works is when you've found a Plan B, a conflict resolution that doesn't involve the other person. (See chapter 9, "Problem-Solving," for more on using a Plan B.)

Avoiding offers an advantage unique among the conflict-management strategies: the other person may not realize when you're using it. Unlike the other strategies, avoiding can be invisible—as in the earlier airline-passenger example.

Avoiding does have pitfalls. First, if you need the other person to help you fulfill your content goal, then completely disengaging from her probably won't help. Second, if you frequently avoid conflicts instead of addressing them with a different strategy, they'll probably persist. Sometimes a conflict will dissolve with time, but you can't count on it. Third, avoiding can be frustrating for the other person who wants to resolve a conflict, but can't engage with you. If you continue using this strategy over the long term, your ongoing relationship is likely to suffer under the weight of unresolved conflicts and growing resentments. Finally, if you use this strategy out of fear or because you don't know how to advocate for your content goals, you'll probably feel resentful. When you really care about your content goal, avoiding wouldn't be a useful strategy.

Understanding which strategies work best in particular situations gives you more options for managing conflicts skillfully. If you use the strategy that best fits with your goals, it's more likely you'll be able to resolve the conflict in a way that suits both you and the other person. Keep in mind that no one strategy is effective in all situations. Be flexible in selecting the one that fits your circumstances.

Also keep in mind that just as no single strategy fits every conflict, no single solution fits every situation. The useful solutions you find today might need to be updated tomorrow, as your goals and those of the other person evolve.

Conflict Resolution for Parents: Be Willing to Adapt

Parents often use the strategy of competing during conflicts with their young children. But as children get older and develop the ability to think for themselves, many parents find that compromising or collaborating better supports their long-term relationship goal of developing cooperative, mutually respectful relationships with their children. If parents stay with competing, over time they might inadvertently reinforce qualities they wouldn't have wanted for their children, such as poor listening and a lack of empathy, compassion, and mutual respect. (For more on skillful communication for parents, please see chapter 16.)

Frequently Asked Questions

Our students often have questions as they begin putting the concepts of this chapter to use in their own lives. Here are some they frequently ask and how we respond.

What can you do if you think the other person—intentionally or unintentionally—isn't taking your goals into account? There are several options. First, how do you know the other person isn't taking your goals into account? Perhaps she hasn't taken certain actions that you think show she understands them. But did she explicitly say she's not interested in what you want? Or are you assuming she's not interested? If it's your assumption, you need to determine whether it's accurate. You could say, "I'm not sure I've described my goals clearly enough. I'd like to know which ones I have made clear. Could you let me know?"

The other person's response may reveal that she's interested in your goals but doesn't fully understand what they are. In this case, try restating them using different words. Make sure you're not flooding her with too much information. Using I-language, state your goals in a positive way (what you want, rather than what you don't want) and be specific. After you've shared your goals, let the other person tell you what she thinks about them. Use reflective listening to ensure you understand her.

If you're relatively sure the other person isn't interested in your goals, you might need to reassess your conflict-management strategy. Perhaps competing or avoiding would be more useful. Or you could turn your efforts to finding a Plan B solution to your conflict (see chapter 9).

What can you do when you and the other person are pursuing different conflict-management strategies? First, confirm that you and the other person are indeed using different strategies. People often don't carefully choose their strategies, but habitually default to one. Sometimes they pursue a strategy that has worked well for them in the past or in a different context. For example, a successful competitive athlete might automatically approach conflicts with their new romantic partner as competitions. They might not even realize they're doing so, much less how that strategy is affecting their personal relationship.

You can initiate a frank discussion about strategies with a frame such as, "I'd like to find a compromise where we both can feel satisfied." or "I'd like to have a conversation where each of us gets what we want and our friendly relationship can continue." From there, each of you can determine what strategy best supports your goals.

You may find you need to switch to another strategy. Once the athlete realizes they've frequently been competing with their partner (perhaps after their partner expresses frustration about seldom getting what they want), they might feel more willing to consider collaborating or compromising, especially if their long-term relationship goal is to maintain mutual trust and goodwill.

If you both share a spirit of goodwill and want to resolve the conflict constructively, just having a conversation about strategies may help you align them. This conversation might even yield new potential solutions.

Your discussion about strategies may reveal that you are indeed pursuing different strategies and neither of you is willing (or able) to shift to a different one. If that's the case, resolving the conflict constructively will probably be more difficult. Then you'll have to deal with the effects an unsatisfying resolution might have on your relationship.

How can you employ the two conflict skills (identifying your goals and choosing an appropriate conflict-management strategy) in the heat of the moment? When you're emotionally triggered, it's often hard to remember what your goals are, let alone what strategies could help you achieve them. So if your conflict has triggered strong emotions, you might need to take a break. Otherwise, you might escalate the conflict and say things that will require cleanup work later. You can say to the other person, "I'm feeling really worked up right now and having a hard time listening. I can't find any solutions at the moment. I need to take a break and calm down so I can think straight." You should also suggest a time to resume the conversation—in an hour, the next day, or a later date.

During the break, calm yourself down. Then review your goals and the conflict-management strategy you've been using so far. Would a different strategy work better? If your content and relationship goals are equally important, you'll probably first try collaborating or compromising. If your relationship goal is more important than your content goal, accommodating might work. You can also think about what other communication skills—such as reflective listening, creating a four-part-message, or framing—might help you when you resume the discussion.

And remember, it takes practice to be able to communicate skillfully in the heat of the moment. You may find it helpful to practice your communication skills in less contentious conversations before you come back to your conflict conversation.

What's the best way to address a conflict that isn't about differing goals (something you want), but about differing points of view (such as opinions, beliefs, or assumptions)? This question comes up frequently in our classes, workshops, and personal coaching sessions. You're sitting at the dinner table with your new girlfriend's family, and it quickly becomes clear that their political opinions are the polar opposite of yours. Or your new client strongly expresses an absolute belief that you definitely don't share. What can you do?

Several skills from this and previous chapters can prove useful in these situations. If you feel a strong reaction to the other person's point of view (or how they express it), your best first step is to calm yourself, if you can (perhaps using the tips offered in chapter 4). Once you're feeling calmer, consider your options: Are you willing to hear the other person's point of view? Can you activate your curiosity and listen to a point of view that might challenge your beliefs? Do you think you can set your judgments and reactions aside? Do you want the other person (or people) to hear and potentially accept your point of view? Would this conversation be a good opportunity to practice your communication skills? Do you want to avoid an argument, yet not completely disengage from the other person? How you answer these questions will help you determine what you want from the conversation.

Also remember to consider your relationship goals and whether they're short or long term. How important is it for you to maintain goodwill with this particular person or group of people? If you want to stay on good terms with your girlfriend, you may decide it's worth making an effort to understand her family's political views. If you foresee spending the next several holidays with her family, fostering goodwill now might lay the foundation for a less contentious long-term relationship. Though you don't share your new client's belief, you may want to continue working with them.

As we've noted before, you can't control what people think or feel, but you might be able to influence them. So while you might be tempted to come back to the conversation with a goal such as,

"I'm going to show them they're wrong" or "I'm going to set them straight," you could spark a polarizing conflict instead.

Let's say, based on your goals, you decide to continue the conversation. Using a frame can help you reopen it, set the tone, and share your intention. You might say something like, "I'd like to discuss _____ so I can better understand what you think." Or, to invite a fuller dialogue, "I'd like to discuss our different views—not to argue or to try to convince you of anything. Just to understand each other. Is that something you'd be up for?"

If the other person agrees to continue the conversation as you've framed it, you can start by using reflective listening to take in their point of view. Remind yourself that reflective listening requires you to set aside your judgments only temporarily so you can focus just on understanding the other person. Also remember that understanding them doesn't mean you have to agree with them. Using reflective listening can help you maintain goodwill.

Listening to the other person and demonstrating that you've understood what they've said might be your sole intention for the conversation. But in the process, you might establish a rapport with them. And in light of that rapport, they may become open to hearing what you have to say. They may pick up on the frame you used and ask you about your viewpoint. Or you might utilize another frame, such as, "I appreciate you letting me know what you think. I have other thoughts on the subject. Would you like to hear some of them?"

Conveying your thoughts in I-language often helps the other person stay receptive to your views. Being ready to shift back to reflective listening if they interrupt or begin to argue will also help you maintain loop communication. And don't take it too personally if the other person doesn't want to hear your views, even after you've heard theirs.

On the other hand, you might not be able to maintain your emotional equanimity when discussing a controversial or challenging topic. You may be disinclined to listen to a point of view you don't agree with or that runs counter to an absolute belief you have. Fair enough. Sometimes you're just not up for it. Or you may recognize that this isn't a time when you can communicate skillfully about a controversial topic. If you're flying home after attending a friend's funeral, for example, you might not be up for discussing an opposing political view with the passenger next to you. In these cases, your best option may be to end the conversation as politely as possible. Or, if you wish, you could introduce a topic that's less likely to trigger strong emotions in either of you.

What Are Your Beliefs About Conflict?

Your beliefs strongly influence how comfortable you are with interpersonal conflict and how you approach disagreements with other people. For example, some people believe that arguing is the sign of a healthy partnership, while others believe exactly the opposite.

Our beliefs usually have their roots in our personal and social history. If you're like many people, however, you may not be aware of your beliefs about conflict, much less how you developed them.

As you begin practicing this chapter's skills, we invite you to look at what you believe to be true about conflict and how to resolve it. As you do, notice whether any of your beliefs are too absolute. If so, could they be adjusted with some provisional language? For instance, if you notice yourself thinking, "People who really love each other don't have conflicts they can't ultimately resolve," you might revise the thought to say, "Even people who love each other sometimes argue and can't find resolutions."

Recognizing your beliefs about disagreements and conflicts—and revising them, if appropriate—can help you navigate conflicts with more ease and skill. It's also helpful to remember another person may be operating under beliefs quite different from yours.

Practice

Preparing for a Conflict Conversation

You can prepare for a conflict conversation by thinking through your own goals and those of the other person, and then considering which conflict-management strategy you'd like to pursue. This exercise breaks your preparation into clear steps. At the end, it asks you to create a frame you could use to open your conversation. We've used Alisha's example from earlier in the chapter to demonstrate each step.

For the sake of brevity, this exercise assumes that you already have a clear understanding of the other person's goals. If you don't, you may need to have a preliminary conversation in which you can use reflective listening to uncover their implicit goals.

1. Think of a conflict you're having with another person but haven't constructively resolved yet. If you can't think of a current unresolved conflict, use one that you experienced in the past. Describe the conflict in a nutshell.

   Example: Alisha describes her conflict with Jacob this way: "Jacob and I are getting divorced and disagree on several issues."

2a. Identify your *content* goals and write them down as a list.

   Example:

My Content Goals (Alisha)
Keep the house
Have enough money to support Alex and myself
Ensure Alex is a happy, healthy child

2b. What do you know or think the other person's content goals are? Write them down as a list next to your own.

Example:

My Content Goals (Alisha)	Jacob's Content Goals
Keep the house	Sell the house
Have enough money to support Alex and myself	Divide our financial assets in a mutually beneficial way
Ensure Alex is a happy, healthy child	Ensure Alex is a happy, healthy child

3. Identify your respective *relationship* goals. Write them down just as you did your content goals, listing yours next to those that you think the other person has.

Example:

My Relationship Goals (Alisha)	Jacob's Relationship Goals
Be more independent from Jacob	Maintain a close relationship with Alex and me
Make my own financial decisions	Make financial decisions together
Make plans with friends without consulting Jacob	Make plans together with friends
Work together for Alex's benefit	Work together for Alex's benefit

Review your respective goals. As you do, note:

• Which goals are essential, important, and less or least important to you?

- Which goals are short-term goals? Which are long-term goals?
- How do you believe the other person would prioritize their goals?
- Where do your goals overlap with the other person's goals?

Example:

My Goals (Alisha)	Jacob's Goals
Keep the house—*important, at least until Alex is out of grade school*	Sell the house—*important*
Have enough money to support Alex and myself—*essential*	Divide our financial assets in a mutually beneficial way—*important*
Ensure Alex is a happy, healthy child—*essential, shared goal*	Ensure Alex is a happy, healthy child—*essential, shared goal*
Be more independent from Jacob—*less important in the short term, more important long term*	Maintain a close relationship with Alex and me—*essential to maintain a close relationship with Alex in short and long term*
Make my own financial decisions—*less important in the short term, very important long term*	Make financial decisions together—*important in the short term, may not be as important in the long term*

Make plans with friends without consulting Jacob— *less important in the short term, more important long term*	Make plans together with friends— *important in the short term, may not be as important in the long term*
Work together for Alex's benefit—*essential, shared goal*	Work together for Alex's benefit—*essential, shared goal*

Based on the importance of your goals, what conflict-management strategy seems suitable for you to use?

> **Example:** Since she and Jacob have quite a few shared goals, Alisha may think that collaborating would be worth trying. But because she and Jacob might not find much middle ground on some goals they differ on, one or both of them might have to give up something. Compromising looks like the most realistic strategy for her.

6. Create a frame to start a conversation with the other person about your conflict.

   Your frame might express your desire to maintain goodwill during the conversation and/or seek a constructive outcome. It might also state your goals and which conflict-management strategy you think would work well.

> **Example:** Alisha might begin her conversation with Jacob with this frame: "I'd like to discuss some of the logistical issues we're facing during this transition. I hope we can find compromises that satisfy both of us."

Part III

Applications
and Additional
Information

Chapter 15

Conflict Management
for Couples

More Skill, Less Fallout,
Closer Relationships

C ommunication can make or break relationships. One of the top reasons people seek out our coaching services is that they want to communicate better with their partner—especially during conflicts and when they need to have conversations about difficult topics.

Some couples boast that they never have conflicts, as if that were an indicator of a vibrant, enjoyable relationship. Other couples become overly reactive at the first whiff of conflict. Both responses—avoiding conflict or getting emotionally triggered by it—can hamper a couple's ability to work with conflict constructively. In this chapter, we'll show you how to apply the communication skills you've learned so far to the conflicts that inevitably come up when you and another person are in a close relationship. The goal is not to prevent all conflicts (that would be impossible), but to help you work with conflicts that are threatening to get heated. Skillful communication in these situations can support and even enhance your relationship instead of damaging it. We'll also discuss helpful ways to handle conflicts that simply can't be resolved.

Although this chapter is focused on couples, the guidance here can also be applied to many other types of close relationships. On a broader scale, this chapter can help you navigate most interpersonal disagreements with more confidence and clarity.

Trust, Communication, and Conflict

Trust affects the way two people in a close relationship handle conflicts. Trust typically involves a sense that the other person will be there for you and vice versa. "Being there for you" can mean different things to different people. In terms of communication, it usually means the two of you are responsive to each other's requests for attention and engagement.

Suppose you say to your partner during breakfast, "Did you hear that Nick's finally getting married?" If your partner ignores your question and continues to read the newspaper, you might feel less connected to them. Later, if you try to begin another conversation—again with no response—your connection to your partner might start to weaken. Or if they reply, "Everybody knows that. You're always the last one to know what's happening," that criticism could diminish trust. On the other hand, if they say, "Really? What happened?" you'll feel more connected to them. They've shown you they're interested in what you're saying. If they continue being responsive when you bring up other topics, your trust in them will likely grow.[1]

Trust often takes a long time to develop, but it can be destroyed quickly. A bank account of trust is built from many small deposits of trust made over time; it can be almost emptied in a careless comment or an unskillful conversation.

Trust provides a social lubrication to help smooth the friction that often comes with having differences. Two people who trust each other are more likely to use communication that confirms each other. In other words, they are more likely to at least consider what the other person is saying, even if they disagree. When there is mutual trust, each person is more likely to be interested in what the other person wants as they look for solutions to their conflict.

Conflict Conversations: Putting Your Communication Skills to Use

When you're in a close relationship, you probably have a good idea what topics can trigger conflict between the two of you. While it might be tempting to just avoid those topics, it's possible to have conversations about difficult, contentious topics *and* still preserve your relationship. Many of the communication skills you've been practicing so far can help you do just that.

Please note that it's not always necessary to take all the steps or employ all the skills we'll describe here. Your conflict conversations with your partner can benefit from whatever skills you're able to apply.

Before the Conversation: Do Some Prep Work

When you're talking with your partner frequently, preparing for one particular conversation might seem unnecessary. But the more significant or potentially contentious a conversation is, the more preparing for it can help. Thinking through in advance how best to approach the topic and what you want to say can help you stay calm and focused during the conversation itself. Being prepared can help you feel more confident.

There's no perfect amount of preparation. You certainly don't need to be 100 percent prepared or use all the following recommendations all the time. When it comes to consequential or potentially triggering conversations, any amount of preparation is often better than none.

Consider Your Goal(s) and Conflict-Management Strategy

When preparing for your conversation, start by asking yourself:

1. What are my content goals? What do I explicitly want?

2. What are my relationship goals? How do I want to treat my partner, and how interdependent do I want to be?

Next, identify what you know about your partner's content and relationship goals. If the two of you have clashed about the topic before, you might already know or be able to accurately guess what their goals are. If it's a new conflict, you can plan to focus part of your forthcoming conversation on learning what their goals are. (See chapter 14 for ways to discern other people's goals in a conflict.) Also consider whether each of your goals is a short- or long-term goal.

Your goals will inform your choice of conflict-management strategy. For example, if one of your goals is to develop a cooperative relationship with your partner over time, competing, which could damage trust and goodwill, isn't the best choice. Collaborating, compromising, and accommodating typically build more trust and cooperation, and are more likely to yield mutually satisfying outcomes.

Relinquish the Need to Be Right

It's natural for two people to have different perspectives about a topic. Recognizing and acknowledging that fact from the get-go will help you steer away from believing your partner shouldn't think or feel the way they do. We also recommend you skip arguing about whose perspective is right or wrong. Rather than trying to relentlessly persuade your partner to agree with your perspective, focus on finding solutions that work for both of you.

Not arguing about who's right or wrong may seem minor, but it can make a difference. If either of you adamantly believes your perspective is the *only* right way to view the topic, you're probably holding your belief in an absolute way. As discussed in chapter 6, an absolute belief can limit options for resolving a conflict. When someone insists they're right in an absolute way, they're more likely to pursue a conflict strategy of competing. Then the only way forward would be for one partner to give in to the other—a solution that might well leave the capitulating partner feeling resentful and dissatisfied. You may have resolved the conflict at hand, but at a cost to your ongoing relationship. On the other hand, if neither you nor your partner insist on being right, the strategies of accommodating and compromising become more available.

Holding beliefs in a more relative way opens the door for multiple possibilities of defining, viewing, and solving a problem. You can acknowledge that your view is not the only perspective. Doing so typically makes it easier to listen to the other person's perspective during a disagreement. Even so, remember that you don't need to discard your absolute beliefs, especially those based on core values. Just be prepared to examine the usefulness of your absolute beliefs when they seem to interfere with resolving a conflict.

Sketch Out a Four-Part Message

A four-part message is a handy way to launch a conflict conversation constructively. Thinking through the four parts before your conversation will help you make sure you're giving your partner complete information.

When addressing difficult topics, aim to keep the referent (what you're talking about) focused on a specific situation or topic. In challenging conversations, it's easy to start bringing up one problem after the next. But too often it can sound like a litany of all the ways your partner has screwed up, which can trigger a defensive reaction. Identifying a specific, relatively narrow referent can help keep the conversation from spiraling into a truckload of other conflicts.

Remember to include your intention—what you want. And remember to state it in a positive way. Let's say your conversation is going to be about money and finances. Rather than phrasing your intention negatively, "I don't want to drown in debt," say what you do want: "I want to create a realistic savings plan that both of us can easily follow."

Your intention may also encompass your relationship goals. You might say, "I'd like us to create a realistic savings plan that we can easily follow. Even if we don't agree about some points, I hope that ultimately we'll both feel satisfied with the plan. And we'll better understand each other's feelings and priorities."

Opening the Conversation

How you open a consequential conversation can strongly influence its tone and whether loop communication develops. If you're feeling emotionally charged or a strong sense of urgency, you might be tempted to say something like, "I won't beat around the bush" or "Let's cut to the chase." But slowing down and applying your communication skills early on increases your odds of having a constructive, mutually satisfying discussion.

Choose Your Timing Carefully

Staying attentive and composed and maintaining goodwill can be difficult if you're feeling hungry, tired, or stressed. If possible, initiate the conversation when you and your partner are relatively calm.

Finding a time and place where you won't be interrupted—by phone calls or children for instance—is also helpful. Take the setting into account too. For example, would discussing your challenging topic in a public place support or inhibit a constructive conversation?

Check in with Yourself

Are *you* ready to have a challenging conversation with your partner? It's worth asking yourself this question and answering honestly. Sometimes when people feel agitated, impatient, or uncomfortable with a topic or conflict, they dive into a conversation before they're actually ready. It's easy to become emotionally triggered and communicate unskillfully at such times. So before you initiate a conversation on a potentially difficult topic, check in with yourself: Do you feel sufficiently ready to talk? Are you in a receptive frame of mind and able to hear what your partner might say?

Maybe you aren't ready for a conversation about the topic. Or maybe you don't think you'll be able to communicate skillfully. In these cases, consider whether more prep work would help. You might also look at your current self-talk and see whether any cognitive distortions or assumptions are stirring up your emotions. If so, you could review chapter 10 for ways to regain more equanimity.

What if your partner initiates a conversation you may not be ready for in that moment? The section on "Listening When You're Feeling a Strong Emotional Reaction" in chapter 4 offers suggestions for what to say.

Check in with Your Partner

Even though *you* may be ready to start a challenging conversation, your partner may not be. When in doubt, ask. You might say something such as, "I'd like to discuss _____ with you and see if we can find a solution that we're both comfortable with. Is now a good time to talk?"

Asking to find a future time for the conversation is a good option when one of you isn't ready at that particular moment. "I've been feeling anxious since our last conversation. I'm hoping we can talk again and find a satisfying resolution. Would you be up for that? If so, when's a good time?" is one way to ask for a future discussion.

Use an Inviting Frame

Your frame should tell your partner what you want to discuss and, ideally, set the stage for a constructive conversation. "I want to discuss how your irresponsible spending is driving us into more debt" is a poor frame for a conversation about money. A better frame would be, "I'd like to discuss a concern I have about our savings." Your partner still might not be pleased to hear that you'd like to talk about this topic. Nevertheless, keeping your negative judgment out of the frame will invite them to listen rather than quickly push back.

Skillful frames can also be handy when opening a new conversation about an ongoing disagreement. Often frames express your content and relationship goals. (Remember, frames start a conversation, but don't fully state the rest of what you want to say.) For example:

- I hope we can resolve our disagreement in a satisfying way and keep the goodwill flowing.

- I hope we can find a solution that satisfies both of us.

- I'd like to work together to resolve this conflict as quickly and easily as possible.

- It's important to me that we come to a resolution that we both like, even if it's not what we originally expected.

- Overall, I hope we can stay open to each other's ideas as we resolve this conflict.

- Since we last talked about our goals, I've thought of some solutions that might work for both of us.

- In thinking about our goals, I realized that _____ is the most important thing for me. I'd like to hear what's most important for you too.

Sometimes it's difficult to come up with a frame before you know what your four-part message is. If so, write out your message first, as directed earlier in the chapter, before creating your frame.

Start Gently and Calmly

Notice the tone of your voice. If you start with a harsh tone, your partner is more likely to feel defensive. If you want to calm yourself and alter your tone, you can use the suggestions offered in chapter 4.

During the Conversation

The communication skills from part II can help you pay attention to loop communication and maintain goodwill even during difficult conversations on contentious topics. Here are some recommendations. Again, you don't need to use all the skills described here or employ them perfectly. And here's a tip: the more you practice these skills during neutral, less consequential conversations, the easier it will be to use them during more challenging ones.

Share Your Goal(s)

If your frame didn't mention your goals, include them in the conversation. Be sure to phrase your goals so you're saying what you do want, rather than what you don't want. Goals such as, "I'd like us to track our spending so we can save enough to buy a house in five years" is an example of a positively stated goal. A negatively stated version is, "I don't want to be still wasting money on rent in seven to ten years" or "I don't want us to spend so much that we can't buy a house in five years."

If you aren't sure what your partner's goals are, use the recommendations in chapter 14, under "Discerning the Other Person's Goals," to check (or double-check) them.

Keep Your Common Ground at the Forefront

During a conflict, recognizing where your goals overlap with your partner's can lead you to find solutions. You might acknowledge some common goals by saying something such as:

- It's seems like we both want _____. If that's true, I feel hopeful we can find a solution soon.

- Now that we understand some of our differences, I think our mutual goal of _____ can help us find a solution that will work for both of us.

- I think our previous discussions might not have brought us closer to a resolution, and I feel a little frustrated. At the same time, I feel encouraged that we seem to be on the same page about _____.

Reminding both yourself and your partner of your common goals can also help you when the conversation stalls or tensions mount. Your common goals can function like bridges between you; loop communication can keep flowing over these bridges even when the distance between your goals seems to be widening.

To show you what we mean, let's return to Alisha and Jacob, the divorcing couple you met in chapter 14. The italicized text indicates specifically where Alisha speaks of their common goal—the wellbeing of their son, Alex—as they discuss their conflicting housing goals.

Alisha: (framing the conversation) I wish we could
            find a way to resolve some of our differences.
            *I'm hoping that our love for Alex and desire to see
            him do well can help us find solutions that we can
            agree on.*

221

Jacob: Okay. What are you thinking of?

Alisha: Maybe we can find some compromises, even though we want different things right now.

Jacob: Compromises such as . . . ?

Alisha: I want to stay in the house so that Alex can have the stability of staying in the same school and neighborhood while we get divorced. If I agree to sell the house later on, would you consider renting until then? *We both agree that we want Alex to feel secure and happy.* I think he'll have a more stable home if he and I can continue living in the house for now.

Jacob: I'd rather buy a condo than rent. But I can't afford it unless we sell the house. How long do you think you want to stay in the house?

Alisha: Until Alex is done with middle school.

Jacob: Until he's done with middle school? That's—what?—six years from now. That's too long!

Alisha: (reflecting Jacob) Sounds like you're hoping to buy a condo sooner than that.

Jacob: Yes. I hate throwing money away on rent.

Alisha: What if we agree to keep the house until Alex finishes elementary school? That will be in three years. Then we can decide whether he needs the stability of living in the same place or if he might be ready to move out of this school district.

Jacob: That might work. I know we both want Alex to feel stable. But I really want to stick to a definite deadline for deciding whether he's ready to move.

Alisha: I'll agree to a strict deadline. I do think he
            might be ready to adjust to a new neighborhood
            by the time he finishes elementary school. Then
            we can sell the house. But I'm fine with selling
            sooner if Alex seems ready to move before then.
            I'm glad we both want the best for Alex.

Use I-Language

You-language is a red flag that often invites defensiveness: "You're irresponsible. You buy things we don't need. You're driving up our debt." Instead of labeling and characterizing your partner or their behavior, use I-language to describe the problem you're having, what you think about it, and how you feel: "When I think that we won't be able to afford to buy a house in five years, I feel disappointed."

Don't use the phrase "makes me feel"—as in, "You're making me feel insecure" or "Our extra spending makes me feel frustrated." This phrase implies that the other person or the situation is *causing* your emotions. As you know from chapter 8, thinking this way and using this language easily leads to blaming and counterattacks. Better to say, "When I think about our extra spending, I feel frustrated (or insecure)."

Remember to Listen

Listening is a crucial step in resolving conflicts. It's essential for learning how your partner thinks and feels. Yet during disagreements listening too often falls by the wayside. It's easy to become so fixated on what you want to say next that you neglect listening.

After you've said what you want to say, give your partner the opportunity to respond. Use reflective listening to let them know you're taking in what they're saying.

Be ready to shift to reflective listening at any point in the conversation. Reflecting will confirm that you understand your partner. It's also a great way to maintain loop communication and goodwill as the conversation continues.

Be Willing to Have Multiple Conversations, if Necessary

Resolving tough conflicts often requires several conversations. Although you and your partner may both want to end your conflict, you might not find a constructive resolution in just one sitting. If so, you might need to alter your expectation that the conflict should be resolved in a single conversation.

You can acknowledge this possibility at the start of the conversation. For example:

- I'd like to first talk about our goals, so we both have a sense of what we each want. Then maybe we could each take some time to think about solutions that might work for us before we meet again. What do you think?

- Even though I want to resolve our disagreement quickly, I think finding a resolution might take more than one conversation. I'm okay with having several conversations so we can both feel good about the outcome and each other.

- I'm not sure we'll be able to completely resolve this conflict before we go to bed. If we can't, let's schedule a time later this week to talk again.

When Things Get Heated: Addressing Emotional Triggering

Disagreements can be messy. It's common for people to get emotionally triggered during a conflict, even when everyone involved has positive intentions. It's also easy to slip into unskillful habits, such as flooding, stating opinions as facts, blaming, and using you-language. You can easily end up saying things you'll need to clean up later.

As your conversation proceeds, be on the lookout for emotional triggering in yourself or your partner. When either of you gets swept up in emotions, or when tensions run so high that the conversation falters, here are two recommendations.

Switch to Reflective Listening

The more heated a conflict gets, the less likely partners are to listen to each other. Instead, most people typically start defending their own positions or attacking their partner. They may interrupt one another with accusations and denials or inflame angry feelings with criticisms and judgments. At such times, loop communication can quickly spiral downward or fall apart entirely.

Tensions can also escalate quickly when one partner doesn't think the other has heard or understood them. That partner might be tempted to withdraw from the conversation, thinking, "They clearly don't want to hear what I have to say. So what's the point of continuing?"

One person shifting to reflective listening can often keep a conflict conversation from turning into an unconstructive, hurtful fight. Using reflective listening is especially helpful when one partner is upset. People are often more willing and better able to continue the conversation when they know their partner has understood them.

Pause and Reset

Be ready and willing to pause when emotions start to flare up. Sure, hitting the brakes on an emotional conversation can sometimes feel as jarring as hitting the brakes on a car zooming downhill. But it's better to do that than allow the conversation to crash completely, leaving you and your partner with injuries to treat and wreckage to clean up afterward.

However long your pause is—a few minutes, a couple hours, a couple days—you can use the time constructively. Have your favorite self-soothing techniques in your mental back pocket and be ready to use them to recover your emotional equanimity. (See chapters 4 and 5 for suggestions.) Revisit any preparatory steps you did, reminding yourself of your goals and making adjustments to your language as needed. Let's say your partner had a strong emotional reaction to your initial frame or message. After your break, you might restate what you said, but use different words. Sometimes rephrasing your message can invite a more receptive response.

The message you use to open the conversation could acknowledge the potential for strong emotions. We recommend using I-language, implying that you might be the one who gets upset. Avoid using you-language that characterizes your partner. Your message could also set the stage for taking pauses. For instance:

- One of my goals is to stay calm during our conversation. That said, I feel strongly about _____ and could get caught up in my emotions. If I do, I might have to pause to calm down. I hope that's okay.

- I want to listen carefully and give you my full attention. But I might get too emotional to do that. I'd like to pause if that happens. I'm okay with you doing that too.

- Just so you know, I have had a lot of different feelings about _____ since we last talked. I might get upset (or impatient, or irritated) in this conversation. If I do, I might want to take a break to calm down.

- What we're talking about is very important to me. If I start getting too worked up, I might have trouble listening to you. If I need to take a break, I hope you'll understand. I hope you'll also take a break if you need one.

Skillful Communication in Action: Conflict Conversations

As you've probably realized, conflict conversations often require more skills than just identifying your goals and choosing a conflict-management strategy. Be ready to reach into your communication toolkit and pull out additional skills as needed. Bringing more than one skill into your conversations usually becomes easier with practice. And the more practice you get in lower-stress, lower-stakes conversations, the more likely you'll be able to mix and match skills when needed during more intense conversations.

The examples in this section show people doing just that. Each begins with the basic conflict. Then we suggest how each couple could move forward, as if they'd come to us for communication coaching to help them manage their disagreement.

Money is one of the most common things couples argue about. That's perhaps not surprising, given how many unspoken, unseen beliefs and assumptions people hold about it. When we were considering examples of difficult conflict conversations, several money-centered conflicts quickly came to mind. Also fresh in our memories were real-life conflicts that came up in our online workshops and practice groups during 2020, as people were navigating the unique challenges and restrictions of the coronavirus pandemic. So we've also included an example derived from those discussions with our students.

Example 1: Is There Really a Problem?

Laura is attempting to talk with her partner, Rebecca, about their finances. "We need to do something about our dwindling savings," she says. "I think we should start eating out less often and put the extra money we'd usually spend on restaurants into our savings account."

Rebecca disagrees. "Given your new job and my raise, I'm not worried. I don't plan to eat out less often," she says with a shrug.

How can Laura and Rebecca move forward when one of them thinks there's a problem and the other doesn't?

By dismissing Laura's concern, Rebecca is, perhaps unwittingly, using avoiding as her conflict-management strategy. To her, the problem doesn't exist, so there's really nothing to talk about. It's a risky strategy, however, given how interdependent they are. Plus, her view of their finances might not change Laura's view of them. Trying to avoid a conflict now could lead to a bigger one later.

Listening to and understanding each other's perspectives is key to managing differences. If Rebecca wants to influence Laura to see the situation as she does, she first needs to understand how Laura views the problem. Reflective listening can ensure that each partner has the opportunity to share her perspective and be understood by the other.

Let's say Rebecca comes back to Laura and says, "I think I responded too quickly when you brought up our savings and eating out less often. I'd like to hear more about what you're thinking. Then I can consider the situation more carefully. What do you say?" Rebecca has shifted away from avoiding in order to reconnect with her partner. She's also used I-language to reopen the conversation.

Laura agrees to resume their talks. Relieved that Rebecca is willing to hear her out, she feels more willing to listen to Rebecca's point of view. As they listen to each other's perspective, Laura and Rebecca soon discover where their goals overlap and differ. They learn that even though earlier in their relationship, they'd established a common goal of buying a house, they hadn't specified a precise timeline for reaching that goal. Rebecca had assumed they'd continue to rent for at least ten years. She believes their current income was enough to support their lifestyle as they slowly grow their savings for a down payment. Laura believes they'll be priced out of the housing market if they wait more than five years to buy a home. Therefore, they have to accumulate enough money for a down payment in a shorter amount of time.

Aha! Laura and Rebecca had unknowingly been working under different assumptions. Now that they recognize it, they can do some research on the housing market in their area, then assess their assumptions in light of what they discover. Both of them can also stop and consider what conflict-management strategy they want to pursue as talks continue. We'd suggest that they keep their mutual goal of buying a house at the forefront of their ongoing conversations.

Both partners are willing to amend their assumptions. As they learn more about their local housing market, Rebecca agrees that buying a house in five years makes sense, given rising home prices. She also agrees to eat out less often and find additional ways to save money. But she still worries that trying to save excessively might dampen their fun together—something she sees as important for their relationship. They compromise by agreeing to eat out half as much and finding more low-cost fun activities to do together. Both feel satisfied with their compromise.

Example 2: A Clash of Priorities

Judy and Robert, who have been married two years, bought a home using money from Judy's trust fund as a down payment. Although both have jobs, they could not have afforded the house from their earnings alone. Judy would have been happy with a smaller house, but Robert persuaded her that a bigger house in a good neighborhood was a better investment. Now they've begun to quarrel over the cost of the furnishings. Robert wants to buy top-of-the-line furniture. He sees high-quality furniture, like the house, as a long-term investment, and it's worth dipping into Judy's trust fund again to buy it. Judy, on the other hand, thinks they should limit themselves to more modest furniture choices, purchased with their earned income.

As the tension between them escalates, the couple falls into a familiar pattern: the more argumentative he becomes, the more she withdraws. When Judy insists on a moratorium on buying furniture, Robert accuses her of playing power games. That's the last straw for Judy; she stops talking to him all together. How can they not only break their deadlock, but also repair the strained connection between them?

If we were coaching Judy and Robert, we'd suggest they focus as much on *how* they're managing their disagreement (process) as *what* they're disagreeing about (content). And we see a few important skills that would likely enhance their process.

A good first step would be for the couple to reopen the conversation with an intention to better understand each other's perspectives. Either partner might begin an opening frame that states that intention. (See chapter 14 for examples.)

Next they could look at the assumptions influencing their argument. When two people are in a close relationship, each brings their own assumptions about important topics. Conflicts can easily arise from these differing assumptions, as well as the assumption that your partner operates under the same assumptions you do! One of the biggest stumbling blocks to working out disagreements is failing to recognize what assumptions are at play. When two partners identify and discuss their key assumptions, the basis of their disagreement typically becomes clearer.

As you know from chapter 7, it can be challenging to uncover your assumptions about an issue you feel strongly about. It's also typically not easy to examine the accuracy of those assumptions. For these reasons, we'd recommend Judy and Robert examine their assumptions together only when they're relatively calm. Waiting until their emotions are less triggered might allow them to approach the discussion with more curiosity. We'd also recommend they initially stick to unearthing their own assumptions, rather than guessing what their partner's might be. Reflective listening can be useful for identifying assumptions that are hard to recognize or put into words. Both partners should be careful not to let their own opinions or judgment sneak into their reflections. Staying focused on understanding each other is crucial.

Following our suggestions, the couple begins talking again and quickly discovers they're operating from different assumptions. Robert assumes that, as married partners, he and Judy should have equal say in how they spend their money. And "their money" included Judy's trust fund. Judy assumes her trust fund was just that—*her* trust fund, not theirs. She could take Robert's point of view into consideration when making decisions about her trust fund money, but ultimately, any decisions were hers alone. In addition, both partners had assumed their positions were obvious and so reasonable that they didn't need to be stated explicitly. They both realize it's time to update their assumptions.

Judy decides to rethink her assumption that she's under no obligation to share her trust fund's resources since they're legally hers. She decides to revise that assumption to a new, more relative one: she will share her trust fund's resources with Robert more often. She also recognizes that sharing her money will help balance the power in their relationship, especially as they become more interdependent over time.

Robert realizes he's holding an absolute prescriptive assumption: Judy *should* share her trust fund with him now that they're married. He also recognizes that she isn't obligated to share her funds. So he decides to shift his ironclad rule to a preference: he *would like* to have an equal say in what Judy's trust fund is used for. And he also adjusts his expectation about how much money he has access to.

Their conversations continue over the course of the week. They again use reflective listening to keep the discussion progressing. During conflicts, people often forget to include intentions in their messages, or they state their intentions as what they don't want, rather than what they do want. So Judy and Robert use reflective listening to discern the positive intention in each other's messages, as demonstrated in chapter 12.

Example 3: Whose Fair Is Fair?

Bill and Ted have lived together for four years. From the start, they pooled their money and shared their living expenses equally. When they earned approximately the same amount, the arrangement had worked well. Last year, however, Bill accepted a new position in a high-growth company. Between bonuses and salary increases, his income more than doubled. Feeling flush, he began buying more expensive clothes and talked of moving to a larger apartment. Ted balked. As a social worker, he can't afford such extravagances. More-over, as long as he's working for his current nonprofit organization, his income isn't likely to increase substantially.

Given the growing discrepancy in their financial situations, Bill and Ted figure they have a few options: they could keep their present arrangement and live at the same standard, they could stop pooling their money, or they could work out a new arrangement. Both of them also want a "fair" arrangement. Unfortunately, that's all they can agree on.

"You earn twice as much as I do now, so I think you should put twice as much as I do into our pool," Ted tells Bill.

"That's not fair," Bill says. "It's not my fault your job pays less than mine. Why should I be penalized for that? I also have more personal expenses than you do. I need to spend more on clothes now that my job has changed, and I just bought a new car."

"Well, I have student loans to pay off, and you don't," Ted says. "I only spend money on things I really need. A lot of the things you spend money on are luxuries, not essentials. New suits, a new car, a bigger apartment—do you really need all that stuff to be happy?"

"Hey, I work hard for my money!" Bill replies, his temper rising. "I don't think there's anything wrong with wanting to spend some of it on some things I enjoy."

"I don't have a problem with you spending money on 'enjoyable' things. The problem is that you spend money on them, then claim you don't have enough to put more into the pool for our shared expenses. If I could put in the same amount that you can, I would. But I can't afford it."

"Here we go again! Poor Ted has no money. He can't afford anything nice. Everyone feel sorry for him. You know, sometimes I think it's your attitude that's keeping you from earning more. If you'd just . . ."

The longer their discussions continue, the more frustrated Bill and Ted become. Instead of getting closer to a plan for their shared expenses, their perspectives only seem to be growing further apart. What's more, their talks have started to devolve into personal attacks.

Here are the skills we'd suggest the couple use to de-escalate the tension and shift to more constructive conflict conversations.

First, they can make sure they start new conversations only when they're both feeling relatively calm. Next they could use more reflective listening to better understand each other's positions.

We'd encourage them to use more I-language, rather than characterizing each other. Their previous conversations were peppered with you-language, such as, "A lot of the things you spend money on are luxuries, not essentials"; "The problem is that you spend money on them, then claim you don't have enough to put more into the pool for our shared expenses"; and "Poor Ted has no money. He can't afford anything nice. Everyone feel sorry for him. You know, sometimes I think it's your attitude that's keeping you from earning more."

Finally, we'd point out that having different ideas about fairness and sharing money is common. It would be useful for Bill and Ted to recognize that their ideas about fairness make sense only from their *own* perspectives. There are no absolute standards for fairness to apply to this situation. So they need to figure out a resolution that seems fair to each of them. They could begin by looking at their assumptions about fairness in their relationship. Bill's assumes each person gets to keep what he earns and they will split costs evenly. Ted assumes that if one partner's income improves, it's only fair that he share his money with his partner.

If Bill and Ted were working with us, we'd help them recognize and update their assumptions in the light of Bill's increased income. They might, for example, also take into account nonmonetary contributions to the shared household. Maybe Ted can't contribute the same amount of money that Bill can. But perhaps he could take over tasks that Bill doesn't like doing, like paying the bills, doing more yard work, cooking, or walking their dog more often. Their options for finding a "fair" resolution might expand if they broaden their idea of contributions to include more than just money.

Example 4: One Event, Two Points of View

Cleo has decided to host a birthday party for her six-year-old son at her father's house. Though they don't live together, she's been helping her eighty-nine-year-old father take care of himself throughout the coronavirus pandemic. In addition to inviting several local friends, she's invited some out-of-town family members. They feel comfortable flying in for the event, despite the fact that coronavirus vaccines aren't yet available.

Tyler, her brother, lives in a different city. He's decided not to attend the party, though he knows it would mean a lot to Cleo to have him there. He's also raised several concerns about whether it's safe to hold an indoor party during the pandemic. He's worried that people gathering at their father's house will put their dad, as well as everyone else attending, at risk for catching the coronavirus.

The siblings have already had two conversations about it. In light of Tyler's concerns, Cleo has agreed to ask out-of-town visitors to get

COVID tests after they fly. She plans to take everyone's temperature when they arrive at the house. She'll also keep the windows open to allow in fresh air. But she's leaving it up to guests to decide for themselves whether or not to wear masks. Insisting they have to would infringe on their personal liberties, she believes. She also doesn't want to offend them by suggesting she doesn't trust them to monitor their own health and keep her family safe. And since her guests are the ones who will actually be there, their preferences take priority over her absentee brother's.

For Tyler, Cleo's precautions don't go far enough. He values his relationship with his sister and wants family harmony. But he thinks the party is a super-spreader event in the making.

"I know you think it's important for David not to miss out on having a birthday party because of the pandemic," he says in their next conversation. "I know it would be hard for him to understand why it's not possible. But I've heard of too many people getting sick from going to parties like this. This virus is serious, and I just don't want anyone there to risk coming in contact with someone who has it. And I especially don't want Dad to end up in the hospital on a ventilator."

"That's not going to happen. That's just your anxiety imagining the worst-case scenario," Cleo says. "Dad isn't afraid to have David's party here, and neither am I. And the people I've invited aren't afraid to come. Just because you're living in fear doesn't mean we all have to."

With her last statement, Cleo has attempted to negate Tyler's position, a signal that she's adopted the conflict-management strategy of competing (intentionally or unintentionally). How could Tyler respond in a skillful way and, hopefully, move the siblings to a constructive resolution?

First, he could decide to reboot the tone of the conversation by using a different frame. He might say, for instance, "I'd like to understand more about how you think about Dad's safety. Is that okay?"

If Cleo says yes, he could introduce collaborating as an alternate conflict-management strategy. First, he can identify their overlapping content goal of keeping their father safe and healthy: "It seems like we're both concerned about Dad's safety."

"Of course," Cleo would probably say.

Tyler can then reflect what Cleo had previously said to ensure he accurately understands her thinking. "You believe you're going to do enough to protect him and your guests. And you feel confident nothing bad will happen," he reflects.

Cleo might then confirm his understanding: "Exactly! Nothing bad is going to happen. No one's getting sick from this party."

"You also think the precautions you've mentioned will keep everyone safe," Tyler could reflect.

"Definitely."

Tyler can then say what he thinks. "That's possible, and I hope you're right," he might say. Then he could add to her position: "I'm wondering if there are other precautions we could take to protect Dad."

"Between the testing, taking temperatures, leaving windows open, and social distancing, what else could we do?" she might ask.

Now Tyler can propose a solution that he hopes will add an extra layer of protection: "How about having Dad stay outdoors for the whole party? Everyone could stay socially distanced from each other and wear masks. We could send an email to let the guests know that we're taking this extra precaution since Dad is in a very high-risk group. And you could have extra masks on hand for guests who don't bring them."

He can also be ready to add to his ideas, if Cleo sees any potential problems. For example, she might say, "Seems like if it's too cold, Dad could get sick just being outside." To which Tyler could respond by offering to buy an outdoor heat lamp to keep their father warm.

Hopefully, Cleo would be willing to go along with his ideas, in the spirit of accommodating. If one of her relationship goals is to maintain a close connection with her brother, abandoning her strategy of competing in favor of accommodating might well appeal to her.

"Okay. It seems like all this is unnecessary," she might say. "But if it helps you feel better, I'll do it."

Tyler could then summarize their agreement so they both know what they're agreeing to.

This resolution would come about only if Cleo's relationship goal of maintaining a close relationship with Tyler is stronger than her content goals. Otherwise, it's unlikely that she'd accommodate or compromise. If her relationship goals aren't as strong as her content goals, she might persist in her competing strategy. That means even with skillful communication, Tyler may not be able to secure a resolution that alleviates all his concerns. As you know from earlier chapters, it's unrealistic for someone to expect to fully control or change another person's behavior; they can only hope to influence it.

When Conflicts Can't Be Resolved

Sometimes no matter how well intentioned you and your partner are, and no matter how skillfully you communicate, you're still at odds with one another. Some differences between partners never get fully resolved. In his book *The Relationship Cure*, psychologist John Gottman, says, "[A] full 69 percent of marital conflicts never go away."[2] These conflicts are most often about money, housework, and sex.

You might think that unresolved conflicts would doom intimate relationships, but this isn't necessarily the case. What's important is how couples treat each other as they deal with their differences. For some couples, it can be quite a revelation to learn they can still continue to love each other and thrive together even though they can't work out some of their differences. Although they might find themselves in conflict again and again due to different content goals, they can still accomplish their shared relationship goal of staying together and enjoying each other.

How might you stay connected and manage conflict even if you have differences you can't resolve?

First, you need to recognize when a conflict might be unresolvable. Here are some of the signs:

• You keep repeating the same argument without any progress or resolution over time.

- You keep blaming each other. In other words, blaming, instead of looking for a mutually acceptable solution, stays the main focus of your conversations.

- Each of you insists the other person, not you, should change. Neither of you can imagine a viable Plan B that would resolve the conflict.

- Each of you has made all the changes you can think of making to resolve the conflict, yet it persists.

- You agree that both of you are unlikely to change how you think and feel about this issue.

- After fighting, you usually feel more alienated from each other.

- You start wondering whether this issue is a deal-breaker.

If some of the above signs are present, find a time to initiate a new conversation when you're calm enough to listen to each other. Instead of talking about the upsetting issue, discuss how the two of you are handling the conflict about it. It's crucial that you not have this talk when you're actually fighting about the issue. (Unfortunately, once you've started fighting, it can be extremely hard to stop—especially as the fight progresses.) Consider whether both of you can agree on the following three things:

- It's futile to continue having the same disruptive fight when you're not making any progress.

- You want to stop this particular fight.

- The next time you feel the repetitive fight coming on, you're willing to try a new approach to stop the fight from escalating.

If both of you agree on all three of these points, then you will have established a new, shared relationship goal: to reduce arguments about the issue before they can derail your relationship. Here's one strategy for doing just that:

1. Agree on a prearranged signal to stop a fight from beginning or expanding. For example, you could raise your hand and say, "I'm starting to fight. I want to stop before it gets worse." Find a signal or phrase that works for both of you that will interrupt the fight before it escalates too far. Usually, it's easier to interrupt a fight before it intensifies.

2. If one of you uses the stop signal, the other will, ideally, follow your mutual agreement to stop the fight.

   Don't be surprised, however, if one or both of you find it difficult to shift out of fight mode. Perhaps your desire to express your side in the argument is too powerful to hold back. Or perhaps your emotions are running so high that it's hard not to express them. Whatever the reason, it might be very tempting to continue the argument even though one person has used the stop signal.

   If you find yourself in this situation, try step 3.

3. Tell the other person you need to take a break. You can say something like, "I want to calm down right now so I can continue our conversation." (See chapter 14 for other examples of what you might say.)

   It's important the other person know your intention is to pause the conversation only temporarily. Otherwise they might assume you're abandoning the conversation all together.

4. Once you're by yourself, write down what you'd like your partner to understand about the issue. If possible, use I-language. Just write until you've said what you want to say and you begin to feel calmer. Afterward, set aside what you've written.

   Once you've calmed down, reread what you wrote. (Don't read it to your partner.) Then you can decide whether you must say anything to your partner. Many people find that what they urgently needed to say in the heat of the moment isn't that relevant later, after they've cooled down. If you decide not to say anything, destroy the paper.

You still might not feel calmer after following these steps. If so, you and your partner may have other approaches to limit or interrupt your repetitive, divisive fights. Feel free to use them.

If you've tried the recommendations in this chapter, but you've still reached an impasse, perhaps a skilled third party could help you resolve the conflict. You might also consider that you and your partner may never resolve it. You may find that you can "agree to disagree" and still maintain your close, connected relationship.

You might feel comforted to know that even though a conflict can't be resolved now, that doesn't mean it can never be resolved. Human beings often grow, change, and learn. Personal beliefs, desires, goals, and priorities naturally evolve over time. Life circumstances change. New potential resolutions may present themselves down the road. Maybe you and/or your partner's feelings or thoughts on the matter will change. Maybe circumstances around you will change in ways that bring the conflict to an end.

For several years, Lane and Marco have had a recurring argument over how much time Lane spends at work. Marco argues that when they don't spend enough time together, he doesn't feel as close to her as he'd like. Lane argues that while she loves spending time with Marco, she also finds her work deeply fulfilling. Plus, her income supports the lifestyle they both enjoy.

Then, over time, Lane realizes she's outgrown her job. Her work just isn't as fulfilling as it once had been. She's itching to go in a new professional direction. "I have an idea," she says to Marco. "I'd like to start a new company. Actually, I think *we* could start this company." After describing her idea, she asks, "What do you think? Do you think we could work well together?" Lane's dissatisfaction with her work has opened up a new potential resolution to their longstanding argument about spending time together—an option that hadn't existed in the years before.

Regardless of how you limit your repetitive arguments, just doing so will allow you and your partner to feel less drained and demoralized. You'll have more time for richer conversations that go beyond just solving problems, such as sharing your interests and savoring good times together.

Chapter 16

Applications for Parents

Communication Intelligence Meets Emotional Intelligence

Raising children is one of the most challenging endeavors people can sign up for. In this chapter we highlight how parents can use particular communication skills from part II to help their children develop a critical form of intelligence: *emotional intelligence*.

The Importance of Developing Emotional Intelligence in Children

Psychologists Peter Salovey and John D. Mayer define emotional intelligence as "[t]he ability to monitor one's own and others' feelings, to discriminate among them and to use this information to guide one's thinking and action."[1] Emotional intelligence is what allows people to identify and regulate their own thoughts and feelings. (As you've been learning and practicing new communication skills, you may have realized just how crucial emotional intelligence is for communicating skillfully with others. [2]) Research shows that children who develop emotional intelligence are more able to calm down when they're upset. They're also better able to focus their attention, relate to and understand other people, develop good friendships, and perform well academically.[3]

Children can be a handful when they're upset. They have over-whelming feelings but don't know what to call them, how to talk about them, or what to do about them. Parents often use punishment to try to modify some of their children's behavior. But they frequently omit a crucial first step: acknowledging their children's feelings. Psychologist John Gottman says parents who dismiss their children's feelings "are noticeably critical and lacking in empathy when they describe their children's emotional experiences. They don't just ignore, deny, or trivialize their kids' negative emotions; they disapprove of them. Consequently, their children are often reprimanded, disciplined, or punished for expressing sadness, anger, and fear."[4]

When children can name their emotions, they tend to feel calmer.[5] Over time, they can become more emotionally intelligent when their parents stop telling them they shouldn't feel as they do, and instead help them label their emotions and find solutions to whatever problem they're upset about.

Using Reflective Listening to Nurture Children's Emotional Intelligence

Parents can use a slightly modified form of reflective listening to help their kids develop and refine their emotional intelligence. By listening to your children and demonstrating that you understand them, you can help them manage their emotions and become better at solving problems, both of which can help them calm down when they're upset.

Suppose Calvin, age six, is playing with his beloved train set. His sister, Emily, age two, grabs it and pulls it out of his hands. Calvin gets angry and pushes her. She falls backwards, hits her head, and wails. Mom immediately comforts Emily and checks to make sure she's okay. Then she takes Calvin aside.

If Calvin were older, Mom might begin by noting what she thinks he's feeling ("You seem really upset") and allowing him to confirm or correct her understanding. But six-year-old Calvin is still getting to know his feelings and develop his feeling vocabulary. She wants to help him learn to identify what he's feeling and put words to it. So she begins with a simple observation about what his body is doing.

"I see that your cheeks are red, you're making fists, and your voice got louder," she says. "Looks like you've got some pretty strong emotions going on."

"I'm mad. It's my train. I was playing with it," Calvin says.

Calvin gave Mom the basic information about how he's feeling: mad. Mom knows that being mad, or "angry," generally involves the theme of injustice. A lack of fairness is also implied by the rest of what he said. So she includes "unfairness" in her reflection.

"Yeah, that didn't seem fair to you, did it?" she responds in a sympathetic tone. "It's your train, you were playing with it, and you feel mad that Emily pulled it away from you. Maybe you're frustrated too?" By acknowledging Calvin's sense of injustice, she's checking her understanding and helping Calvin feel more understood, while also helping him build more knowledge about the feeling word *mad*.

"Yeah—frustrated." Calvin not only confirms his mom's understanding of his emotion, but also applies the label she used: *frustrated*. Mom has helped him name his feelings, and she's implicitly acknowledged and accepted them. He's beginning to feel calmer.

It's important to be as accurate as possible with the feeling words. Many emotions look quite similar in their expression. For example, if Calvin's little sister had kept jumping in front of the TV when he was trying to watch a special show, and he'd asked her many times to move, he might look and sound "mad." But, more specifically, he'd probably be feeling frustrated.

Now Mom turns her attention to his response to Emily stealing his train—a response she's deemed unacceptable. She sets a limit and coaches him to find a better solution when he's frustrated with his sister.

"I know it's hard for you when Emily takes your toys. But you can't push Emily like that. She's smaller than you and might get badly hurt. And she's only two years old and doesn't understand about fairness." Mom says. "What's another way that you can feel better without pushing her?"

Calvin thinks for a moment. "I'd ask you to get my toy back," he suggests.

"I could do that," Mom says. "What if I'm not home? Any other ideas?"

"Maybe I could play somewhere else or give her my old train to play with."[6]

Our friend Kathryn Lee, of the Yale Center for Emotional Intelligence, says sometimes parents think they know exactly how their children feel. They tend to prematurely reflect their children's implicit feelings, without bothering to investigate if their assumptions are accurate. In doing so, they miss the opportunity to let their children discover and express their own feelings. Also, when parents misidentify their kids' feelings, they may start trying to solve the wrong problem. So a key to using reflective listening to help children develop their emotional intelligence is not to prematurely put words in their mouths. Instead, let them find their own words. You can also ask questions, but don't cross-examine them. And be careful not to overwhelm them with too many questions.

"I Wish": Another Skill for Affirming Kids' Feelings

Many years ago, my young daughter was tired and grumpy and wanted Cheerios, which we didn't have. Earlier in parenting, I (Mudita) probably would have denied her feelings, saying, "There's nothing to feel upset about. We have other cereals." And she'd have probably become more upset. This time, I tried a different strategy.

"I wish I'd finished work earlier yesterday. Then I could have bought a box of Cheerios so you could eat it today," I said. I opened the cupboard door and added, "I wish there were boxes and boxes of Cheerios so you could have as much as you want."

My daughter smiled. "Me too," she said. And she calmed down.

I was amazed how something so simple could get such wonderful results. I knew I'd just gained a powerful tool for my parenting communication toolkit.

This strategy, which I learned from the book *How to Talk So Kids Will Listen and Listen So Kids Will Talk,* by Adele Faber and Elaine Mazlish, is called giving kids their wish in fantasy.[7] A useful supplement to reflective listening, it's especially handy when you want to affirm your kid's feelings but can't come up with a reflective listening response immediately.

Modeling Healthy Self-Talk

Another way to help children manage their emotions and develop emotional intelligence is to model healthy ways of dealing with uncomfortable emotions. As explained in chapter 10, self-talk has a strong influence on emotions. Noticing, labeling, and, if necessary, adjusting the way you talk to yourself can shift your feeling experience.

Imagine that you've misplaced your car keys. Feeling frustrated and upset, you search through the house. "I can't believe I've lost my keys! Now I'm running late. Why can't I put them in the same place? What's wrong with me?" you mutter, as your kids look on. Your derogatory self-talk doesn't help you feel calmer—a fact your kids will take note of, consciously or not. If this is how you, an adult, talk to yourself, this is how they should talk to themselves too, right?

Now imagine you're in the same scenario, but this time your self-talk is different. Instead of characterizing yourself or your actions as bad, you simply say what's going on and how you feel about it. For instance, "I can't find my keys. If I can't find them soon, I might be late. I'm getting worried." Not only is this self-talk more benign, but you've also modeled using a specific feeling word: *worried.* (The "List of Feelings" in chapter 12 can be useful for finding the specific words to describe your feelings.) Perhaps you also give yourself a gentle reminder: "If I just take three deep breaths, I'll calm down. Then I'll have a better chance of finding them." Very likely, you'll begin to feel calmer, or at least your worrying isn't likely to escalate. Moreover, you've just given your kids a firsthand, real-life example of emotional intelligence and feelings vocabulary in action. You are their role model. Your children watch and learn from you. You are teaching these emotional-regulation skills from the time your child is born. The more they see you using a variety of feeling words and using supportive self-talk to help manage uncomfortable emotions, the more likely it is that they'll develop these skills too.

Managing Conflicts While Supporting Emotional Intelligence

Good news, parents! If you want to practice communicating skillfully during conflicts, your kids will provide you with ample opportunities. In fact, your kids might well be some of your best, most dynamic practice partners. They're constantly developing mentally and emotionally, which means that you'll need to frequently reevaluate your content and relationship goals in light of their developmental age and changing needs. Plus, you can factor in an additional type of goal: your parenting goals—what things you'd like your children to learn or skills you'd like them to develop (such as emotional intelligence). All of this suggests that you adjust your goals and pivot to different conflict-management strategies depending on your child's development.

It's your three-year-old's bedtime. "Please start picking up your toys so they're back in your room before you go to bed," you tell her. If you're lucky, your daughter picks up her toys. On the other hand, she may decide to assert a short-term content goal of her own: to keep playing with her toys.

Now you have a conflict. How you proceed depends on your goals.

Many parents with children of this young age choose to pursue the strategy of competing. In this strategy, you, the parent, get your way and your child doesn't. This strategy could work if you have a short-term goal of getting the toys picked up. It could also work if your longer-term goal is to teach your child that she needs to comply with your wishes.

But what if you have a different longer-term goal? Maybe you want to teach your child to take responsibility for her things. Maybe you want her to learn that everyone in your family can do their part to keep the home clean. Maybe you want to nurture the early seeds of self-reliance and the pride of doing a job well. Maybe you want to lay the foundation for a cooperative, mutually respectful long-term relationship with your child. Maybe you just want to establish a consistent bedtime routine that includes your child picking up her toys without you having to remind her. The strategy of competing wouldn't likely support any of these goals.

Instead, you might say, "Okay, you can take ten minutes more to play. After that, put your toys away." With this compromise, your child gets some of what she wants (more playtime, though not unlimited), and you get some of what you want (the toys picked up, though not immediately). Another compromise could be to incorporate the task into part of an extended playtime: "How about we play a game? Let's race to see who can pick up the toys the fastest in their half of the room" or "How fast can you get all your toys put away? I'll time you tonight, and then tomorrow we'll see if you can beat that time."

Many parents forget their longer-term goals in the heat of their compelling short-term ones. But remember, what your children learn from you now will affect their lives and your relationship with them for years to come.

Each of the conflict-management strategies has benefits and drawbacks. Ordering your child to accede to your wishes (competing) may work when children are very young. As children get older and start thinking for themselves, they're more likely to push back against their parents' orders. If you stay with the strategy of competing, over time you might inadvertently reinforce qualities you don't want in your children, such as poor listening and diminished empathy.

Your child's ability to engage the different conflict-management strategies will depend on their development. Competing and compromising call for your child to understand your goals along with her own, a task that requires emotional intelligence. Your three-year-old may not yet have developed the emotional intelligence needed to care about your goal of putting her toys away. Also, in a successful compromise, your child must be mature enough to feel satisfied (or at least tolerate) not getting everything she wants. How receptive your three-year-old is to the idea of picking up her toys as a game may depend, in part, on whether she can be satisfied with not getting more playtime in exactly the form she wanted.

Fortunately, as children get older, many parents find compromising and collaborating actually support the development of emotional intelligence, plus other desirable personal qualities, such as creativity. (Creativity is usually needed to find solutions that work for both parties.[8])

A willingness and ability to employ different conflict-management strategies will serve you well as your kids grow and develop. Fortunately, some problems that seem unsolvable in one phase of your child's life can become more solvable in another.

The Beliefs Underlying Your Parenting Goals

As you become more adept at identifying your goals during a conflict, you might begin to notice beliefs lurking behind your goals—including beliefs you may not have known you had. Beliefs about parenting and the relationship between parents and their children can be especially influential during conflicts with your kids.

If you believe that children must be taught to obey their parents, you're more likely to pursue the strategy of competing, where one person (in this case, the parent) gets their way while the other (the child) does not. If you believe constantly forcing children to do their parents' bidding crushes their spirit, then you may choose the strategies of collaborating, compromising, or accommodating.

In the throes of a conflict with your child, you probably won't be able to scrutinize how your beliefs help shape your goals. However, it may be worth taking some quiet time to think about what beliefs are fueling your parenting goals, how you prioritize your goals, and your choices of conflict-management strategies.

One of our goals here in part III is to show you how to apply skillful communication in specific contexts. To that end, we've focused on using skills from part II—including reflective listening, skillful self-talk, identifying goals, and choosing suitable conflict-management strategies—to support the development of your children's emotional intelligence. But children's emotional intelligence is a rich topic, and there are many creative ways parents can help kids learn to notice, label, and regulate their emotions. For more information and ideas, please check out the books and online sources listed in our "Recommended Resources" section, as well as the books listed in this chapter's notes.

We believe that along with skillful communication, the best parenting involves both kindness and firmness. Being warm and responsive to your child's feelings and providing appropriate structure also helps nurture their emotional intelligence.

Chapter 17

Health Challenges

Skillful Support for Tough Times

Illness and injury are almost inevitable experiences in life, especially as we age. When your physical health is seriously compromised, it's often difficult to appreciate much; illness, injury, and pain can eclipse almost everything else. Such circumstances can leave you feeling stressed, vulnerable, and emotionally triggered—and less able to communicate skillfully.

How skillfully you communicate, with both yourself and others, can play a role in how much suffering you experience during a health challenge. Suffering is different from pain. Pain is a form of physical or mental discomfort that signals something's off; suffering is the way you relate to these unpleasant sensations, including mental patterns and emotions you experience in relation to pain. Suffering can be amplified or reduced by your assumptions and beliefs, your self-talk and stories, as well as your sense of compassion, gratitude, and wholeness.

Using skills from this book can help you reduce communication problems and suffering while you're facing challenging health situations. They might even help you find pockets of peace along the way.

Most of the guidance in this chapter is for those who are going through an illness, recovering from injury, or navigating any other type of health challenge. However, watching someone you care about go through these times is also difficult. So this chapter includes suggestions if you're helping others who have health challenges. Please remember that skillful communication is not a substitute for professional medical care, including mental health care.

Notice and Change How You Talk to Yourself

Self-talk, as discussed in chapter 10, consists of thoughts that arise without much choice on your part. They are the unspoken assumptions, judgments, and beliefs that pepper your consciousness. You usually assume them to be true when they appear frequently. The problem is, sometimes those thoughts can intensify your experience of pain so that you feel even worse.

The first step in addressing your self-talk is to observe it and notice what it's telling you. If your self-talk is heightening your suffering instead of helping it, you can begin to shift it in the following ways.

Use Provisional Language

If your self-talk sounds negative or extreme, you can modify it with provisional language, which acknowledges that people and circumstances change over time.

"It's been three days since I started this treatment, and if anything, I feel worse. This treatment will never work" is an example of a non-provisional thought. Not only does it set a discouraging tone, but it also may not be accurate. A provisional thought—such as, "Although I don't feel better yet, the doctor assured me this treatment often takes time to work"—is less discouraging and more accurate.

Even if your condition is not likely to improve, or you're still researching pain management tools, using provisional language in your self-talk might help you feel more resilient. Thinking "I'll never be able to bear this pain" adds more stress than "Right now I can't bear this pain." Just adding "right now" acknowledges that the pain you're feeling could change later.

Revise Your Stories

Sometimes your inner voice tells you a story or puts a certain spin on the situation. That story or interpretation can add to or reduce your suffering, depending on the details.

When Maureen tripped on a throw rug and fractured her wrist, she felt a lot of pain. Initially, she told herself, "This is going to take forever to heal. I should have gotten rid of that throw rug long ago. Keeping it was stupid." On further consideration, she recognized that this particular story led her to feel discouraged. She also noticed she felt more hopeful when she thought differently: "My wrist hurts, but it will heal. I'm going to look around the house to make sure there's nothing else I can trip on." Even though she still felt pain, changing her story helped her feel less disheartened and somewhat happier.

Identify and Amend Cognitive Distortions

Cognitive distortions—inaccurate, limiting thought patterns—can crop up very easily during health challenges. Here are some tips for counteracting them when you notice they're affecting you.

Filter in the positive. A significant illness or injury can bring limitations to your life. When they do, it's easy to focus solely on these limitations and filter out any potentially positive aspects of your situation.

Suppose you have surgery on your spine, and your mobility will be severely limited for several weeks while you recover. Even amidst your pain and limitation, you can recognize and appreciate that you're still able to work and you have a job that doesn't require standing for long periods of time. It may be a cliché, but counting your blessings often adds up to a better day-by-day experience, especially during a tough time.

Please note, we're not suggesting you focus *only* on positive things or deny the difficult aspects of what you're going through. Instead, you're countering the natural human tendency to hyperfocus on the negative (a tendency known as the negativity bias). You're filtering in the positive to *balance* the difficult aspects of your experience, not cancel or deny them.[1]

Diffuse imagined catastrophes. Catastrophizing is a form of overgeneralizing. When catastrophizing, you envision a worst-case scenario about the future—"I'll never recover from this accident"— to the exclusion of all other potential outcomes. Unfortunately, when you imagine the worst, you're likely to feel worse. Modifying your thinking with provisional language opens the door to considering other possible outcomes. Thankfully, many people *do* recover from accidents. You can remind yourself of this fact with a thought such as, "Even though it's taking me longer than I'd like, my doctor did say my chances for recovery are good."

Another thing that can help is to remember that you're only *imagining* the future. Despite whatever good or bad you conjure up, your future is yet to be seen. A well-circulated saying captures this truth: "my life has been filled with terrible misfortune, most of which never happened."[2]

Leave the land of "should." Thinking that your symptoms or illness shouldn't be happening can leave you feeling drained, especially when your energy is already low. When what you want to be happening is at odds with what's actually occurring, you usually experience more stress.

Suppose you were struck by a car while you were crossing the street in a crosswalk. You're likely to think that you shouldn't have been hit because you were crossing on a green light, and cars should yield to pedestrians in these circumstances. Even though those facts are true, continually dwelling on them adds stress beyond the pain of your physical injuries and gets you nowhere. As much as possible, avoid dwelling in the land of "this shouldn't be happening." It's probably not a country you'd want to live in permanently.

A good way to take yourself out of this land is to modify your self-talk's *should* statements with relative ones. For example, you might say, "That car shouldn't have hit me when I was in the crosswalk, but some drivers are careless. Sometimes pedestrians get hit even when they're doing nothing wrong. It stinks, but that's what happened." Although you're now in the land of a more accurate, if unfortunate, description, at least you're no longer being drained by dwelling on circumstances you can't change.

Acknowledge that life isn't always fair. The fallacy of fairness is another cognitive distortion that pits you against your current circumstances. You might think getting struck by a car is unfair because you were crossing with the light. Dwelling on what's unfair can intensify your distress. If possible, instead of repetitively thinking, "Life should be fair," remember that life isn't *always* fair.[3]

Notice When You're Self-Critical

Overly critical self-talk triggers stress and reduces your compassion for the difficulties you're enduring. How do you feel when your inner voice says, "I shouldn't be whining; I should be stronger"? Now how would you feel if it said, "I wish I felt stronger right now, but I'm doing what I can do"? The second statement is more compassionate and less self-blaming. You accept what you're able to do, rather than focusing only on what you're not doing well enough.

Important note: Be kind to yourself if you become self-critical about how well you're regulating your self-talk. Just being aware of how your inner voice affects you shows that you're paying attention. Meanwhile, cut yourself some slack!

Treat Yourself with Compassion

When you can't change your condition, a little compassion can go a long way towards giving you more ease. Fortunately, you don't need to wait for someone else to show compassion to you; you can give it to yourself. Replacing self-critical judgments with tender feelings can be comforting.

For many people, compassion for others comes easier than compassion for themselves. Feeling compassion for both yourself and others means you realize "that suffering, failure, and imperfection [are] parts of the shared human experience," says Kristin Neff, PhD, an expert and leading researcher on self-compassion.[4] Instead of dismissing or ignoring what you feel, you can acknowledge your feelings and comfort yourself the way you would a beloved friend who was going through the same thing. "When we soothe our agitated minds with self-compassion," Neff says, "we can orient ourselves towards that which gives us joy."[5]

Neff's extensive research, and that of her colleagues, shows that extending compassion toward yourself during difficult times allows you to maintain a healthier, more balanced perspective. Self-compassion can also counteract the isolation that many people feel when they're suffering. As noted, part of self-compassion is recognizing that many people in the world also suffer, that suffering is a normal part of being human. That thought can help you feel more connected to others even when you feel somewhat isolated.

Consider How Things Could Be Worse

Unless you have a dire situation, you can sometimes feel a little better when you recognize that your circumstances could be worse. Suppose you're struggling with an illness, and you have the full support of your family and friends. Imagine how much harder your circumstances would be if you lacked their support. Even during the coronavirus pandemic that began in 2020, when you may not have been able to be physically present with family and friends, you could still connect to them and feel their support via video chat and on the phone. Virtual connections may not have been ideal, but not being able to communicate with loved ones at all would be worse. Reminding yourself of the good things you still have can give you a boost when negative self-talk begins to wear on you.

Express Gratitude

In her book *Self-Compassion*, Kristin Neff says, "Studies show that grateful individuals tend to feel more happy, hopeful, vital, and satisfied with their lives. . . . Luckily, research also suggests that gratitude is something that can be learned."[6]

After Maureen was diagnosed with Parkinson's disease, it became harder for her to do mundane tasks, such as cooking and writing legibly. Her husband, Eric, began helping her with these tasks more often. Despite her increasing challenges, Maureen feels lucky that she has Eric's loving support and reassurance that she's still important to him, even with her current limitations—and she frequently tells him so. She also still enjoys having lively conversations with family and friends, being in nature, eating tasty meals, and watching movies, among other activities. When she expresses gratitude for these things, both she and the people around her feel lighter.

In addition to countering negative self-talk, expressing gratitude can help you go beyond rigid ideas about caregiver and care-receiver roles. Typically, caregivers are seen as mostly giving, and ill or injured people as mostly receiving. Caregivers can easily feel overburdened by their role. Sometimes they overlook what they can receive from caregiving: opportunities to be useful and contribute to someone's wellbeing in simple and profound ways. Expressing gratitude is a means by which the care-receiver can give something to the caregiver. Maureen's husband, Eric, felt gratified that he could help her with tasks. Feeling useful and appreciated has often given him an added sense of purpose.

Remind Yourself of Your Wholeness

Disabilities, injuries, and illnesses can change your sense of who you are. When so much of your time is spent managing your health and not engaging in many of your usual activities, it's easy to fall prey to limiting stereotypes and labels. You might start to identify yourself as your health problem—"I'm a cancer patient"—and forget your fuller sense of self.

When you notice that you're beginning to define yourself only in terms of your malady, consider aspects of your life that go beyond it, such as your family relationships, your spirituality, or contributions you've made to others. Then add these positive elements to your self-talk. If your self-talk says, "I'm a cancer patient," you could add, for example, "I'm also a loving aunt, an alto in my neighborhood choir, and a huge fan of John Grisham novels. And I cook a fantastic risotto." No one is just one thing. Acknowledging all of these details is not only encouraging, but also presents a more complete picture of you.[7]

Change How You Talk with Others

When you're experiencing a health issue, the way you communicate with others is as important as how you talk to yourself. The following guidance can help prevent the friction that often affects relationships during these difficult times.

Replace Complaining with Reporting

When your health is compromised, the urge to complain can be very strong. Your pain and discomfort may be so intense that they occupy almost all of your attention. You may also feel frustration, anger, vulnerability, fear, and other uncomfortable emotions. Sharing your feelings with others can be a way of coping with the emotional overload. But it can sometimes veer into unconstructive, repetitive complaining. Frequent complaining can not only amplify your unwelcome feelings, but also impact your relationship with others and their ability to help you.

Reporting is an effective alternative to complaining. As explained in chapter 10, reporting communicates what's happening with you right now, including your thoughts and feelings about it. It doesn't zero in on just the negative things. It also incorporates provisional language and recognizes that circumstances can change.

Maureen has found that how she talks about her Parkinson's makes a big difference to both herself and others. For example, when she notices that her balance is worsening, she's sometimes said to her husband, Eric, "This is so unfair! I used to be athletic. My balance is awful. I can't live like this." The more often she says these words, the more true they seem, and the more she gets caught up in self-pity and dissatisfaction. Her grievances tend to eclipse what's still enjoyable and meaningful in her life. And they don't help her solve her problems. Eric and her other loved ones, meanwhile, often feel burdened and even bored when she keeps complaining.

Continual complaining can turn people off. On the other hand, reporting is often easier to listen to. It can also help others support you. While complaining tends to foster impatience, reporting usually encourages empathy.

"When I'm turning around, I sometimes have trouble keeping my balance. I feel unsteady," Maureen reports to Eric. "Holding onto your arm helps me keep my balance and feel more secure. I'm glad I don't feel off balance that often." Though she still feels vulnerable when she describes what's happening physically, reporting reduces her catastrophizing and feelings of discouragement.

Eric, meanwhile, finds her reports are less draining than her complaints. Plus, her reports let him know what she's experiencing and what may have changed—details that can help him find new ways to assist her, if needed. Together, they've worked out a gentle way he can alert her when she slips into complaining: if he tells her in a friendly tone, "The complaint department is now closed until the morning," she knows he's reminding her that reporting might be more useful for both of them.

Utilize Frames and Four-Part Messages

Danni has been working with a physical therapist (PT) for three months to address pain in her shoulder. It hasn't yet improved as much as she'd hoped. She doesn't think the home exercises the PT prescribed have been working well for her. Yet she's reluctant to bring up her concerns, lest the PT think she's just complaining. Or worse, the PT could label her a "nonprogressing" or "noncompliant" patient. Either designation might prompt her doctor or her insurance company to reduce the scope of PT sessions.

To allay some of her anxiety, Danni might find it useful to sketch out a four-part message before her next PT appointment. It could look something like this:

Referent: When I practiced the new exercises each day and didn't feel better, I remembered how the earlier exercises *did* help.

Thought: I'm wondering how I can get more benefit from these new exercises.

Feeling: I feel cautiously optimistic.

Intention: I'd like you to double-check how I'm doing the exercises to ensure I'm doing them correctly.

She might also include an opening frame for her message. A frame such as "The exercises you gave me aren't working" could sound like complaining or blaming. "I wish I had good news to report about the last set of exercises you prescribed" sounds more positive.

Four-part messages give listeners key information in a relatively succinct way—something that's useful when talking with busy health professionals. But this skill can be just as useful when having important conversations with loved ones, friends, or others about your health situation and decisions. For example:

Frame: I'd like to keep you up to date on a decision I've made.

Referent: Unfortunately, the antidepressants I'm taking haven't helped much. I remember you saying a while ago that strong people shouldn't need therapy.

Thought: Despite what you said, I think seeing a psychologist could help me.

Feeling: I feel hopeful.

Intention: I'd like you to support my decision.

Say What You Want Clearly and Directly

When what you want or need is obvious to you, it's easy to assume it's obvious to others too. But others cannot read your mind.

Moreover, when you're navigating a health challenge, your needs often change. Clearly updating your family and friends will keep them more aware of these changes. For example, when someone asks you if you'd like to go for a walk, just saying yes or no doesn't let the other person know the reason you're doing so. Instead, fill them in: "I want to walk with you in the morning, but I'm too weak to do that by late afternoon."

Being explicit about what you want is particularly important when seeking help from others. Many people, not wanting to inconvenience, impose on, or burden others, are reluctant to make direct requests. Instead, they might drop hints or beat around the bush. While respecting others is admirable, indirect requests for help can create confusion, which might interfere with others' ability to help you.

Martin needed biweekly rides to and from his doctor's office to have his emphysema monitored. His brother, Arthur, who was already helping with Martin's shopping, offered to drive him. Martin was grateful, but not wanting to inconvenience Arthur too much, he looked to his friends for rides.

One day, Martin's ride cancelled on him on the morning of his doctor's appointment. Not knowing whom else to turn to, he reluctantly called his brother.

"Hey there, Arthur," he said casually. "I'm wondering what your plans are for the day."

Arthur could tell Martin was being indirect, and he felt impatient. "If you need a ride today, just say so. I told you I'd drive you," he said.

Arthur and Martin shared a tense drive. And, Martin realized, it could have easily been avoided.

"Arthur's repeatedly asked me to tell him when I needed rides. I guess I wasn't as direct as he asked me to be," Martin thought. Though he still felt uncomfortable asking Arthur for rides, he resolved to tell his brother well in advance when he might need him for his doctor's appointments. That way, he could ask directly for what he needed while hopefully making things more convenient for Arthur.

Be Understanding of Others' Mistakes

Even when you think you've clearly communicated what you need or want, sometimes people misunderstand what you've said or don't hear it all. And when trying to help and support you, people will sometimes miss the mark.

For instance, some friends might still bring you sweet desserts even though you've told them you're now on a low-sugar diet. When they do, you can remind them what your situation is, but also be understanding. You could calmly say, "Thanks for the pie. I wonder if I've mentioned I'm on a low-sugar diet. But my kids will love it—as would I, if I could eat it."

You're less apt to get upset if you see your friends' present as a sign of their good intentions, even though they didn't remember what you said about your food restrictions.

Say What Works For You

You can appreciate others' good intentions, but you don't have to feel obligated to accept the help they're offering. Let's say a couple of friends had asked if they could stop by and cheer you up after your gallbladder surgery. You'd said yes gladly. But when they arrive, you find that you're much more tired than you'd expected to be. Decide how much interaction works for you and tell them clearly. You might say, "I'm glad to see you, and I know I told you this would be a good time to visit. But I'm starting to get really tired, and I think I need to cut short our conversation. Let me call you when I'm feeling stronger." Or perhaps, "I'm feeling woozy and really need to sleep. Thanks for thinking of me. Let's chat in a couple of days." It's better to say what works for you than to compromise your health.

How to Communicate Your Support

When someone you know is facing a health challenge, you might want to help them. At the very least, you don't want to say something that will add to their suffering. At the same time, it can be hard to know what to say, what not to say, and how to say it. Here are some general suggestions to help you communicate in a supportive way.

Respect the Person's Communication Choices

Just as there's no single way to navigate a health challenge, there's no single way to communicate with others about it. Everyone shares information about their experience in their own way. Some people feel most comfortable disclosing details only to those they're close to. Others feel comfortable reaching out to their larger community, perhaps using social media.

If you want to be supportive, respecting what others choose to share is a sensible first step. Even if you don't fully understand or agree with those choices, you can still acknowledge them and put your unspoken judgments aside for the time being.

Respecting their communication choices includes not sharing details about their condition or experience without their knowledge or permission. Allow them to decide how, when, and with whom they share their experience. (If they aren't able to give permission, then you have to rely on your own sense of what they'd want. Take into account how private they typically are and how much they have wanted their family or friends to reveal about them in the past.)

Pause Before Giving Advice

It's tempting to give unsolicited advice to someone who is ill or injured. After all, you care about them and want them to feel better. But having to field unasked-for ideas or suggestions can feel draining to someone who's already struggling. Suggestions of the "Have you tried . . . ?" variety can carry an unintended tone of judgment about how the person is approaching their treatment. Be cautious about thinking you know what's best for someone else. If you want to share suggestions or ideas, first ask if they want to hear your advice. Give it only if they say yes.

Listen, Understand, and Affirm

One of the most helpful things you can do is to allow the person to talk about their experience while you listen attentively. Then you can tune in to what they're going through and how it's affecting them.

Reflective listening is the perfect tool for such conversations. In addition, reflective listening allows you to temporarily put aside judgments that could limit the conversation. By listening with attention and confirming that you've understood, you're demonstrating empathy (without pity). After they've confirmed that you've understood them, you can decide whether it would be useful to offer your own, possibly different perspective.

Another advantage of reflective listening is that you can learn exactly what type of support the other person wants. It's an opportunity for them to clarify what kind of help would be most valuable. Then you're less likely to make inaccurate assumptions or get lost in what you imagine they want.

Listening, understanding, and affirming are not the same as trying to convince someone their experience is different from what they're expressing. It's not unusual for people to try to change, dismiss, or ignore someone's experience before fully understanding it.

Katherine is dying and feels at peace with it. She wants to talk with her adult children about her funeral plans and burial preferences. But the kids, struggling with the fear of losing their mom, cut short conversations about the matter. They say things like, "We don't need to think about those things now. Just focus on getting better" and even "You're not going to die. Everything is going to be fine." Katherine feels frustrated. Instead of listening, understanding, and affirming her experience of dying, her family is denying it. They might mean to be encouraging, but their denial is working against Katherine's goal of settling her affairs in the way she wants.

Adjust Your Conversational Expectations

Conversations with someone who's experiencing a serious health condition can be less reciprocal than the usual, day-to-day conversations. It might be unrealistic to expect them to listen attentively to your problems when they're focused on serious ones of their own. The exception would be if they specifically invite you to share your problems so they can temporarily put their own aside. Just be aware that they might not necessarily want to hear your problems but could say yes out of a sense of obligation.

It's normal to have feelings of uncertainty and fear when someone you care about is facing a serious health issue, as Katherine's children did. It might be tempting to talk about your difficult feelings with the person in question. But most people with serious health issues won't have the capacity to help you with your fears. (If they can, you're lucky to know them!) Instead, recognize that you have these feelings and extend some compassion to yourself. Most people have fears about pain, loss, suffering, and death. You might decide you could use some outside help, such as talking with a friend, family member, or mental health professional.

Finding Peace in Tough Times

If it's highly unlikely you'll recover, or recover fully, from your illness or injury, the communication skills and guidance offered in this chapter can help you in this new phase of your life.

When Ethan was diagnosed with stage-four pancreatic cancer, he realized he probably had a short time to live. As his pain intensified daily, he knew he'd die soon.

Knowing how easy it would be to succumb to his suffering, Ethan began to pay closer attention to his assumptions, beliefs, and stories. Sometimes he noticed his inner voice whispering to him, "This isn't fair. I'm a good person. I tried so hard to live a healthy life. This shouldn't have happened to me!" At such times, he realized he could gently revise his inner story: "I'm a good person and did the best I could to keep myself healthy. I still don't think it's fair that I have cancer, but some things are beyond my control."

When Ethan felt his pain increasing, he paid particular attention to how his friends and family were showering him with support and love. He frequently reminded himself, "I'm so lucky to have such a wonderful community around me." He also made expressing gratitude to them a regular practice, which felt uplifting. A week before he died, he told his wife, "I hadn't realized how much my friends and family love me. I've felt more love in these past few weeks than I could have imagined."

Even though Ethan wasn't able to control the course of his illness, he recognized that how he responded to his circumstances could make a difference in how much he suffered. In doing so, he discovered that a kind of acceptance and peace was still possible amidst his painful cancer.

We hope that the guidance offered in this chapter can help you lessen your suffering and find peace, as Ethan did.

Chapter 18

Diversity and Social Context

Recognizing and Respecting Differences

All communication occurs in a context, and actual or perceived differences between people are part of that context. Broadly, these differences can be called *diversity*. Maybe the most common differences we notice are skin color and speech. Others include social categories such as culture, gender identity, religion, socio-economic status, race, age, health, ability and disability, and experience. All of these factors can strongly influence how people see the world and how they communicate.

In casual conversations, such differences may not be an issue. But in more important, consequential, or contentious conversations, they're hard to ignore. Their influence is perhaps more noticeable when people are talking *about* them—when differences themselves are the topic.

The potential for miscommunication increases when people overlook such differences, no matter how skillfully they may communicate otherwise. This chapter will help you better appreciate how actual and perceived differences may be influencing your own communication and that of others. "Actual differences" and "perceived differences" is a key distinction. Some differences are factual, and some differences are perceptual. In other words, some differences are based on facts, and some are based on opinions. As you know from chapter 6, distinguishing between facts and opinions is an important aspect of critical thinking. Whether or not you do so influences how you think and communicate about differences.

Recognizing and respecting differences is useful for working toward mutual understanding and for having constructive, satisfying conversations in general. But when you're talking specifically about differences, it's essential.

In many ways, conversations about differences are subject to the same potential disruptors that play a role when you're talking about other topics. Yet there are some contextual factors unique to conversations about differences. If you aren't aware of these factors, or if you don't take them into account, you may struggle to have constructive conversations about differences, even with skillful communication. We'll discuss several concepts that often play a role in contemporary conversations about differences, including power differences, implicit bias, gender-based communication styles, gender identity and fluidity, generational differences, and cultural differences. These are by no means all the social differences that might influence your communication or contribute to contentious conversations. Rather, they're representative examples illustrating just how influential differences can be and the risks of not taking them into account. We recognize that we have not addressed other important differences, such as physical disabilities, mental health stigmas, neurodivergence, and sexual orientation. There are, however, many wise people thinking and writing about these topics. We encourage you to review their work. The sources in our "Recommended Resources" can give you some solid starting points.

All the skills from part II, and the rest of the information we've shared in the book so far, can be used to have more constructive conversations about differences. Detailing how specific skills could be used in various contexts could quickly turn into another book. So we've included just a few targeted examples to illustrate how the skills can be used in connection with this chapter's concepts. We trust you'll be able to see how you could apply these and other skills to your unique circumstances.

Unskillful Communication Habits Often Disrupt Conversations About Differences

Differences—and the prejudices and discrimination that often accompany these differences—are often tough to talk about. These topics are even more difficult to discuss without skillful communication. Here are some of the unskillful communication habits we've observed that can interfere with having constructive, satisfying conversations about many kinds of differences.

Inattentive listening. When you're discussing differences with someone, inattentive listening keeps you from understanding them in a complete and accurate way. It could also lead you to think the two of you have even more differences than you originally assumed.

"I've heard it before" syndrome. How often do you hear someone say certain words or phrases and immediately think you know all about their point of view? If you tune out, thinking you've "heard it all before," you might miss hearing a new, more nuanced perspective.

Premature, unsolicited, and clumsy expressions of judgment. It's easy to form judgments about someone without sufficiently understanding them first. And many people express judgments before considering whether doing so might be useful.

Mistaking opinions for facts. How often do you assume you're stating facts without realizing that you're actually expressing opinions? Not distinguishing between the two can lead to more difficulties when discussing differences.

Inflexible beliefs and assumptions. Bringing strong beliefs and unexamined assumptions into conversations about differences is quite common. You might or might not be aware of these beliefs and assumptions. Plus, holding an absolute point of view (such as, "My understanding about _____ is the right/only/best way to understand it" or "The way I experience the world is how everyone experiences it") can keep you from examining or adjusting other beliefs and assumptions.

Power Differences

Many factors can contribute to power differences between people: money and access to resources, gender and gender identity, race, social status, positions in a hierarchical system, mental and physical health, and disability are just some examples. Power differences in communication, specifically, are the actual and perceived disparities regarding the degree of influence people have with each other.

An example of an *actual* power difference is the one between a manager and employee. An employee might not be able to easily challenge a manager's decisions, owing primarily to the manager's formal position in an organization's hierarchy. A *perceptual* power difference occurs when someone believes another person has more influence than they do, regardless of whether or not that belief is accurate. An employee might believe their manager is the sole person deciding whether they'll get a promotion, for instance, even though other people's input might also play a role. The employee's perception of their manager's power would likely influence what they say and don't say to their manager.

Skillful communication can help counter uneven power dynamics (actual or perceived) and foster a balanced, reciprocal conversation. We believe the person in the higher-power position, having greater influence in the communication context, bears more responsibility for regulating conversational power imbalances. So if a manager aspired to have more balanced conversations with employees, the onus would be on the manager to use their communication skills to address the power imbalance. For example, the manager could practice restraint by initially talking less and listening more, giving an employee opportunities to add their voice to the conversation. The manager could also use reflective listening to confirm their understanding before trying to influence the employee. Doing so at least may give the employee some satisfaction that their views are understood. Even so, how much the manager is influenced by the employee depends on other factors, like the manager's goals and constraints. Let's say an employee suggests hiring someone to resolve a problem the team has. Though the manager may agree that a new person would help the team, they may not have the budget to hire someone. In this case, the employee's influence can't override the manager's financial constraints.

Unfortunately, some people in higher-power positions do exactly the opposite: they ignore others' perspectives and make little effort to understand people with less power. A catch-22 quickly develops: the communication imbalance highlights the unequal power dynamic, which further imbalances the talking-listening exchange. In the business example, the employee, having less formal power according to the organization's hierarchy, can do little to counter power imbalances influencing their communication with their manager. In fact, if they try, the manager has the power to demote them, give them poor performance reviews, or even fire them. A typical result? The employee might grow frustrated, dissatisfied, and more disempowered. Lacking alternatives, they eventually may abandon attempts to communicate skillfully about important concerns.

The same general principle applies to groups of people: we believe the onus is on members of higher-power, dominant groups, who have more privileges in society, to learn about power imbalances and take them into account as part of their skillful communication. Historically, groups with less power have had to struggle and work harder to survive and thrive in society than dominant, higher-power groups. They've typically had to pay closer attention to and learn more about the higher-power groups in order to survive and get along.

Curiosity is key for anyone interested in learning to communicate more skillfully about differences. However, members of higher-power, dominant groups sometimes have less motivation to be curious about the differences and issues we discuss in this chapter. The status quo is usually comfortable for people in these groups. Their success, their jobs, and other important aspects of life are not on the line in the same way as they are for people in lower-power groups. To communicate skillfully about differences, it's important to recognize that your curiosity might be inhibited if you're part of a higher-power, dominant group.[1]

It's important to note that any one individual can—and often does—belong to more than one group. And you might belong to lower- and higher-power groups simultaneously. These overlaps can make power dynamics even more complex. Yes, a manager's formal position in a business hierarchy confers a certain degree of power. But their gender identity, sexual orientation, race and ethnicity, or other factors may mean they're also members of groups that traditionally have less power in the workplace and in society.

Given how nuanced and complex power differences can be, you might be tempted to try to ignore them all together. Doing so might even seem like a good way to level the communication playing field. But ignoring power imbalances doesn't make them go away. And doing so is a luxury usually only those with more power can afford. Instead, you can focus on *allyship*, which involves using power and privilege to promote equity, inclusion, and justice while being accountable to marginalized people's needs.[2]

What You Don't Notice: Assumptions and Implicit Bias

Difficulties can arise when you're unaware of your assumptions about others and the ways you may see them as different from you. As discussed in chapter 7, assumptions are ideas you take for granted and, therefore, are difficult to detect. You usually acquire assumptions early in life. Assumptions are inevitable and eliminating all of them is unrealistic. You can, however, become more aware of and scrutinize many of them for their accuracy and usefulness. Recognizing and evaluating your assumptions is a valuable communication skill in general. But if you'd like to have constructive conversations with people you perceive as different from you, or constructive conversations about differences, it's also essential to learn about *implicit biases*.

Diversity and equity educator Shakil Choudhury describes implicit bias as "a hidden or unintentional preference for a particular group based on social identity such as . . . gender, age, class, ability or sexual orientation. It's a form of prejudice that is indirectly expressed."[3] Developing implicit biases is a natural part of growing up in any society. Virtually all people have implicit biases—even people who don't want to have them or don't think they have them.[4]

Whether you realize it or not, implicit bias can affect how you think, behave, and communicate with others. When you hear someone speak in not-very-fluent English, for instance, implicit bias may lead you to assume they're not that intelligent. Therefore, you might not take their message seriously. Or suppose you're at a coffee shop and see an older person sitting alone at a table that has extra seats. An implicit bias about older people might prevent you from sitting down at their table and talking with them. Even though you weren't aware of your implicit bias, it affected where you sat nevertheless.

Implicit biases are so hidden from your everyday awareness that it's possible to have implicit biases that don't align with your known beliefs and values. Suppose you need cataract surgery. The ophthalmologist you're referred to is a Black woman who graduated from Harvard Medical School. When you meet, you catch yourself wondering if she's a good surgeon. In the back of your mind, you might wonder whether she got into Harvard based on affirmative action. Or you might find yourself thinking you'd be more comfortable with a male surgeon. Realizing you have one or both of these implicit biases would probably come as a shock if you hold egalitarian values and firmly believe gender and race play no role in someone's intelligence. Though you might feel uncomfortable with this discovery, recognizing your implicit biases allows you to adjust your behavior. If you'd remained unaware of them, you might have asked for another doctor. Or you might have listened with discomfort and skepticism to what this doctor said.

Implicit biases can create assumptions that become stereotypes about people. A stereotype is "a standardized mental picture that is held in common by members of a group and that represents an oversimplified opinion, prejudiced attitude, or uncritical judgment."[5] These stereotypes shape what you say and what you can hear in conversations. They can act like blinders that limit constructive conversations about differences. When you're aware that you might be stereotyping others, you're more likely to notice how your implicit biases affect your conversations. You can then be more open to new information.

Even when you've identified your implicit biases, they can still continue to arise. However, identifying them means you can more readily notice how and when they're affecting you.[6]

Metacognition and Implicit Biases

As you might remember from chapter 3, metacognition involves paying attention to your experience in a relatively neutral way. Metacognition is particularly useful when talking about differences. It can help you recognize your implicit biases for what they are, as well as how they can influence your communication.

Impact and Intent: Recognizing Your Influence

Distinguishing between impact and intent is very important if you want to reduce potential friction with others, encourage mutual understanding, and be accountable for how your words and actions influence others. Specifically, your communication can inadvertently highlight the perception of differences in a way that has a negative impact. So while you might say something innocently or with what seems to you to be a positive intent, the impact could be very different. If you're unaware that intention and impact are distinct, it might take some education to recognize how your communication can be inadvertently offensive.

It's common to assume that if your intention is good, your impact will also be good. Let's say you're white and think a Black coworker has beautiful hair. You might ask her, "Can I touch it?" Or perhaps you see that one of the baristas at your local coffeehouse uses forearm crutches. As he sets your latte on the counter, you say, "Wow, you really get around well!" In both cases, your intent is to compliment the other person. But in their eyes, your request highlights how different you think they are from you, implying that they are "other."

Many people also assume that their intentions are what matters most in an interaction. Unfortunately, having a positive intention won't necessarily lessen the negative impact your communication can have.

Imagine that Will, a white man, is talking with a new colleague, Ken, who is Asian American, born and raised in the Midwest, like his parents and grandparents. Somewhere in the conversation, Will asks Ken where he's from. For Ken, Will's question highlights a way Will perceives Ken as different from him; it singled out Ken for looking or seeming different or other. If Will assumes intention is the more important element in communication, he might take issue with how Ken perceived his question. He was simply trying to get to know Ken better, he might argue; therefore, any negative impact his question had should be forgiven. In essence, Will believes Ken should give him more credit for his intention than the impact of his question. Doing so, however, would center the conversation on Will's intention rather than on how Ken was impacted.

Even with a clear understanding of impact and intent, you can't always prevent your communication from having an inadvertently negative impact, especially considering how common implicit bias is. What's essential is recognizing when you don't know something. (See stage 1 of the "Four Stages of Learning Skillful Communication" in chapter 3.) That recognition opens you to the possibility of learning something new and correcting your mistakes, misconceptions, and inaccurate assumptions. If you think you're already competent in a skill, you might not be as motivated to learn something new that could challenge what you already know. In this situation, Will might recognize he has more he could learn. Then he may be curious about how his question to Ken came across as offensive, despite his positive intent. Perhaps he'll ask Ken questions, use reflective listening, or express interest to discover more. Ken can then consider whether he's up for educating Will.

Microaggressions: Many Small Things
That Add Up to Big Impact

Even when people recognize that implicit bias is silently influencing their communication, and even when they're considering the impact of what they say, they still might say things that could be taken as *microaggressions*. Kevin Nadal, a psychology professor who's studied the effects of microaggressions, defines them as "everyday, subtle, intentional—and oftentimes unintentional—interactions or behaviors that communicate some sort of bias toward historically marginalized groups."[7] Here's how skillful communication and the information covered so far in this chapter can help address microaggressions.

First, if you're in a higher-power position, you can be aware of how social context influences your assumptions about the interaction. If you're in a socially dominant group, remember that those with less power might have different ways of interpreting what you're saying. Being sensitive to loop communication can help you notice your listener's reactions to what you say. When someone gives you subtle or explicit pushback, you can use reflective listening to understand what's happening for them. Stay curious about how your communication might have a different impact than what you had intended.

If you're in a lower-power or minority group, be aware that microaggressions you hear may be unintentional. Perhaps you'll consider cutting them some slack as they learn more about what they're doing. Or you may not. Ultimately, what people think and say about the importance of intent versus impact is still evolving.

If you experience what sounds like a microaggression, here are some steps you can take from a communication standpoint. First, pause to decide whether or not you want to say anything. If you decide you do, what would you like to accomplish? How you answer this question can help you shape a four-part message with a frame. In your message, you can advocate your perspective. For example:

Frame: I want you to know how I was affected by your comment.

Referent: When you said that my English was unaccented and asked me where I'm from,

Thought: I started thinking of other times I've been asked the same question. I'm a third-generation Mexican American. I lived here my whole life. I can't believe people still ask this question.

Feeling: I feel exhausted.

Intention: I'd like you to remember that BIPOC—or Black, indigenous, and people of color—are often U.S. citizens born in this country.[8]

What's a skillful way to respond when someone alerts you to a micro-aggression you've committed? We recommend reflective listening. First you'd reflect what you've heard them say: "You want me to remember that it's off-putting when a white person asks a BIPOC where they're from or makes comments about their English. You'd like me and others to recognize that many BIPOC are American citizens." If the person says, "Yes, that's right," you can respond, "I appreciate you telling me this so I don't say things like this in the future."

After using reflective listening, you might also acknowledge the impact you've had. In addition, apologizing after you've understood your impact can be helpful. Last, say how you'll act differently. Remember that emphasizing your intention ("I just wanted to get to know you better," for example) can sound defensive if you haven't sufficiently addressed the impact you've had.[9]

Let's say you're getting to know someone, such as a new coworker or acquaintance. Recognizing that you're still learning, you can tell them that you're open to hearing if you've said something that sounds like a microaggression. For example:

Frame: I'm wondering if you could help me with a sensitive issue.

Referent: I've recently been learning more about microaggressions,

Thought: I've realized that some things I've said may have had a negative impact on others. I know I still have a lot to learn about how I come across.

Feeling: I feel concerned.

Intention: If something I say sounds offensive, could you let me know? I want to be more aware of how I impact others and avoid committing microagressions.

Keep in mind that you're proposing a Plan A, asking another person to help you solve your problem. They might be willing; then again, they might say no to your request.

The Challenge of Talking About Racism

Racism is a highly charged phenomenon that influences our communication, as well as society as a whole. Prejudice is different from racism. Being prejudiced involves having preconceived opinions about others that aren't based on reason or actual experience. Anyone, whether they're in a majority or minority group, can be prejudiced against others. But the same isn't true of racism. Racism is not just individually held prejudice. It's an institutionalized form of oppression, where some members of society lack access to the power, privileges, and resources that other people have. Sociologist Allan G. Johnson explains, "Racism refers to the patterns of privilege and oppression themselves and anything—intentional or not—that helps to create, enact, or perpetuate those patterns."[10] The unequal treatment of BIPOC in the United States has grown from many historic, economic, political, and social conditions.

Aspects of racism are often perpetuated when people aren't sensitive to the difference between intent and impact in communication. For example, it's not unusual for a white person to say, "I don't see color." Their intention might be to say that they see all people as equal and don't discriminate. They think they're being egalitarian. But from a BIPOC's perspective, "I don't see color" often comes across as a microaggression. Ironically, the white person is highlighting a difference by saying that they're not highlighting it.

Neuroscience research shows that everyone is wired to see differences like skin color.[11] By saying, "I don't see color," you're discounting this fact. You're also ignoring the inequality, oppression, and discrimination of the past (such as slavery) and the present (including how often BIPOC Americans face police brutality compared to white Americans). In addition, saying, "I don't see color" can also ignore someone's heritage or a group's accomplishments, such as the acquisition of civil rights.

Moving towards social equity and inclusion can be harder to do when people say things like, "I don't see color." Seeing color differences doesn't automatically mean you're a racist. On the contrary, you're noticing an element of someone's life that has an important personal and social impact.

If a white person says, "I don't see color" and gets a negative reaction, they could take it as an opportunity to learn more about their implicit biases and undetected assumptions. They can use reflective listening to ensure they accurately understand the other person's pushback.

"Report" and "Rapport" Communication Styles

Deborah Tannen, a linguistics professor and author of *You Just Don't Understand: Women and Men in Conversation*, writes that boys and girls typically learn to use communication for different purposes as they grow up. She's labeled these styles of communication "report" and "rapport" talk.

Report talk focuses on solving problems, disseminating information, and getting things done. It tends to be prevalent in the workplace. The tone of report talk is often characterized as assertive. Report talk is not the same as reporting, a skill in which the speaker simply describes what's happening.

Rapport talk focuses on establishing and maintaining connections with others. Expressing emotions goes with this style. The tone of rapport talk is often characterized as somewhat tentative.[12]

Many people use both styles, regardless of their gender identity. However, misunderstandings can still occur when people assume they're using communication for the same purpose in a conversation. If you aren't aware of these two communication styles, it's easy to assume different meanings and intentions about what someone says. These inaccurate assumptions can lead to a clash or conflict.

Let's say Jennifer, using rapport talk, says to her male manager, "I'm having difficulty closing the Hart account." Though not obvious, her relationship goals might be to gain support and build rapport as she brings this issue up. Her manager, using report talk, gives advice. He thinks he's being helpful. But she thinks he's trying to prematurely shut down the conversation and feels frustrated.

When Jennifer comes home from work, she says to her husband, Jason, "I had a hard day at work. My new manager cut me off when I tried to update him on a difficult account of mine." Using report talk, he immediately tries to solve her problem: "Did you speak to his manager or Human Resources? You need to start documenting this." Like her manager, he might think he's being constructive and helpful. But she was hoping to further explore her feelings with him. When he started giving solutions, she thought he, like her manager, was also cutting her off.

Reflective listening, loop communication, identifying positive intentions, detecting assumptions, and using frames are all skills that can help prevent misunderstandings that often crop up when two people aren't using the same conversational style. For example, if Jennifer had previously recognized that Jason often used report talk, she might have anticipated that he'd launch into problem-solving before she was ready. To prevent this, she might have used a frame to let Jason know what she wanted: "I want to tell you about an issue I had with my manager. I'm hoping you can first just listen and understand how I feel before you help me solve the problem." If Jason were aware of the different styles, he might hear Jennifer out before giving her advice. He might also think to use reflective listening to help her clarify her thoughts and feelings.

Tannen's observations don't tell us all there is to know about gender-based conversational styles. Some of her ideas are generalizations that several linguists have disputed.[13] Nevertheless, it's still useful to remember that conversations can be used for different purposes, depending at least in part on how people are socialized.

From a larger social perspective, different conversational styles tend to mirror people's unequal access to resources and power. Even though women have gained more credibility and power socially, they still are paid less than men and have less access to higher-level jobs. Their conversational styles demonstrate not just early socialization, but also the power dynamics of a society in which women still face sexist discrimination.

The Language of Gender Fluidity and Identity

Historically, many people have seen gender as binary: someone is either male or female. But these days, more and more people view gender identity as distinct from someone's sex. Increasingly, *gender* refers to a person's social identity rather than the sexual biological characteristics assigned at birth. Someone who looks like a woman or a man may not identify as female or male gender. As people have become more openly fluid regarding their gender identities, the language people use to think and talk about gender is changing.

One sign of this shift is the wider range of pronouns people use to refer to themselves and others. If you identify as a traditional male or female, you may not think it's important which pronoun you use to refer to someone else's gender. However, when you talk with people who no longer identify as strictly male or female, using more fitting pronouns is often a sign of respect and inclusion.

Paying attention to gender-identity pronouns is becoming increasingly common. The Associated Press's 2017 stylebook, a standard reference for journalists, includes using third-person plural pronouns (*they, them, their*) for gender-fluid individuals who don't identify with traditional male or female pronouns.[14] Many universities have also adopted the use of gender-fluid pronouns.[15] Some new nonbinary pronouns are also gradually coming into use, including *ze/hir, co/cos, xe/xem/xyr,* and *hy/hym/hys.*

Many people initially feel uncomfortable using the new, unfamiliar pronouns. You're not alone if you feel puzzled or frustrated by them. If you want to update your nonbinary pronoun vocabulary, many internet sites provide detailed descriptions of what they are and how they're used[16] The more you use gender-neutral pronouns, the less strange it becomes. That's the language principle at work: How you use language conditions your mind. Changing what you say and how you say it can change how you see others and the world.

If you want to know what pronouns someone uses, ask them. An easy way to do so is to say what pronoun you use: "Hi, I'm Mudita. I use *she* and *her* pronouns. What pronouns do you use?" We don't recommend asking, "What pronouns do you prefer?" Many people don't consider pronoun use an optional preference. If you use an incorrect pronoun and the person corrects you, simply apologize and use the correct one. Also remember, if someone's gender identity changes over time, their pronoun use can also shift.

You can include your own or other people's preferred pronouns in social media posts or profiles. In the workplace, using pronoun-specific nametags is becoming more common. Many people now include their pronouns after their name in their email signatures or Zoom names.

It may take some practice to learn to refer to people by the pronouns they say most accurately represent their gender identity. Making the effort will foster trust and goodwill.[17]

Generational Differences

What makes you part of a specific generation? Typically, it's when you were born, along with the key historical events and social trends you shared with others as you grew up. For example, the Great Depression, World War II, the social unrest of the Sixties, and the development of personal computers, the internet, and smartphones are all events that have shaped each generation's sensibilities—and in turn, influenced how they communicate.

Currently, there are at least five living generations:

1. The Silent Generation (traditionalists): born before 1945

2. The Baby-Boom Generation (boomers): born between 1946 and 1964

3. Generation X (gen Xers): born between 1965 and 1980

4. Generation Y (millennials): born between 1981 and 1996

5. Generation Z: born between 1997 and 2012[18]

People who have a sense of belonging to a generation often share similar reference points. However, sometimes people from one generation can identify with aspects of other generations. For example, a millennial might feel drawn to the boomer music of the Sixties.

Each generation measures its worth in different ways. For example, some traditionalists and boomers believe that having more life experience makes them wiser and more capable than the younger generations. Some gen Xers and millennials assume they can be more innovative than previous generations due to their greater familiarity with technology. When people hold absolute beliefs about the value of one generation versus other generations, they're more likely to clash with or stereotype others.

Different generations may share the same values, but express and interpret them in different ways. Both a millennial and a boomer may value respect in the workplace, for example. But then a younger manager may clash with their older employee about whether it's respectful to text during an in-person meeting. The boomer might believe texting during the meeting is disrespectful. The millennial might believe not replying to texts immediately is disrespectful.

Being curious about generational differences can help you go beyond your implicit biases and modify some of your absolute beliefs and assumptions (see chapters 6 and 7). Understanding generational differences and taking them into account can help you communicate more skillfully with people of many different ages.

Cultural Influences

Culture constantly influences how people communicate—whether or not they know it. Culture includes the shared attitudes, values, and communication practices of a society. People in different cultures think differently about these factors.

Here's one example of how cultural norms can impact communication. In many Asian cultures, it's typical for individuals to harmonize with a group, to create unity. Consequently, one member of a business team may avoid expressing a viewpoint that diverges sharply from those of other team members. However, their silence doesn't necessarily indicate agreement. In contrast, individuals in the United States often feel freer to express differing views within a group. At a team meeting, a member might say, "I think we can all agree that this policy will work in the future." Even as other team members nod, one person declares, "I don't agree. I think the policy will be problematic." Although her statement might create conflict in the group, she feels more comfortable about disagreeing.

Culture, says Shakil Choudhury, "encompasses all the learned patterns of behavior, thinking and being in the world that are passed down between generations."[19] People from the same culture have shared ways of communicating that people from other cultures might not recognize. A simple example: slurping noodles in Japan is a sign of appreciation to the chef, whereas in the United States, it's often considered rude. There are many cultural dimensions that affect how people express themselves.[20]

Owing to cultural differences, you can mistakenly think, for example, that you don't have the same values as someone who acts differently than you. Suppose two college students both respect their professor. However, due to cultural differences, they communicate their respect differently. In the first student's culture, asking questions during a lecture is a sign of respect and engagement. So they raise their hand frequently as their professor is talking. In the second student's culture, respect is demonstrated by remaining silent and not asking questions unless invited. So they sit quietly and take notes while the professor talks. Only when the professor concludes and asks, "Are there any questions?" do they bring their questions forward.

The behaviors you see are like the small one-tenth of the iceberg that's above water. Cultural attitudes, beliefs, and norms are like the nine-tenths of the iceberg that's under water and practically invisible. People usually notice the observable behavior, the visible part of the iceberg, not the underlying values below the surface that they might share. Yet ignoring the bottom nine-tenths can lead to miscommunication. The less you take cultural differences into account, the more likely you are to make inaccurate assumptions about others' values, beliefs, and motivations. If you're the professor in the previous example, you might assume that the quiet student is uninterested in your class if you don't recognize they're demonstrating respect based on their culture's etiquette.

Low- and High-Context Communication Styles

In his 1976 book *Beyond Culture*, anthropologist Edward Hall categorized cultures on a scale of lower to higher context, as a way to understand their different communication styles.[21] Context is the situation in which an event occurs that partially shapes how you perceive that situation, whether it's a family dinner, a board meeting, or a sporting competition.

In *low-context* cultures, people typically assume fewer shared reference points regarding the situation they're in. Therefore, they use communication, and especially language, to directly clarify their thoughts, feelings, and ideas. "Say what you mean and mean what you say" summarizes a low-context communication style. People often expect explicit clarification when something is unclear.

In *high-context* cultures, people usually assume they share many similar reference points and overlapping background knowledge. Communication is less direct, meaning it's often more ambiguous, understated, implied, and nuanced. Listeners are expected to read between the lines to understand what's left unsaid. In a high-context culture, people understand that different rules govern interactions in a particular context, such as a family dinner or a company meeting. In addition, people's status and nonverbal cues influence communication. For instance, in a company meeting, a high-status manager might signal a subordinate with a glance to close an open door. In a low-context culture, the manager would explicitly say, "Please close the door."

Neither communication style is better than the other. The key thing to know is that people have different expectations based on their cultural context. In high-context cultures, meeting group expectations and maintaining group harmony are more the norm. Countries with high-context cultures include Turkey; France; Greece; Portugal; Brazil and most other countries in Latin America; Japan, China, Nepal, Pakistan, and many other Asian countries; and many African countries. In low-context cultures, individual expectations can take precedence over collective ones, sometimes disrupting group harmony.

Low-context-culture countries include Israel, the United States, Germany, Denmark, Finland, Australia, Canada, and Switzerland.

We've observed that cultural context can affect how people use the communication skills we teach. We've noticed, for example, that many of our students from high-context cultures, like Japan and China, initially have more difficulty practicing reflective listening. If you're from a high-context culture and your message is somewhat indirect, hearing your listener reflect your message can be jarring in its directness. And, if you're the listener, putting someone's message (including implicit ones) into your reflection can feel too direct and almost rude. However, once these students practiced reflecting and became more comfortable with it, they frequently reported how beneficial it was. While they were in the United States, using reflective listening kept them more engaged in conversations, helped them comprehend other people, and helped them decide what to say when it was their turn to talk. They enjoyed the clarity and rapport that reflective listening engendered. However, not all of them continued to use reflective listening after they returned home to their high-context cultures.

Differences in low- and high-context communication styles can lead to misunderstandings when you're talking with someone from a different culture. Suppose you're a manager presenting a budget projection that seems unrealistic to your financial team. In a low-context culture, some team members might directly criticize it. In a high-context culture, a team member might respond less directly. They might say, for instance, that the budget presents many details that could be studied further.

Here's another example: Imagine that an instructor in a U.S. graduate program is teaching a team dynamics class. He notices that a young Japanese student rarely speaks in an intergenerational group. Since he's sensitive to cross-cultural communication, he asks her privately whether the group is interesting to her. She says that she's interested in the group discussion, but doesn't want to say anything until the people who are older than her have spoken. Japanese culture has historically conferred a higher status to elders. This student still believes she would have been rude to speak before older people have spoken. Had he not asked, the instructor might have assumed her lack of participation in the discussion meant that she wasn't interested.[22]

Low-context communicators interacting with high-context communicators should be aware that:

- Nonverbal cues and gestures are as important as spoken words in conveying a person's status, identity, and message.
- Being frank shouldn't overshadow using tact and restraint.

High-context communicators interacting with low-context communicators should be aware that:

- What people say isn't necessarily suggesting other nuanced meanings.
- People often try to understand what you're saying by making comments or asking questions. Don't assume they're being disruptive or rude.
- You might need to say what you mean more directly rather than relying on indirect signals if you want to be understood.

Erin Meyer, an expert on international business, has written an excellent book on cross-culture communication: *The Culture Map*. In it, she says that one way to figure out whether someone is a more low- or high-context communicator is by their native tongue. Languages like French and Japanese lend themselves to higher-context conversations. A French speaker might say, for example, "That movie gets out very late." But what they really mean is, "You look tired and probably need to get more sleep. So let's go to an earlier show."[23] Languages like English are more direct. It wouldn't be unusual to hear a U.S. speaker say, "You look really tired. Do you want to go to an earlier show?"

In both low- and high-context styles of communication, being aware of the loop aspect of the conversation will help you assess how the other person is understanding you. Their verbal and nonverbal signals will provide a great deal of information. The first time Mudita went to Bali, she didn't know about low- and high-context communication styles. Coming from a low-context culture herself, she thought the Balinese were like her, mostly saying what they meant. She often took their messages quite literally. Over time, she realized they often said what was socially appropriate rather than overtly saying what they were thinking or feeling, which might have been bad form in that culture.

For example, a Balinese friend sometimes came to her home, and Mudita asked them if they'd like to eat. Even if they were hungry, they'd first say they'd already eaten. It would have been bad form to say they're hungry after being asked only once. But when she continued to ask them, they'd know she was serious about offering food and say yes.

It's easy to make inaccurate assumptions about someone's intentions if you don't take into account the communication style they're using. Say you're from a low-context culture and think someone isn't giving you "a straight answer." If you automatically assume they're trying to deceive you or have a hidden agenda, you might feel upset. But if you know the other person is from a high-context culture, you might understand they probably think it's impolite to state something too directly. Knowing that, you might make more of an effort to read between the lines of what they've said.

Preventing Cross-Cultural Misunderstandings

Given how communication styles can vary between cultures, it's very easy to misinterpret someone's meanings and motivations when they're from a different culture. The following tips can help you recognize how some of your automatic assumptions might exacerbate cross-cultural misunderstandings:

- When cultural differences exist and communication problems occur, don't automatically assume that others have negative intentions. Not knowing about cultural communication styles may be the culprit.

- If you want to increase your influence, adapt your communication to other people's cultural communication styles rather than expecting them to change their styles for you.

- How trust is built varies across cultures. Friendly relationships often promote trust in high-context cultures. A person's accomplishments and skills tend to build trust in low-context cultures (although friendly relationships also help).[24]

Navigating cultural communication differences can be challenging, yet doing so will enrich your connections to others. And when you're more cognizant of cultural differences, you can gear your communication to better build rapport and influence.

Regional Differences Can Be Cultural Differences Too

Cultural differences not only exist between countries, but also within various regions of a country. In the United States, for example, people from the South tend to have a higher-context communication style than people from northern states. People on the East Coast tend to have a lower-context style than people on the West Coast.

We really came to appreciate how different regional communication styles could be when we were first getting to know each other. As a former New Yorker, Dan had a lower-context communication style that was more direct than Mudita's Minnesotan way of speaking. Over time, we found ways to take these regional differences into account. Dan recognized that he needed to pay more attention to loop communication and to chunk his messages more frequently. Mudita realized that she had to be more direct when expressing what she wanted. She also discovered she could interrupt Dan more often than she did her Minnesota friends, and he wouldn't consider her rude for doing so.

We realize this chapter only begins to touch on the myriad personal and social differences that can influence communication and contribute to misunderstandings if people aren't aware of them. We encourage you to stay curious and maintain a learning mindset. Our "Recommended Resources" provides several directions you can explore. The key takeaway is this: No conversation occurs in a social vacuum. Many contextual factors inform how people see the world and how they communicate. Recognizing this fact will help you communicate more skillfully. And it will help you foster clarity, mutual understanding, harmony, and trust with others.

Chapter 19

Electronic Communication

Where Conversation Meets Technology

A s technology has progressed over the past century, it's expanded the ways we can communicate with each other. Prior to the internet, personal computers, and smartphones, having conversations face-to-face, over the phone, or in written letters was the norm. Today, text, social media posts, and video have become prevalent and somewhat unavoidable communication mediums.

Each medium offers unique advantages and disadvantages. Understanding their relative merits and drawbacks can help you discern which ones might be most useful in light of your communication goals. With so many communication mediums available, it pays to be selective about which ones you use and when. The good news is, the communication skills we've presented can be as useful in electronic communication as they are in face-to-face conversations.

Besides expanding your communication options, new mediums impact your ability and desire to converse one-on-one, verbally with others. At the end of the chapter, we'll touch on that topic and share what we think is the value of face-to-face conversations in an increasingly digital world.

Instrumental Communication and Evocative Communication

To help you appreciate the nuances of various communication mediums, let's look first at two common types of communication: instrumental and evocative. Understanding the difference can help you figure out what communication medium would be most appropriate for particular conversations.

Instrumental communication focuses on exchanging information to achieve a goal or a purpose. In instrumental conversations, the information exchanged is often specific and factual. An employee asking the accounting department to send them fourth-quarter statistics for a report, or a friend confirming the time you'll meet at a restaurant exemplify this type of communication.

Instrumental exchanges can also be more complex, requiring collaboration or negotiation, such as when your manager wants to negotiate a compensation agreement with you. The more complex instrumental communication is, the more important it is that information be accurate and complete. If your manager doesn't tell you whether your vacation time can accrue year to year, for instance, you won't be able to tell whether or not the compensation package they're offering you is sufficient.

Evocative communication tends to stimulate an emotional response that can inspire, move, influence, or persuade people to think, feel, and act differently. Words, metaphors, and images, as well as voice tone, body language, and other nonverbal signals, can all be used to arouse these responses in others. While evocative conversations might include an exchange of information to accomplish goals and purposes, they tend to do so in a more emotionally engaging way.

Evocative communication can be useful during negotiations, conflicts, and decision-making situations that involve more than just facts, such as when values or emotional reactions are involved. For example, discussing a divorce settlement that involves a decision about child custody can trigger intense emotions. Your values might come into play when you've recognized a mistake you've made and feel compelled to make things right. A decision about whether or not to get married can involve both values and strong emotions.

You can move your communication from strictly instrumental to more evocative in different ways. You can play with your delivery, such as varying the pace, rhythm, and volume of your speech or using gestures, body language, and facial expressions. You can introduce attention-grabbing words, phrases, and metaphors. Rebranding the inheritance tax as a "death tax" is an example of evocative language use. The *way* you deliver your message can evoke a variety of thoughts, feelings, and behaviors in yourself and others, and that's an aim of evocative communication.

Pros and Cons of Different Communication Mediums

Once you recognize the difference between instrumental or evocative communication, you can probably begin to see that specific communication mediums are better suited to each type.

High-tech mediums like texting, email, or instant messaging (IM) are convenient and easy to use, particularly for instrumental communication. Email would be a convenient and sufficient way for an accounting department member to send fourth-quarter statistics to their supervisor. Text is a quick, efficient way to let your friend know you'll meet them at 7 p.m.

Electronic communication mediums offer myriad advantages. You can initiate a message at any time you choose. Your messages can be composed, saved, and easily shared. You can respond when you're ready. These mediums can also help you avoid the unpredictable and, at times, messy consequences of face-to-face or phone conversations. For example, in face-to-face conversations, you might flood listeners with excessive details and repetitions. Texting, on the other hand, encourages you to compress information into concise chunks that are easy to take in.

Texting is less effective for communicating about complex issues, such as marital problems, parent-child conflicts, and contractual agreement details. It's also often less effective for conveying subtle emotional nuances that may be relevant to the information. Listeners can usually discern evocative elements, such as changes in voice tone and nonverbal communication signals, more easily and accurately during phone, video, or face-to-face conversations. In general, these mediums are better suited to emotionally evocative communication.

Let's say Jessica texts her mother, Linda, about problems she's having with her new boyfriend. Linda feels frustrated with their exchange. Without seeing Jessica's face or hearing her voice, she's less able to grasp the nuances of Jessica's concerns. She thinks she may not be getting a complete picture. She'd likely feel more satisfied if Jessica had chosen to communicate with her in person, over the phone, or via video chat.

The evocative aspects of communication are often overlooked as people increasingly focus on exchanging information through texting and text-centered forms of social media. Emoticons (or emojis), creative punctuation use (!), animated gifs, photos, and videos allow you to add evocative elements to a certain extent. They can also reduce ambiguity and heighten a message's intensity. Still, they usually lack the nuance of nonverbal expressions. They also frequently can't replace the intimacy of phone, video, and face-to-face conversations. Although you can get things done with these mediums, if they're all you use, you're probably underusing evocative communication. You might also miss the delights of face-to-face evocative conversation. Saying, "I love you" with a text and an emoticon has a different impact than saying, "I love you" as you hug your sweetheart.

Face-to-face, phone, and video conversations are often less predictable than more composed texts and emails. That unpredictability could be problematic or useful, depending on your aims. On the one hand, you can choose your words carefully and ensure you're giving complete information when writing an email or text message. On the other hand, the spontaneity and immediacy of verbal, real-time conversations can bring forth unexpected information and lead to unanticipated themes. In addition, you can refine your social skills within the give and take of a verbal, real-time conversation by:

* recognizing and responding to nonverbal body language
* noticing and responding to verbal nuances, such as changes in vocal tone and speaking pace
* developing an emotional sense of rapport
* cultivating mutual understanding and empathy

During the coronavirus pandemic, many people gained a new appreciation for both the usefulness and drawbacks of video communication. On one hand, video platforms like Zoom and apps like FaceTime allowed people to have real-time conversations and see each other's faces, without masks, while observing social distancing protocols. Being able to see, as well as hear, others was especially useful for people who couldn't safely visit hospitalized loved ones. Video conferencing also allowed coworkers to carry on business meetings while many people worked from home.

On the other hand, recognizing and interpreting nonverbal signals over video is very different from doing so in person. Video doesn't usually show people's full body posture, which means some nonverbal signals can get lost. Research shows that "Zoom fatigue" is related to the difficulty people have interpreting nonverbal communication displayed on flat screens.[1] Having to maintain eye contact with others for longer periods of time and stay seated in one position also make video conversations more exhausting than face-to-face ones.[2] And certainly video offers no opportunity to use touch to build greater intimacy when appropriate.

Choosing the Optimal Communication Medium for Your Goals

When choosing a communication medium, it's useful to consider your content and relationship goals. Omar and Ryan are both team members in a start-up. Recently they've disagreed about their team's strategic initiatives for the next year. Omar texts Ryan that he'd like to meet in person to discuss the conflict. Ryan texts back that he doesn't have time to meet for the next two weeks and suggests they discuss their differences using texts and email. While Omar has no problem discussing content goals using these mediums, he believes they aren't ideal for supporting his relationship goal, which is to reestablish goodwill with Ryan.

How you view different mediums can shape how well you think they support your content and relationship goals. Linda appreciates that Jessica texts her throughout the week to stay in touch. She likes being up to date on her daughter's life. But communicating primarily by text doesn't fully satisfy her relationship goal of feeling close to her daughter. Jessica, meanwhile, enjoys being able to communicate in short bursts with her mother. To her, frequent texting allows them to stay close when they don't have time for lengthier phone or face-to-face conversations. So she's surprised when Linda tells her, "I worry that we're drifting apart. We hardly talk anymore."

"We text every day," Jessica says. "I communicate more with you than anyone else."

Jessica and Linda's goals overlap: they both want to stay close (relationship goal) and keep current about what's happening in each other's lives (content goal). But where texting helps Jessica feel a sense of closeness, Linda sees it creating distance.

In these situations, we recommend taking into account each other's preferred medium and being flexible about using it. Jessica was willing to accommodate her mom's preference for face-to-face and phone conversations, especially for involved conversations. At other times, Linda goes with Jessica's preference for texting.

Using Skillful Communication with Technology

Even if you've chosen the optimal communication medium for your conversation goals, your communication can still go awry, especially if you're not communicating skillfully.

Justin and his younger sister, Megan, co-own an office furniture store they inherited from their father. They live an hour's drive from each other and sometimes have conflicts as they try to run the business together. Megan thinks Justin doesn't take her ideas as seriously as she'd like. There are many ideas she'd like to discuss with him, but he's rarely available for face-to-face meetings. Justin thinks they can use texts or emails to share all the information they need to. Although Megan finds texting convenient for most instrumental communication, she finds it too limited for conversations that involve brainstorming. Without skillful communication, their text exchanges too often turn into conflicts.

MEGAN

Hey—We need to meet this week

JUSTIN

Why?

To discuss my new marketing ideas

We don't need new ideas—no time to meet—Let's text and email

That won't work—Dinner's better—I never see you—We need to get together

I'm overloaded with vendor accounts—we don't need new ideas right now—just need to manage what's on our plates

Typical! You never take me seriously—You just think I'm your inept little sister!

You'll always be my little sister ☺

Can't you take me seriously—Dad made us equal partners

> Yeah, but Dad knew that I had
> the business chops 😊

> Excuse me?! Being older doesn't
> make you a business expert

This text exchange turned contentious as Megan and Justin fell back on the same unskillful communication habits that can interfere with any conversation. One problem is that they're inadvertently speaking for each other by saying *we* rather than *I*. When Megan says, "We need to meet," she means, "I want to meet with you." Justin does the same thing, saying, "We don't need new ideas." instead of saying, "I don't need new ideas." If they'd used I-language instead, it would be more evident that they have different perspectives.

Megan could have also used provisional language instead of the nonprovisional *never* and *only*. Justin, meanwhile, could have activated his listening skills at any point. But instead he ended the conversation without acknowledging her requests to make time for her ideas or affirming that he sees her as an equal partner. Perhaps if he'd been able to see her face or hear her voice, he would have picked up on her rising frustration and used reflective listening, rather than making jokes about her concerns.

Let's look at how their texting exchange might have gone with more skillful communication.

MEGAN

> Hey—I need to meet with you this week

JUSTIN

> What's up?

> I want to discuss my new marketing ideas

> I'd like to hear your ideas—I don't have
> time to meet in person for a couple of
> weeks. How about over text and email?

> That won't work for me—I'd like to have dinner—Haven't seen you for a month

Got it! You want to discuss marketing ideas over dinner together

> Yes, exactly!

Sounds good—me too. FYI, I'm still overwhelmed with vendor accounts. Much to update. I can discuss your ideas over dinner in two weeks. Okay with text and email until then?

> I'm okay with text and email until we can meet—Any chance you can finish in a week?

OK. I'll do my best

> Great! Feels important to discuss my new ideas. Feels like we're partners.

Yes, equal partners! I want to hear your new ideas.

> Great!

OK. Let's schedule dinner in a week or two. Until then let's text and email

In this version of their text conversation, Megan and Justin both use I-language more skillfully than they previously did. At the beginning, Justin also states his positive intention ("I'd like to hear your ideas") so Megan knows he's taking her seriously. Megan trades in her nonprovisional statement "I never see you anymore" for a more specific one: "I haven't seen you for a month." Justin reflects her content goal ("new ideas") and relationship goal ("dinner together" and "equal partners"). Later, he repeats his positive intentions ("I want to hear your new ideas," "Let's schedule dinner . . .").

This is just one example of how some of the communication skills can be used with texting. Another example of using the skills with electronic communication is using frames and four-part messages to be concise and add clarity to emails. We believe that as you become more confident using the skills, you'll be able to put them to use in whatever medium you choose.

Technology Warrants Some Critical Examination

We believe innovations in communication technology can expand or limit how people relate to each other, depending on how skillfully or unskillfully the new technology is used. We aren't anti-technology, but we don't think technology is necessarily neutral either.

Consider smartphones, for instance. Besides allowing people to carry on conversations via text and social media, these small devices have had a big impact on face-to-face conversations. These days it's become socially acceptable to text and check your phone when you're talking with someone in person. The problem is, doing so can send an implicit message that what's on your phone might be a higher priority than the person you're with. It can also fragment your focus, making it harder to attentively listen. Smartphones can even disrupt loop communication when they're not turned on. Sherry Turkle, a longtime researcher on humans' relationship with technology, says, "Studies of conversation both in the laboratory and in natural settings show that when two people are talking, the mere presence of a phone on a table between them or in the periphery of their vision changes both what they talk about and the degree of connection they feel. People keep the conversation on topics where they won't mind being interrupted. They don't feel as invested in each other. Even a silent phone disconnects us."[3] Even though you might want to reduce your smartphone use, it's often difficult to do. They're literally addictive. Research has shown that when people check their phones less often, they have withdrawal symptoms such as an increased heart rate, increased blood pressure, and a rise in cortisol levels in the brain.[4]

A full consideration of how technology impacts other means of communication is beyond the scope of this chapter. So we've shared a list of our favorite sources on this topic in our "Recommended Resources." We also think it's important to consider how your use of technology affects not only your communication, but your life overall as well. As psychologist Nancy Colier says in *The Power of Off*, "Technology offers the potential for everything we can imagine, but when we do make the effort to get quiet, we often discover that what we really want, 'the most important thing,' is to experience a good life, one filled with contentment, love, meaning, and depth, a life filled with rich experiences and relationships—not more of everything virtually possible."[5] How does communication technology fit into your ideas about "a good life"?

A Case for Face-to-Face Conversations

It will probably come as no surprise, but to us, a good life involves plenty of face-to-face conversations. Our preference is built on our experience as communication teachers, as well as our membership in the Baby Boomer generation, who grew up without email, texting, and social media. By this time in our lives, we've had so many productive and enjoyable face-to-face conversations that we've experienced their wide range of benefits.

We're not the only ones who see the value of face-to-face conversation. "[A]ll forms of socialization aren't equal," says Alan Teo, MD, MS, an associate professor of psychiatry at Oregon Health and Science University. "Phone calls and digital communication, with friends or family members, do not have the same power as face-to-face social interactions in helping to stave off depression." His observation is based on a 2015 study for which he was the lead author. In that study, researchers found that having limited face-to-face contact nearly doubles an older adult's risk of depression.[6]

Sherry Turkle observes that face-to-face conversations are crucial for learning about each other. Digital forms of communication, she says, just don't allow us to connect to others in the same way. "[W]e have found ways around conversation—at least from conversation that is open-ended and spontaneous, in which we play with ideas and allow ourselves to be fully present and vulnerable," she says. "But it is in this type of conversation—where we learn to make eye contact, to become aware of another person's posture and tone, to comfort one another and respectfully challenge one another—that empathy and intimacy flourish. In these conversations, we learn who we are."[7]

One of the reasons we wrote this book is so that more people could more easily experience those benefits for themselves. We believe the skills in this book can improve your communication across any communication medium. We especially hope they'll lead you to richer, more satisfying face-to-face conversations with those who are important to you.

The Spiritual Side
of Our Approach

Throughout most of this book, we've focused on practical aspects of the communication skills. We now conclude this adventure by exploring some of the spiritual implications of our method.

Spirituality can be experienced in many ways. For some people, it's the feeling of communion in a house of worship. For others, it's the sense of wonder that comes from looking at the night sky or hiking in the wilderness. And for many, it's the serenity that comes when they feel fully and deeply understood by another.

As long-time students of Buddhism, we recognize the connections between what we teach and important concepts that run through various spiritual and philosophical traditions, including:

- How language can be used to evoke or inspire
- Impermanence
- Interdependence
- Self-knowledge
- The limitations of knowing
- Service to others

Just as these concepts inform many people's spirituality, they also affect the way we practice communication.

How Language Can Be Used to Evoke or Inspire

The way people use language can conjure new perspectives and possibilities. For example, you may think of death only as a morbid event until a friend quotes Emily Dickinson's evocative line, "Dying is a wild night and a new road."[1] Suddenly, you realize that death could also be an unexpected adventure. Dickinson's metaphorical language has given you a profoundly altered vision of death.

Taoism, Sufism, and some schools of Buddhism teach that language has the power to evoke or inspire. The Mādhyamika school of Buddhism, in particular, has a sophisticated examination of the ways language creates people's ideas about what's real. Contemporary philosophers of language, such as Ludwig Wittgenstein and Richard Rorty, also focus on the evocative nature of language.

Our language principle is an expansion of this concept. It recognizes the important role that language plays in shaping beliefs, thoughts, feelings, and experiences.

Impermanence

According to Socrates, the Greek philosopher Heraclitus taught that "everything gives way and nothing stands fast" and "you cannot step in the same river twice."[2] Life is flux, or everything is always changing, was one of Heraclitus's key teachings. The Buddha conveyed a similar idea when he said, "'All conditioned things are impermanent'—when one sees this with wisdom, one turns away from suffering."[3]

When you embrace the idea that life and circumstances are constantly changing, you're able to have more equanimity amidst the rising and falling tides of your life, instead of getting stuck thinking that change shouldn't be happening. Using provisional language helps you remember that change is inevitable and to more easily adjust to shifting circumstances.

Interdependence

Buddhism teaches the idea of "dependent arising," or that every-thing takes form in relation to everything else. Not recognizing this interdependence, says the Buddha, is a form of ignorance. A saying from Zen Buddhism echoes this idea of dependent arising: "The bell doesn't ring. Nor does the stick. The 'between' is ringing." The yin-yang symbol in Taoism visually describes the concept of mutu-ally defining opposites. Cold cannot exist without hot; good cannot exist without bad; light cannot exist without dark. The presence of one depends on the other, and opposites form a dynamic unity. Many Pagan, Wiccan, druidic, shamanic, and other nature-centered spiritual traditions also hold that the universe consists of a vast web of interconnected living beings and conditions. One thing affects another, *ad infinitum*.

The concept of interdependence is the twin of the systems principle: both recognize that people's thinking, behavior, and communication are influenced by many, many different factors. Sometimes you can easily see what's influencing your conversations; more often you can't.

The loop-communication principle takes into account how inter-dependence affects your ability to build a shared understanding with another person. When you're "in the loop," the two of you mutually affect each other as your conversation progresses.

Self-Knowledge

Western philosophy, particularly the Socratic tradition, places a high value on self-knowledge. "Know thyself" read the inscription on the famed temple of Apollo at Delphi. Buddhism presents a systematic methodology for understanding the elements that comprise who you are (and aren't). A central question in Hinduism is "Who am I?" The Judeo-Christian traditions emphasize knowing who you are in relation-ship to God.

I-language reveals the beliefs and stories that shape your identity and, in doing so, can increase your self-knowledge. Exploring your beliefs and assumptions, your thinking and self-talk, your talking and listening habits, all add to your bank of self-knowledge too.

The Limitations of Knowing

If it's true that life and circumstances are impermanent and that everything in life is interdependent, then it follows that there are limits to what humans can know, in general or in a given moment. With so many factors and forces operating on so many different levels at once, it's impossible to control or predict with certainty the outcome of every circumstance, every situation, every interaction. There are simply too many possibilities in every moment.

Zen author Ray Grigg recognizes and urges us to respect these limitations when he says, "Place the smallness of what is known beside the greatness of what is not known. . . . There is a limit to a lifetime but not to the mystery in a lifetime."[4] In Buddhist philosophy, there are many references to the limitations of knowing (particularly in regard to relative and absolute truth).[5]

It can be humbling to realize that there's only so much about life or circumstances that you can know or control. At the same time, recognizing these limitations can allow you to more fully appreciate how surprising and mysterious life can be. Plus, not knowing what will happen next isn't inevitably a problem. While predictability might add comfort to your life, unpredictability allows what's new and fresh to arise in creative ways.

When you're conversing with another person, you don't always know where a conversation is heading and what the other person will say. You can think through what you want to say before a conversation; however, once you're actually engaging with the other person, you can't necessarily plan out your exact words from one moment to the next. We think this unpredictability can be a beautiful aspect of communication. With an exchange of ideas, you and your conversation partner together can build a new, shared understanding.

The limitations of knowing also extend to what you know about yourself. While cultivating self-knowledge is both possible and worthwhile, to some extent you'll remain enigmatic and indefinable even to yourself. As the Zen expression says, "The eye cannot see itself." You can speak authoritatively about yourself, but you can't exhaust all you might say. Recognizing that your self-knowledge is limited can have a positive impact on your communication with others. When you recognize that everyone, to some degree, is ineffable, you're less likely to characterize and stereotype yourself and others.

Speaking provisionally helps you incorporate the limitations of knowledge into your communication.

Service to Others

Service involves helping others and is integral to many spiritual traditions. Jesus exemplifies a leader who uses the power entrusted to him to serve others. Charity (*zakat*) is one of the five pillars or acts of worship in Islam. The Jewish concept of *tzedakah* encompasses the concepts of generosity, charity, and philanthropy, as well as the compassion, empathy, and caring that often motivate someone to share.

If being of service to others is important to you, skillful communication can support that intention. Perhaps you want to help others but don't exactly know how. Listening, an essential component of skillful communication, builds a foundation for understanding what others are experiencing. Reflective listening helps people clarify what they're going through, both for you and for themselves. While it's tempting to immediately offer someone advice, help, or information to alleviate their suffering, providing understanding and empathy through listening is often the best place to start. When you've taken the time to really listen to and understand others, you can better tailor your actions to fit their situation. Sometimes reflective listening alone is beneficial enough.

The Dalai Lama said, "Our visit to this planet is short, so we should use our time meaningfully, which we can do by helping others wherever possible. And if we cannot help others, at least we should try not to create pain and suffering for them."[6] Skillful communication can help you avoid making a situation worse. Some problematic situations are so complex that adding your point of view can be premature or disruptive, especially when there's no action you can take to help the other person. In these cases, the best you can do is not add to a problem, including not saying something that might intensify someone's suffering.

If your intention is to serve others, it also pays to consider whether *what* you want to say will be useful to them. Perhaps you, like many people, think that being authentic means speaking your truth no matter what. And in our tell-all culture, it can be challenging to keep from expressing what's true for you. Doing so might feel gratifying to you, but it might not be useful to the people you want to help. We're not suggesting you curtail your self-expression completely. Just consider whether what you'll say is likely to help or harm others, given their circumstances.

Finally, the quality of everyone's daily conversations helps shape the quality of society—even in turbulent times. What a difference it makes when those conversations encourage mutual understanding and empathy! People are then more able to blend their differing views in ways that can foster harmony. Your commitment to communicating more skillfully not only serves you and those you interact with every day, but your wider community as well.

Thank you for allowing us to be your guides as you learn to communicate more skillfully. We're delighted to share with you the knowledge we have acquired over the past thirty-five years of teaching. May your conversations continue to plant the seeds for greater understanding, enjoyment, fulfillment, and peace.

Appendix

Nonverbal Communication

Nonverbal behaviors are part of what the anthropologist Edward Hall called the "hidden dimension" of communication.[1] Nonverbal communication is defined by researchers as the transfer and exchange of messages in any form except the spoken or written word.[2]

It's estimated that in a spoken message, between 60 and 80 percent of the information is communicated nonverbally.[3] The nonverbal part of a message might be less obvious than the verbal part, but if you don't pay attention to it, you can miss a lot of important information.

Covering all the nuances of nonverbal communication is beyond the scope of this book. However, we hope the basic information provided here can jump-start your interest in the ways nonverbal communication affects your conversations. If you wish to expand your knowledge and skills, the sources provided in this appendix's notes are great places to start.

Key Forms of Nonverbal Communication

There are many forms of nonverbal communication. Some of the significant ones are:

Facial expressions: A range of expressions often accompanies what someone says or doesn't say.[4] During the coronavirus pandemic, many of us found it harder to read someone's emotion when they were wearing a mask over their nose and mouth. It was a reminder just how great a role facial expressions play in communication.

Personal space: During conversations, the amount of space between you and another person typically indicates the type of relationship you share—intimate, casual, personal, or formal. The amount of interpersonal space people are comfortable with varies across cultures. For example, in a meeting, Japanese people tend to stand farther away from each other than Americans and Europeans do in their meetings.[5] This is another form of nonverbal communication that changed dramatically in light of the social distancing guidelines of the coronavirus pandemic. Needing to keep at least six feet between you and other individuals not in your household or social bubble made it challenging to express affection or intimacy.

Appearance: Your clothing and grooming choices influence how people respond to you. For example, dressing too informally for a job interview at a conservative organization can undermine your credibility, even though you might answer the interviewer's questions intelligently.

Gestures: Whether they're aware of it or not, people use body movements to convey a large range of messages. Professional speakers, lawyers, and actors use movements such as arm waving and finger pointing to accent their words. The meaning of gestures can vary significantly across cultures. For example, the thumbs-up, "everything's okay" gesture in the United States is an uncomplimentary signal in Australia and the Middle East.[6]

Posture: How you position your body when talking and listening can signal a variety of attitudes and feelings. For example, crossing your arms on your chest while you're listening can be a sign that you may not be so open to what's said. Placing both hands on your hips while giving directions can indicate that you're in charge.

Vocal variety: Changes in the tone, volume, and pace of your speaking can add or detract from a spoken message. When someone asks, "How was your day at work?" your voice tone can express different meanings even when all you say is, "Pretty good." A soft murmur conveys a much different meaning than a more robust, rising volume.

The Relationship Between Verbal and Nonverbal Communication

The relationship between verbal and nonverbal communication is complex. Nonverbal communication can confirm your verbal message. For instance, you might say, "I'm tired," as you slouch in your chair with your head in your hands. Nonverbal communication can even be a substitute for verbal communication. Nodding your head can replace saying yes, for example. On the other hand, nonverbal communication can contradict verbal communication, such as when you say, "I'm doing fine" while your facial expression is flat and downcast.

Even though nonverbal communication is so impactful, it's more ambiguous and open to interpretation than words. It sends a powerful message, but the meaning of that message can be unclear. For example, you ask your spouse if it's okay to have your friends over for dinner. She says yes while rolling her eyes. You don't know whether to believe the yes or the eye-rolling, which might imply no. Fortunately, you can clarify what she meant: "When you said yes and then rolled your eyes, I wasn't sure whether or not you felt okay having these friends over. I'm confused." She can then use words to communicate more precisely what she's thinking and feeling.

In this type of situation, sometimes people inaccurately assume that the nonverbal is more truthful than the verbal communication. Typically, both the verbal and nonverbal are important. If, during a consequential conversation, you notice a discrepancy between the two, use verbal communication to clarify what the person is trying to convey. Different cultures allow different ways of commenting on someone's nonverbal communication, depending on whether those cultures are "high context" or "low context." (Please see chapter 18 for more on high- and low-context cultures.)

Notes

Introduction: A New Approach to Person-to-Person Communication

1. Sara Kehaulani Goo, "The Skills Americans Say Kids Need to Succeed in Life, Pew Research Center, FactTank: News in the Numbers, February 19, 2015. Available online at pewresearch.org/fact-tank/2015/02/19/skills-for-success.

Chapter 1: How Communication Goes Awry

1. The difference between facts and opinions may seem obvious, but it's not always. Different sources offer various definitions of each. Here are definitions we think are both accurate and useful: "A fact is a statement of truth that can be verified and is able to be proven as true," while an opinion "is a statement that reflects an author's or the speaker's point of view, beliefs, personal feelings, and values; opinions cannot be verified and proven to be true unless . . . these opinions are based on facts and evidence."

   From Alene Burke, "Basic Terms and Terminology Relating to Distinguishing Between Fact and Opinion, Biases, and Stereotypes," article online, RegisteredNursing.org (July 31, 2021). Available at registerednursing.org/teas/distinguishing-between-fact-opinion-biases-stereotypes/. Accessed January 4, 2022.

Chapter 3: Set Yourself Up for Learning

1. Josh Jones, "Why Incompetent People Think They're Amazing: An Animated Lesson from David Dunning (of the Famous Dunning-Kruger Effect)," Open Culture, December 6, 2017. Available online at openculture. com/2017/12/why-incompetent-people-think-theyre-amazing.html. Accessed April 14, 2021.

2. Merriam-Webster.com Dictionary, s.v. "metacognition." Available at merriam-webster.com/dictionary/ metacognition. Accessed October 26, 2021.

3. Experts who study metacognition define it in various ways, some of which are more detailed than we can discuss here. For sources offering more in-depth information, please see "Recommended Resources."

4. In addition to developing metacognition, the skills will help you develop what's known as *psychological mindedness*. Michael Karson, a psychology professor at the University of Denver, defines it as "the capacity to examine yourself with the accuracy, intelligence, curiosity, empathy, and humor that fosters attachment and growth when it is deployed by one person toward another." For more on this capacity, see Karson's blog posts "Is Your Therapist Psychologically Minded?" *Psychology Today* (November 17, 2015), and "Psychological-Mindedness as a Worldview," *Psychology Today* (September 6, 2016). Available at psychologytoday.com/us/blog/feeling-our-way/201511/ is-your-therapist-psychologically-minded and psychologytoday.com/us/blog/feeling-our-way/201609/ psychological-mindedness-worldview, respectively. Accessed April 14, 2021.

5. For more on the growth mindset and its opposite, a fixed mindset, we recommend Carol S. Dweck, *Mindset: The New Psychology of Success*, illustrated ed. (New York: Ballantine Books, 2007).

Chapter 4: Talking and Listening

1. This suggestion comes from Kristin Neff, *Self-Compassion: The Proven Power of Being Kind to Yourself* (New York: William Morrow, 2015), 148. For more on self-compassion, see our chapter 10, "Self-Talk."

2. The amount of information that's considered flooding varies in different cultures. In some cultures, it's considered rude to interrupt too soon. Chapter 18 will say more about communication differences across cultures.

Chapter 5: Reflective Listening

1. Brigette Hyacinth, "Empathy Is the Most Important Leadership Skill Needed Today," LinkedIn (November 4, 2019). Available online at linkedin.com/pulse/ empathy-most-important-leadership-skill-needed-today-hyacinth. Accessed December 9, 2020.

Chapter 6: Beliefs

1. The human tendency to overlook or dismiss information that doesn't agree with our beliefs is called *confirmation bias*. See note 3.

2. Nisargadatta Maharaj, *The Wisdom of Sri Nisargadatta Maharaj*, Robert Powell, ed. (New York: Globe Press Books, 1992), 102.

3. Raymond S. Nickerson, "Confirmation Bias: A Ubiquitous Phenomenon in Many Guises," *Review of General Psychology* 2, no. 2 (1998), 175–222. Available online at psy2.ucsd.edu/~mckenzie/nickersonConfirmationBias.pdf. Accessed September 27, 2020.

Chapter 7: Assumptions

1. For more on how to think critically about assumptions, we recommend Stephen D. Brookfield's *Developing Critical Thinkers: Challenging Adults to Explore Alternative Ways of Thinking and Acting* (San Francisco: Jossey-Bass, 1991). Brookfield shows how to use what he calls "critical incidents"—normal events in your life—to discover the way your assumptions affect your thinking and actions. Brookfield also discusses critical incidents and the three types of assumptions in "Using Critical Incidents to Explore Learners' Assumptions," a chapter within *Fostering Critical Reflection in Adulthood: A Guide to Transformative and Emancipatory Learning*, Jack Mezirow, ed. (San Francisco: Jossey-Bass, 1990), 177–193.

2. Cambridge Dictionary, "Values," Available online at dictionary.cambridge.org/dictionary/english/values.

Chapter 8: Shifting the Blame Mindset

1. For a detailed discussion of these ideas from a systems thinking perspective, see Marilyn Paul, "Moving from Accountability to Blame," The Systems Thinker, n.d., thesystemsthinker.com/moving-from-blame-to-accountability/. Accessed February 17, 2021.

2. Attributing someone's actions or behavior to their character or an aspect of it is known as *dispositional attribution*. Attributing their actions or behavior to

outside forces, which they may have little or no control over, is called *situational attribution*. Both terms come from attribution theory, a branch of social psychology that examines how people explain the reasons or causes of behavior, actions, or events. To learn more about attribution theory, see our "Recommended Resources."

Chapter 10: Self-Talk

1. Matthew McKay, Martha Davis, and Patrick Fanning, *Thoughts and Feelings: Taking Control of Your Moods and Your Life*, 4th ed. (Oakland, CA: New Harbinger, 2011), 18.

2. Tony Schwartz, "Overcoming Your Negativity Bias," *New York Times*, June 14, 2013.

3. Psychiatrist David D. Burns, MD, for example, has identified fifteen cognitive distortions. For a summary of them, see John M. Grohol, "15 Common Cognitive Distortions" (article online), PsychCentral, updated June 24, 2019. Available at psychcentral.com/lib/15-common-cognitive-distortions/. Accessed September 28, 2020.

Chapter 12: The Four-Part Message

1. Gregory Bateson, "Form, Substance, and Difference," in *Steps to an Ecology of Mind* (Chicago: University of Chicago Press, 2000), 462.

2. The original quote from Epictetus is, "Men are disturbed not by things, but by the views which they take of things." From *The Enchiridion*, Thomas W. Higginson, trans. (New York: The Liberal Arts Press, 1948). Available online at gutenberg.org/files/45109/45109-h/45109-h. htm. Accessed October 27, 2020.

Chapter 13: Framing Your Message

1. For a more extensive description of metacommunication's use in communication, see Kathleen M. Galvin, *Making Connections: Readings in Relational Communication*, 5th ed. (Oxford and New York: Oxford University Press, 2011), 16–17.

2. For a more detailed discussion of the way metaphors frame conflicts, see Joyce L. Hocker and William W. Wilmot, *Interpersonal Conflict*, 10th ed. (New York: McGraw-Hill Education, 2017), 49–60.

Chapter 14: Managing Conflict

1. Hocker and Wilmot, *Interpersonal Conflict*, 80.

2. The concept of content and relationship goals originates in the field of conflict studies. For more on these two types of goals, we recommend the book *Interpersonal Conflict* by Hocker and Wilmot, specifically chapter 3, "Interests and Goals."

3. The well-known conflict-negotiation book *Getting to Yes*, by Roger Fisher and William Ury, discusses *interests* and *positions*. These two concepts are useful when you're trying to work out differences and want to find common ground with the other person.

    An interest is something a person wants that influences them to take a position. In the example with Emily and George, her interests are staying fit and feeling safe as she does. Her position is that she wants to work out outside. George has the same interests (staying fit and feeling safe). But his position is that he wants to work out at the gym.

    Emily and George differ on whether the gym is a safe setting. If they focus only on their differing positions, they could lose sight of their partially overlapping interests of staying fit and feeling safe. Then they might have more trouble finding a solution that works for both of them.

For more on interests and positions, see Roger Fischer and William Ury, *Getting to Yes: Negotiating Agreement without Giving In*, 3rd ed., Bruce Patton, ed. (New York: Penguin Books, 2011), 51–62.

4. The five strategies we describe are based on the five "modes of responding to conflict" developed by Kenneth W. Thomas, PhD, and Ralph H. Kilmann, PhD, in the 1970s, as part of their Thomas-Kilmann Instrument, or TKI. This instrument has since been used by thousands around the world, and other authors have described and used its five conflict modes in various ways. More information on the TKI and its five modes can be found on the website for Kilmann's company, Kilmann Diagnostics (kilmanndiagnostics.com). For additional information on conflict-management strategies, see Hocker and Wilmot, *Interpersonal Conflict*, chapter 5, "Conflict Styles."

Chapter 15: Conflict Management for Couples

1. John M. Gottman, "How Couples Build Trust with Attunement," in *The Science of Trust: Emotional Attunement for Couples* (New York: W. W. Norton & Company, 2011), 176–250.

2. John M. Gottman and Joan DeClaire, *The Relationship Cure: A 5 Step Guide to Strengthening Your Marriage, Family, and Friendships* (New York: Three Rivers Press, 2001), 207.

Chapter 16: Applications for Parents

1. Peter Salovey and John D. Mayer, "Emotional Intelligence," *Imagination, Cognition, and Personality*, 9, no. 3 (March 1, 1990), 185–211. Available online at doi. org/10.2190/DUGG-P24E-52WK-6CDG.

2. For more on emotional intelligence, we recommend Dan Goleman, *Emotional Intelligence: Why It Can Matter More Than IQ*, 10th anniversary ed. (New York: Random House, 2005).

3. Stephanie M. Jones and Jennifer Kahn, *The Evidence Base for How We Learn: Supporting Students' Social, Emotional, and Academic Development* (Consensus Statements of Evidence from the Council of Distinguished Scientists), National Commission on Social, Economic, and Emotional Development, the Aspen Institute (September 13, 2017). Available online at assets.aspeninstitute.org/content/uploads/2017/09/SEAD-Research-Brief-9.12_updated-web.pdf.

4. John M. Gottman and Joan DeClaire, *Raising an Emotionally Intelligent Child: The Heart of Parenting* (New York: Fireside, 1998), 57.

5. Gottman and DeClaire, 100.

6. For more on addressing behavior and setting limits, see Gottman and DeClaire, 103–104, and Marc Brackett, *Permission to Feel: The Power of Emotional Intelligence to Achieve Well-Being and Success* (New York: Celadon Books, 2020), 71–166.

7. Adele Faber and Elaine Mazlish, *How to Talk So Kids Will Listen and Listen So Kids Will Talk*, updated ed. (New York: Scribner, 2012).

8. Erin Clabough, *Second Nature: How Parents Can Use Neuroscience to Help Kids Develop Empathy, Creativity, and Self-Control* (Boulder, CO: Sounds True, 2019), 142–143.

Chapter 17: Health Challenges

1. Barbara L. Fredrickson, PhD, a psychologist, professor, and researcher at the University of North Carolina, has found that people need about three positive thoughts to counter the physiological effects of one negative thought. Greater Good Science Center, "Barbara Fredrickson: The Positivity Ratio," YouTube, June 20, 2011. Available at youtube.com/watch?v=_hFzxfQpLjM. Accessed March 26, 2021.

2. Variations of this saying have been attributed to James A. Garfield, Winston Churchill, Michel de Montaigne, Seneca the Younger, Thomas Jefferson, and Martin Farquhar Tupper, among others. But who, if anyone, said these exact words remains a mystery. For more, see "I Am an Old Man and Have Known Many Troubles . . . ," Quote Investigator (website), October 4, 2014. Available online at quoteinvestigator.com/2013/10/04/never-happened/.

3. For information on progressive relaxation, meditation, visualization, and other means of countering negative distortions, please see the recommended resources for chapter 10.

4. Kristin Neff, "Definition of Self-Compassion," a page on the website, Self-Compassion (self-compassion.org). Page available at self-compassion.org/the-three-elements-of-self-compassion-2. Accessed January 8, 2019.

5. Neff, *Self-Compassion*, 13.

6. Neff, *Self-Compassion*, 277.

7. An informative book about how stories affect your brain and how you can change those stories is Lewis Mehl-Madrona, with Barbara Mainguy, *Remapping Your Mind: The Neuroscience of Self-Transformation through Story*

(Rochester, VT: Bear & Company, 2015). For more on how your narrative affects your sense of meaning, we also recommend Viktor E. Frankl, *Man's Search For Meaning* (Boston: Beacon Press, 2006).

Chapter 18: Diversity and Social Context

1. For more details about power-balancing tactics, see Wilmot and Hocker, chapter 4, "Power: The Structure of Conflict," in *Interpersonal Conflict*, 131–150, and Dacher Keltner, "The Power Paradox," *Greater Good* online magazine (December 1, 2007), greatergood.berkeley.edu/article/item/power_paradox.

2. For more detailed descriptions of what allyship entails, see the following three resources: Michelle MiJung Kim, "Allyship (& Accomplice): The What, Why, and How," Medium (November 10, 2019). Available at medium.com/awaken-blog/allyship-vs-accomplice-the-what-why-and-how-f3da767d48cc. Accessed September 7, 2021. Tsedale M. Melaku, Angie Beeman, David G. Smith, and W. Brad Johnson, "Be a Better Ally," *Harvard Business Review* (November–December 2020). Available at hbr.org/2020/11/be-a-better-ally. Accessed September 7, 2021. Sheree Atchenson, "Allyship: The Key to Unlocking the Power of Diversity," *Forbes* (November 30, 2018). Available at forbes.com/sites/shereeatcheson/2018/11/30/allyship-the-key-to-unlocking-the-power-of-diversity/?sh=2cbae20b49c6. Accessed September 7, 2021.

3. Shakil Choudhury, *Deep Diversity: Overcoming Us vs. Them* (Toronto: Between The Lines, 2015), 49.

4. "The Mind of the Village," a June 20, 2020, episode of the NPR radio show/podcast Hidden Brain, discusses just how ubiquitous implicit bias is: npr.

org/2020/06/20/880379282/the-mind-of-the-village-
understanding-our-implicit-biases. See also Farah
Nasser, "Think You Are Unbiased? Think Again," *Global
News* (June 12, 2019). Available at globalnews.ca/
news/5382584/unconscious-bias-shakil-choudhury/.
Accessed April 6, 2021.

5. *Merriam-Webster.com Dictionary*, s.v. "stereotype."
    Available at merriam-webster.com/dictionary/stereotype.
    Accessed October 26, 2021.

6. Project Implicit, a nonprofit collaboration between
    researchers interested in implicit social cognition, offers an
    online test to help you identify your implicit biases. You can
    find the test at this website: implicit.harvard.edu/implicit/
    index.jsp. Data collected from this Implicit Association Test
    (IAT) supports the group's ongoing research efforts.

7. Quoted in Andrew Limbong, "Microaggressions Are
    a Big Deal: How to Talk Them Out and When to
    Walk Away," NPR (June 9, 2020). Available at npr.
    org/2020/06/08/872371063/microaggressions-are-a-
    big-deal-how-to-talk-them-out-and-when-to-walk-away.
    Accessed April 7, 2021.

8. LGBTQIA+ is another frequently used inclusive acronym.
    Its letters stand for lesbian, gay, transsexual/transgender,
    queer, intersex, and asexual. The plus symbol acknowledges
    that people can have more identities than the acronym
    captures. BIPOC and LGBTQIA+ cannot be used
    interchangeably. They represent different identity groups.
    For a detailed description of the latter acronym, see Jennifer
    Betts, "What Does LGBTQIA+ Stand For? Full Acronym
    Explained," YourDictionary (n.d.). Available at abbreviations.
    yourdictionary.com/what-does-lgbtqia-stand-for-full-
    acronym-explained.html. Accessed September 8, 2021.

9. For a detailed description of what to say when offering an apology, see Hocker and Wilmot, *Interpersonal Conflict*, 341–346.

10. Allan G. Johnson, *Privilege, Power, and Difference*, 3rd ed. (New York: McGraw Hill, 2018), 89.

11. Jason Marsh, Rodolfo Mendoza-Denton, and Jeremy Adam Smith, eds., *Are We Born Racist?: New Insights from Neuroscience and Positive Psychology* (Boston: Beacon Press, 2010), 7–15.

12. Deborah Tannen, *You Just Don't Understand: Women and Men in Conversation* (New York: Ballantine, 1990), 76–77.

13. Alice F. Freed, "We Understand Perfectly: A Critique of Tannen's View of Cross-Sex Communication," in Kira Hall, Mary Bucholtz, and Birch Moonwomon, eds., *Locating Power: Proceedings of the Second Berkeley Women and Language Conference*, Vol. 1 (Berkeley, CA: Berkeley Women and Language Group, 1992), 144–152.

14. Lauren Easton, "Making a Case for a Singular 'They,'" Associated Press (March 24, 2017). Available at blog.ap.org/products-and-services/making-a-case-for-a-singular-they. Accessed September 9, 2021.

15. "More Universities Move to Include Gender-Neutral Pronouns," NPR (November 18, 2015). Available at npr.org/2015/11/08/455202525/more-universities-move-to-include-gender-neutral-pronouns. For additional pronouns and their use see: https://genderneutralpronoun.wordpress.com/tag/xe. Accessed September 9, 2021.

16. For additional info on gender fluid pronouns, see Sassafras Lowrey, "A Guide to Non-binary Pronouns and Why They Matter," HuffPost (November 8, 2017). Available at huffingtonpost.com/entry/

non-binary-pronouns-why-they-matter_us_
5a03107be4b0230facb8419a. Accessed September 9, 2021.

17. Beyond respecting people's pronouns, you can demonstrate respect for gender fluidity by using nonbinary greetings when addressing groups. For example, you could say, "Hi folks/friends/y'all" instead of saying, "ladies and gentleman."

18. "The Generations Defined," Pew Research Center (March 1, 2018). Available at pewresearch.org/st_18-02-27_generations_defined/. Accessed July 21, 2021. Michael Dimock, "Defining Generations: Where Millennials End and Generation Z Begins," Pew Research Center (January 17, 2019). Available at pewresearch.org/fact-tank/2019/01/17/where-millennials-end-and-generation-z-begins. Accessed July 21, 2021. Beresford Research, "Age Range by Generation," n.d. Available at beresfordresearch.com/age-range-by-generation/. Accessed July 21, 2021.

19. Choudhury, *Deep Diversity*, 52.

20. Geert Hofstede, "Dimensionalizing Cultures: The Hofstede Model in Context," *Online Readings in Psychology and Culture* 2, no. 1 (December 2011). Available at doi.org/10.9707/2307-0919.1014. Accessed September 14, 2021.

21. Edward Hall, *Beyond Culture* (New York, Anchor Press/Doubleday & Company, 1976).

22. Seppo Tella, "The High Context Vs. Low Context Cultures," in Seppo Tella, ed., *Two Cultures Coming Together: Part 3, Theory and Practice in Communicative Foreign Language Methodology* (Helsinki: University of Helsinki Department of Teacher Education and University of Helsinki Vantaa Continuing Education Centre, 1996), 22–28.

23. Erin Meyer, *The Culture Map: Breaking Through the Invisible Boundaries of Global Business* (New York: PublicAffairs, 2014), 37–38.

24. For more information on building trust in different cultures, see Meyer, *The Culture Map*, specifically chapter 6.

Chapter 19: Electronic Communication

1. Jeremy N. Bailsenson, "Nonverbal Overload: A Theoretical Argument for the Causes of Zoom Fatigue," *Technology, Mind, and Behavior* 2, no. 1 (February 23, 2021). Available at tmb.apaopen.org/pub/nonverbal-overload/release/1. Accessed March 31, 2021.

2. Vignesh Ramachandran, "Stanford Researchers Identify Four Causes for 'Zoom Fatigue' and Their Simple Fixes," Stanford University News (February 23, 2021). Available at news.stanford.edu/2021/02/23/four-causes-zoom-fatigue-solutions/. Accessed March 30, 2021. Liz Fosslien and Mollie West Duffy, "How to Combat Zoom Fatigue," Harvard Business Review (April 29, 2020). Available at hbr.org/2020/04/how-to-combat-zoom-fatigue. Accessed March 30, 2021.

3. Sherry Turkle, "Stop Googling. Let's Talk," *New York Times* (September 26, 2015). Available at nytimes.com/2015/09/27/opinion/sunday/stop-googling-lets-talk.html. Accessed March 31, 2021.

4. Alice G. Walton, "Phone Addiction Is Real—and So Are Its Mental Health Risks," *Forbes* (December 11, 2017). Available at forbes.com/sites/alicegwalton/2017/12/11/phone-addiction-is-real-and-so-are-its-mental-health-risks/#35ad58b813df. Accessed March 31, 2021. Radiological Society of North America, "Smartphone Addiction Creates

Imbalance in Brain, Study Suggests," ScienceDaily (November 30, 2017). Available at sciencedaily.com/ releases/2017/11/171130090041.htm. Accessed March 31, 2021. "Brain Hacking," *60 Minutes* (original air date June 11, 2017). Available at youtube.com/ watch?v=awAMTQZmvPE. Accessed March 31, 2021.

5. Nancy Colier, *The Power of Off: The Mindful Way to Stay Sane in a Virtual World* (Boulder, CO: Sounds True, 2016), xiv.

6. Quoted in OHSU Communications, "Research: Face-to-face Socializing More Powerful Than Phone Calls, Emails in Guarding Against Depression in Older Adults," Oregon Health & Science University News (October 4, 2015). Available at news.ohsu.edu/2015/10/05/research:-face-to-face-socializing-more-powerful-than-phone-calls-emails-in-guarding-against-depression-in-older-adults. Accessed March 31, 2021.

7. Turkle, "Stop Googling. Let's Talk."

Conclusion: The Spiritual Side of Our Approach

1. Emily Dickinson, letter to Perez D. Cowan (October 1869). Available online at archive.emilydickinson.org/ correspondence/cowan/l332.html. Accessed January 21, 2019.

2. Plato, *Cratylus*, trans. C. D. C. Reeve (Indianapolis: Hackett Publishing Company, 1998), 33.

3. *The Dhammapada: The Buddha's Path of Wisdom*, trans. Acharya Buddharakkhita (Access to Insight, BCBS Edition, 1996). Available at accesstoinsight.org/tipitaka/ kn/dhp/dhp.intro.budd.html.

4. Ray Grigg, *The Tao of Being: A Think and Do Workbook* (Atlanta: Humanics New Age, 1989), 73.

5. Susan Kahn, "The Two Truths of Buddhism and the Emptiness of Emptiness," Emptiness Teachings (September 11, 2014). Available at emptinessteachings. com/2014/09/11/the-two-truths-of-buddhism-and-the-emptiness-of-emptiness/. Accessed September 11, 2021.

6. The Office of His Holiness the 14th Dalai Lama, @DalaiLama, Twitter, January 18, 2019, 3:30 a.m. twitter.com/DalaiLama/status/1086209175900712960.

Appendix: Nonverbal Communication

1. Edward T. Hall, *The Hidden Dimension* (New York: Doubleday Anchor, 1990).

2. David Matsumoto, Mark Frank, and Hyi Sung Hwang, eds., *Nonverbal Communication: Science and Applications* (Thousand Oaks, CA: SAGE Publications, 2013), 4.

3. Allan and Barbara Pease, "The Definitive Book of Body Language," *New York Times* (September 24, 2006). Available online at nytimes.com/2006/09/24/books/ chapters/0924-1st-peas.html. Accessed July 1, 2020.

4. For more information on learning to read emotions from facial expressions, see the Atlas of Emotions (atlasofemotions.org), an educational website created by emotion researcher Paul Ekman, at the request of the Dalai Lama, and Paul Ekman, *Emotions Revealed: Recognizing Faces and Feelings to Improve Communication and Emotional Life*, 2nd ed. (New York: Times Books, 2003).

5. Komal B. Patil, "Understanding the Use of Proxemics in Different Cultures," Social Mettle (website), last modified December 21, 2017, socialmettle.com/ understanding-proxemics-in-different-cultures. Accessed January 30, 2019.

6. Kathleen Elkins and Mike Nudelman, "The Shocking Differences in Basic Body Language Around the World," Business Insider (March 17, 2015), businessinsider.com/body-language-around-the-world-2015-3. For more information, see also Richard D. Lewis, *When Cultures Collide: Leading Across Cultures*, 3rd ed. (Boston and London: Nicholas Brealey Publishing, 2005). Chapter 10 of Lewis's book discusses cross-cultural differences in gestures.

Recommended Resources

Chapter 1: How Communication Goes Awry

Deborah Tannen, *That's Not What I Meant!: How Conversational Style Makes or Breaks Relationships*, reprint ed. (New York: Harper, 2011).

Julia T. Wood, *But I Thought You Meant . . . : Misunderstandings in Human Communication* (Mountain View, CA: Mayfield Publishing, 1998).

Chapter 2: How Skillful Communication Can Help You

The Language Principle. Books that explore how language affects perception, beliefs, and communication:

Jeremy Campbell, *Grammatical Man: Information, Entropy, Language, and Life* (New York: Simon and Schuster, 1973).

Daniel L. Everett, *Language: The Cultural Tool* (New York: Pantheon, 2012).

James Geary, *I Is an Other: The Secret Life of Metaphor and How It Shapes the Way We See the World* (New York: Perennial, 2012).

George Lakoff and Mark Johnson, *Metaphors We Live By* (Chicago: University of Chicago Press, 2003).

James W. Pennebaker, *The Secret Life of Pronouns: What Our Words Say About Us* (New York: Bloomsbury Press, 2011).

Steven Pinker, *The Language Instinct: How the Mind Creates Language* (New York: Harper Perennial Modern Classics, 2007).

Ludwig Wittgenstein, *Philosophical Investigations*, trans. G. E. M. Anscombe, P. M. S. Hacker, and Joachim Schutte, rev. 4th ed. (West Sussex, UK: Wiley-Blackwell, 2009).

The Systems Principle. General introduction to systems thinking, with articles focusing on how to apply systems principles:

Michael Goodman, "Systems Thinking: What, Why, When, Where, and How?" Systems Thinker. Available at thesystemsthinker.com/systems-thinking-what-why-when-where-and-how. Accessed September 19, 2021.

Daniel Kim, "Introduction to Thinking," Systems Thinker. Available at thesystemsthinker.com/introduction-to-systems-thinking/. Accessed September 19, 2021.

Donella Meadows, *Thinking in Systems: A Primer*, Diana Wright, ed. (White River Junction, VT: Chelsea Green Publishing, 2008).

The Systems Thinker (website): thesystemsthinker.com. Accessed on September 19, 2021.

The Critical-Thinking Principle:

Dan Clurman and John Esterle, *Conversations with Critical Thinkers* (San Francisco: The Whitman Institute, 1991).

The Critical Thinking Initiative, "Podcasts." Available at thecriticalthinkinginitiative.org/podcasts. Accessed September 19, 2021.

Peter Facione, "Critical Thinking: What It Is and Why It Counts," white paper, Insight Assessment (2020). Update available at insightassessment.com/wp-content/uploads/ia/pdf/whatwhy.pdf. Accessed September 19, 2021.

The Foundation for Critical Thinking (website): criticalthinking.org. Accessed September 19, 2021.

Marlys Mayfield, *Thinking for Yourself: Developing Critical Thinking Skills Through Reading and Writing*, 9th ed. (Boston: Wadsworth, Cengage Learning, 2014).

Richard E. Nisbett, *Mindware: Tools for Smart Thinking* (New York: Farrar, Straus and Giroux, 2015).

Joshua Rothman, "Why Is It So Hard To Be Rational?" *The New Yorker* (August 16, 2021). Available at newyorker.com/magazine/2021/08/23/why-is-it-so-hard-to-be-rational. Accessed September 19, 2021.

The Beliefs Principle:

Paul Watzlawick, *How Real Is Real?: Confusion, Disinformation, Communication* (New York: Vintage Books, 1976).

Paul Watzlawick, *The Invented Reality: How Do We Know What We Believe We Know* (New York: W. W. Norton & Company, 1984).

Also see the recommended resources for chapters 6 and 10.

The Loop-Communication Principle. For a description of the science and philosophy underlying this principle, see:

Gregory Bateson, *Mind and Nature: A Necessary Unity* (Bantam: New York, 1988).

"Information" (webpage), Information Philosopher. Available at informationphilosopher.com/introduction/information. The rest of the Information Philosopher website provides articles about the history and influence of information theories on epistemology, communication, and problem-solving, as well as short profiles of key theorists. Accessed September 19, 2021.

Bradford P. Keeney, *Aesthetics of Change* (New York: The Guilford Press, 1982).

Paul Watzlawick, Janet Beavin Bavelas, and Don D. Jackson, *Pragmatics of Human Communication: A Study of Interactional Patterns, Pathologies and Paradoxes*, reprint ed. (New York: W. W. Norton & Company, 2011).

Chapter 3: Set Yourself Up for Learning

Useful resources for understanding metacognition as it applies to learning:

Theodore Dimon, Jr., *The Elements of Skill: A Conscious Approach to Learning* (Berkeley, CA: North Atlantic Books, 2003).

Stephen M. Fleming, *Know Thyself: The Science of Self-Awareness* (New York: Basic Books, 2021)

Dilwar Hussain, "Meta-Cognition in Mindfulness: A Conceptual Analysis," *Psychological Thought* 8, no. 2 (2015), 132–141. Available at doi.org/10.5964/psyct.v8i2.139. Accessed October 4, 2021.

Improve with Metacognition (website): improvewithmetacognition.com. Accessed September 19, 2021. This site offers research, articles, and a newsletter focusing on metacognition and its application to thinking, teaching, and education.

Jesse Martin, "Learning Metacognition as Higher Order Thinking," LinkedIn (July 16, 2018). Available at linkedin. com/pulse/learning-metacognition-higher-order-thinking-jesse-martin/?published=t. Accessed September 19, 2021.

Jesse Martin, "Metacognition: Knowing What You Know," LinkedIn (May 16, 2018). Available at linkedin.com/pulse/ knowing-what-you-know-jesse-martin/. Accessed September 19, 2021.

For changing habits see:

James Clear, *Atomic Habits: An Easy and Proven Way to Build Good Habits and Break Bad Ones* (New York: Avery, 2018).

Charles Duhigg, *The Power of Habit: Why We Do What We Do in Life and Business* (New York: Random House, 2012).

Moshe Feldenkrais, *The Elusive Obvious: The Convergence of Movement, Neuroplasticity, and Health* (Berkeley, CA: North Atlantic Books, 2019).

Adam Grant, *Think Again: The Power of Knowing What You Don't Know* (New York: Viking, 2021).

Chapter 4: Talking and Listening

For more information about the use of talking and listening to build and sustain interpersonal relationships, see:

Edward Brodkin and Ashley Pallathra, *Missing Each Other: How to Cultivate Meaningful Connections* (New York: Public Affairs, Hachette Book Group, 2021).

Kathleen M. Galvin, "Listening and Feedback," chap. 6, and "Helpful Listening and Responding," chap. 7, in *Making Connections: Readings in Relational Communication*, 5th ed. (New York: Oxford University Press, 2011).

Daniel Goleman, *Social Intelligence: The New Science of Human Relationships* (New York: Bantam Books, 2006).

Daniel J. Siegel, *Aware: The Science and Practice of Presence* (New York: Tarcher Perigee, 2018).

Chapter 5: Reflective Listening

For articles and videos on the ways listening plays a role in the development of empathy, see:

> "Empathy: Defined" (webpage), *Greater Good* online magazine. Available at greatergood.berkeley.edu/topic/empathy/definition#what-is-empathy. Accessed on September 19, 2021.

> The University of California, Berkeley's Greater Good Science Center also has numerous online resources that connect communication to topics such as community, culture, education, media, technology, parenting, family, politics, relationships, society, spirituality, and the workplace. See greatergood.berkeley.edu.

For constructive ways to receive feedback:

> Douglas Stone and Shelia Heen, *Thanks for the Feedback: The Science and Art of Receiving Feedback Well* (New York: Penguin Books, 2014).

Chapter 6: Beliefs: Undercurrents of Communication

Resources for more in-depth information on cognitive dissonance:

> Carol Tavris and Elliot Aronson, *Mistakes Were Made (But Not by Me): Why We Justify Foolish Beliefs, Bad Decisions, and Hurtful Acts*, rev. ed. (Boston: Mariner Books, 2020).

Resources for understanding factors affecting the accuracy of beliefs:

> Thomas Gilovich, *How We Know What Isn't So: The Fallibility of Human Reason in Everyday Life* (New York: The Free Press, 1991).

> Daniel Kahneman, *Thinking, Fast and Slow* (New York: Farrar, Straus and Giroux, 2013).

Shankar Vedantam and Bill Mesler, *Useful Delusions: The Power and Paradox of the Self-Deceiving Brain* (New York, W. W. Norton & Company, 2021).

Chapter 7: Assumptions

For articles, slides, videos, and questionnaires focusing on the role of assumptions in thinking critically about education, politics, and diversity, see the website for Stephen D. Brookfield, stephenbrookfield.com.

M. Neil Browne and Stuart M. Keeley, "What Are the Value and Descriptive Assumptions," chap. 5 in *Asking the Right Questions: A Guide to Critical Thinking*, 12th ed. (New York: Pearson, 2018).

Chapter 8: Shifting the Blame Mindset

For information about how cognitive dissonance influences people's decisions see:

Carol Tavris and Elliot Aronson, *Mistakes Were Made (But Not by Me): Why We Justify Foolish Beliefs, Bad Decisions, and Hurtful Acts*, rev. ed. (Boston: Mariner Books, 2020).

For information on attribution theory (referred to in note 2 of chapter 8), see:

Gifford Weary, Melinda A. Stanley, and John H. Harvey, *Attribution* (New York, Springer Nature Group: 2011).

For a description of how interdependent influences are viewed from a Buddhist perspective, see:

Jay L. Garfield, "Dependent Arising and the Emptiness of Emptiness: Why Did Nāgārjuna Start with Causation?" *Philosophy East and West* 44, no. 2 (1994): 219–250. Available at doi.org/10.2307/1399593. Accessed September 19, 2021.

Susan Kahn, "Why Cause and Effect Never Met," Emptiness Teachings. Available at emptinessteachings.com/2013/05/14/why-cause-and-effect-never-met/. Accessed September 19, 2021.

For information on how linear cause-effect thinking underlies much of our common and scientific thinking see:

Robert J. Martin, "The Importance—and the Difficulty—of Moving Beyond Linear Causality," *Constructivist Foundations* 11, no. 3 (2016): 521–524. Available at constructivist.info/11/3/521. Accessed October 29, 2021.

Chapter 9: Problem-Solving

For a detailed description of how communication shapes perceptions about problems and their solutions, see:

Paul Watzlawick, John Weakland, and Richard Fisch, *Change: Principles of Problem Formation and Problem Resolution* (New York: W. W. Norton & Company, 2011).

For novel ways to solve problems:

Bill O'Hanlon, *Do One Thing Different: Ten Simple Ways to Change Your Life* (New York: William Morrow and Company, 2019).

Chapter 10: Self-Talk and Cognitive Distortions

Books discussing cognitive distortions and how to work with them:

Tara Bennett-Goleman, *Emotional Alchemy: How the Mind Can Heal the Heart* (New York: Harmony Books, 2001).

David D. Burns, *The Feeling Good Handbook*, rev. ed. (New York: Plume, 1999).

Matthew McKay, Martha Davis, and Patrick Fanning, *Thoughts and Feelings: Taking Control of Your Moods and Your Life*, 4th ed. (Oakland, CA: New Harbinger, 2011).

For more information on Acceptance and Commitment Therapy (ACT), see:

Russ Harris, *An Easy-to-Read Primer on Acceptance and Commitment Therapy*, 2nd ed. (Oakland, CA: New Harbinger, 2019).

Stephen C. Hayes, *A Liberated Mind: How to Pivot Towards What Matters* (New York Avery, 2019). Chapter 9 discusses an ACT method for creating distance from your thinking when there's a cognitive distortion or thought pattern that just can't be changed. Hayes also provides useful ACT tools on his website: stevenchayes.com/my-act-toolkit. Accessed September 19, 2021.

Matthew McKay, Avigail Lev, and Michelle Skeen, *Acceptance and Commitment Therapy for Interpersonal Problems: Using Mindfulness, Acceptance, and Schema Awareness to Change Interpersonal Behaviors* (Oakland, CA: New Harbinger, 2012).

Books on applying philosophy to examining and changing beliefs:

Julian Baggini, *The Edge of Reason: A Rational Skeptic in an Irrational World* (New Haven and London: Yale University Press, 2017).

Lou Marinoff, *Therapy for the Sane: How Philosophy Can Change Your Life* (New York: Bloomsbury, 2003).

Books on changing our life stories:

David Denborough, *Retelling the Stories of Our Lives: Everyday Narrative Therapy to Draw Inspiration and Transform Experience* (New York: W. W. Norton & Company, 2014).

Michael White, *Maps of Narrative Practice* (New York: W. W. Norton & Company, 2007).

Chapter 11: I-Language

For an illuminating description of the ways our internal and external communication shapes our identity, see:

Paul John Eakin, *Living Autobiographically: How We Create Identity in Narrative* (Ithaca, NY, and London: Cornell University Press, 2008).

Chapter 12: The Four-Part Message

For a detailed description of the way thoughts and feelings mutually influence each other, see:

Aaron T. Beck, *Cognitive Therapy and the Emotional Disorders* (New York: Plume, 1979).

Judith S. Beck, *Cognitive Behavior Therapy: Basics and Beyond*, 3rd ed. (New York: Guilford Press, 2020).

Dennis Greenberger and Christine A. Padesky, *Mind Over Mood: Change How You Feel by Changing the Way You Think*, 2nd ed. (New York: Guilford Press, 2015).

An in-depth examination of anger:

Carol Tavris, *Anger: The Misunderstood Emotion* (New York: Simon & Schuster, 1989).

Chapter 13: Framing Your Message

A concise presentation on idea framing:

Deborah Tannen, ed., *Framing in Discourse* (Oxford and New York: Oxford University Press, 1993).

How framing can be applied to leadership and communication in organizations:

Gail T. Fairhurst, *The Power of Framing: Creating the Language of Leadership*, 2nd ed. (San Francisco: Jossey-Bass, 2010).

Also see Fairhurst's website, The Leadership Framing Website, leadershipframing.com, for useful tools, examples, worksheets, and videos. Accessed September 19, 2021.

How frames influence interaction from a sociological perspective:

Charles Lemert and Ann Branaman, eds., *The Goffman Reader* (Malden, MA: Blackwell Publishing, 1997).

How framing affects the way people tell their life stories:

Kim Schneiderman, *Step Out of Your Story: Writing Exercises to Reframe and Transform Your Life* (Novato, CA: New World Library, 2015).

Framing messages in business:

Melissa Raffoni, "How to Frame Your Messages for Maximum Impact," *Harvard Business Review* (April 21, 2009). Available at hbr.org/2009/04/leaders-frame-your-messages-fo. Accessed September 19, 2021.

How to use framing for managing conflicts:

Sandra Kaufman, Michael Elliot, and Deborah Shemueli, "Frames, Framing and Reframing," Knowledge Base and Conflict Fundamentals, online essay, Beyond Intractability, updated June 2017. Available at beyondintractability.org/essay/framing. Accessed September 19, 2021.

Framing applied to understanding politics:

George Lakoff, *The Political Mind: Why You Can't Understand 21st-Century American Politics with an 18th-Century Brain* (New York: Viking, 2008).

George Lakoff, "What Conservatives Really Want," *HuffPost*, February 19, 2011. Available at huffpost.com/entry/what-conservatives-really_b_825504. Accessed September 19, 2021.

Chapter 14: Managing Conflict

Anne Brice, "How Power Corrupts Your Instinct for Cooperation," *Greater Good* online magazine, June 18, 2021. Available at greatergood.berkeley.edu/article/item/how_power_corrupts_your_instinct_for_cooperation. Accessed September 27, 2021.

John Ford, *Peace at Work: The HR Manager's Guide to Workplace Mediation* (n.p.: CreateSpace, 2014).

Diane Musho Hamilton, *Everything Is Workable: A Zen Approach to Conflict Resolution* (Boston: Shambhala, 2013).

Joyce L. Hocker and William W. Wilmot, *Interpersonal Conflict*, 10th ed. (New York: McGraw-Hill Education, 2018).

Dacher Keltner, *The Power Paradox: How We Gain and Lose Influence* (New York: Penguin Books, 2017).

Ian Leslie, *Conflicted: How Productive Disagreements Lead to Better Outcomes* (New York: Harper Business, 2021).

Nichola Raihani, *The Social Instinct: How Cooperation Shaped the World* (New York: St. Martin's Press, 2021).

Sheldon Solomon, Jeff Greenberg, and Tom Pyszczynski, *The Worm at the Core: On the Role of Death in Life* (New York: Random House, 2015).

Chapter 15: Conflict Management for Couples

David Bradford and Carol Robin, *Connect: Building Exceptional Relationships with Family, Friends, and Colleagues* (New York: Currency, 2021).

John Gottman and Joan DeClaire, *The Relationship Cure: A 5 Step Guide to Strengthening Your Marriage, Family, and Friendships* (New York: Three Rivers Press, 2001).

Avigail Lev and Matthew McKay, *Acceptance and Commitment Therapy for Couples: A Clinician's Guide to Using Mindfulness, Values, and Schema Awareness to Rebuild Relationships* (Oakland, CA: Context Press, 2017).

Chapter 16: Applications for Parents

For more about parenting to support emotional intelligence:

Marc Brackett, "Managing Emotions in Times of Uncertainty and Stress," Yale University, free online course available via Coursera. Available at coursera.org/learn/managing-emotions-uncertainty-stress. Accessed September 19, 2021.

"Family Engagement," information page on the website for RULER, "an evidence-based approach for social-emotional learning developed at the Yale Center for Emotional Intelligence." Available at rulerapproach.org/how-it-works/family-engagement/. Accessed September 19, 2021.

Yale Center for Emotional Intelligence's website, ycei.org, offers resources to help families feel better and build stronger relationships. Accessed September 19, 2021.

Yale Center for Emotional Intelligence, "Leading Difficult Conversations with Emotional Intelligence," tip sheet,

June 2020. Available at rulerapproach.org/wp-content/
uploads/2020/06/Difficult-Conversations-1.pdf. Posted in
2020. Accessed September 19, 2021.

For resources that explore and demonstrate how to connect with
young children emotionally, see:

Kenneth Barish, *Pride and Joy: A Guide to Understanding
Your Child's Emotions and Solving Family Problems* (Oxford
and New York: Oxford University Press, 2012).

Maurice Elias, Steven Tobias, and Brian S. Friedlander,
*Emotionally Intelligent Parenting, How to Raise a Self-
Disciplined, Responsible, Socially Skilled Child* (New York:
Three Rivers Press, 1999).

John M. Gottman and Joan DeClaire, *How to Raise an
Emotionally Intelligent Child: The Heart of Parenting* (New
York: Fireside, 1998).

Laura Markham, *Peaceful Parents, Happy Kids: How to Stop
Yelling and Start Connecting* (New York: Perigee Books, 2012).

Erica Reischer, *What Great Parents Do: 75 Simple Strategies
for Raising Kids Who Thrive* (New York: Tarcher Perigee,
2016).

Dan Siegel, *No Drama Discipline: The Whole-Brain Way to
Calm the Chaos and Nurture Your Child's Developing Mind*
(New York: Bantam, 2014).

Shauna Tominey, *Creating Compassionate Kids: Essential
Conversations to Have with Young Children* (New York: W. W.
Norton & Company, 2019.)

The Contentment Foundation is an organization that "offers
evidence-based wellbeing curricula to schools internationally."
For more information, see its website, contentment.
org, and its YouTube channel, youtube.com/channel/
UCLGs8_18siaYSFBiLua0kBg. Accessed September 19, 2021.

Chapter 17: Health Challenges

Barbara L. Fredrickson, *Positivity: Top-Notch Research Reveals the 3-to-1 Ratio That Will Change Your Life* (New York: Harmony, 2009).

Susan Halpern, *The Etiquette of Illness: What to Say When You Can't Find the Words* (London and New York: Bloomsbury, 2004).

Joanne Lynn and Joan Harrold, *Handbook for Mortals: Guidance for People Facing Serious Illness* (Oxford and New York: Oxford University Press, 1999).

William and Nancy Martin, *The Caregiver's Tao Te Ching: Compassionate Caring for Your Loved Ones and Yourself* (Novato, CA: New World Library, 2011).

Annelise Schinzinger, *The Art and Science of Caregiving: Stories of Inspiring Elders with an End-of-Life Guidebook* (Santa Cruz, CA: Noble Books, 2019).

For more information on self-compassion, see:

Christopher Germer, *The Mindful Path to Self-Compassion: Freeing Yourself from Destructive Thoughts and Emotions* (New York: Guilford Press, 2009).

Kristin Neff and Christopher Germer, *The Mindful Self-Compassion Workbook: A Proven Way to Accept Yourself, Build Inner Strength, and Thrive* (New York: Guilford Press, 2018).

Kristin Neff's website, self-compassion.org and Christopher Germer's website, chrisgermer.com, offer resources, videos, and guided meditations.

Chapter 18: Diversity and Social Context

Paul Born, *Community Conversations: Mobilizing the Ideas, Skills, and Passion of Community Organizations, Governments,*

Businesses, and People, 2nd ed. (Toronto and New York: BPS Books, 2008).

Shakil Choudhury, *Deep Diversity: A Compassionate, Scientific Approach to Achieving Racial Justice* (Vancouver, BC: Greystone Books, 2021).

Jennifer L. Eberhardt, *Biased: Uncovering the Hidden Prejudice That Shapes What We See, Think, and Do* (New York: Viking, 2019).

Pamela M. Fishman, "Interaction: The Work Women Do," *Social Problems* 25, no. 4 (April 1, 1978), 397–406. doi. org/10.2307/800492.

Megan Gerhardt, Josephine Nachemson-Ekwall, and Brandon Fogel, *Gentelligence: The Revolutionary Approach to Leading an Intergenerational Workforce* (Lanham, MD: Rowman and Littlefield, 2021).

Rom Harré and Fathali M. Moghaddam, eds., *The Self and Others: Positioning Individuals and Groups in Personal, Political, and Cultural Contexts* (Westport, CT: Praeger, 2003).

Janet Holmes and Miriam Meyerhoff, eds., *The Handbook of Language and Gender* (Maiden, MA: Blackwell Publishing, 2003).

Allan G. Johnson, *Privilege, Power, and Difference*, 3rd ed. (New York: McGraw-Hill Education, 2018).

Ibram X. Kendi, *How to Be an Antiracist* (New York: One World, 2019).

Anthony J. Marsella, George DeVos, and Francis L. K. Hsu, eds., *Culture and Self: Asian and Western Perspectives* (New York: Tavistock Publications, 1985).

Leila Monaghan, Jane E. Goodman, and Jennifer Meta Robinson, eds., *A Cultural Approach to Interpersonal Communication: Essential Readings*, 2nd ed. (West Sussex, UK: Wiley-Blackwell Publishing, 2012).

Richard E. Nisbett, *The Geography of Thought: How Asians and Westerners Think Differently . . . and Why* (New York: The Free Press, 2003).

Helen Riess with Liz Neporent, *The Empathy Effect: Seven Neuroscience-Based Keys for Transforming the Way We Live, Love, Work, and Connect Across Differences* (Boulder, CO: Sounds True, 2018).

Dianne Hofner Saphiere, Barbara Kappler Mikk, and Basma Ibrahim DeVries, *Communication Highwire: Leveraging the Power of Diverse Communication Styles* (Boston: Intercultural Press, 2005).

For a variety of articles and research on the different generations, see:

"Generations and Age" (webpage), Pew Research Center. Available at pewresearch.org/topic/generations-age/. Accessed on September 27, 2021.

For articles and videos on the ways listening and other evidence-based strategies can be used to improve dialogue, understanding, and relationships across social and political divides, see:

"Bridging Differences: Articles and More" (webpage), *Greater Good* online magazine. Available at greatergood. berkeley.edu/topic/bridging_differences. Accessed on September 19, 2021.

Chapter 19: Electronic Communication

Nicholas Carr, *The Shallows: What the Internet Is Doing to Our Brains* (New York: W. W. Norton & Company, 2020).

Nancy Colier, *The Power of Off: The Mindful Way to Stay Sane in a Virtual World* (Boulder, CO: Sounds True, 2016).

Victoria L. Dunckley, *Reset Your Child's Brain: A Four-Week Plan to End Meltdowns, Raise Grades, and Boost Social Skills by Reversing the Effects of Electronic Screen-Time* (Novato, CA: New World Library, 2015).

Paula Durlofsky, *Logged In and Stressed Out: How Social Media Is Affecting Your Mental Health and What You Can Do About It* (Lanham, MD: Rowman & Littlefield, 2020).

Howard Gardner and Katie Davis, *The App Generation: How Today's Youth Navigate Identity, Intimacy, and Imagination in a Digital World* (New Haven, CT: Yale University Press, 2013).

Cal Newport, *Digital Minimalism: Choosing a Focused Life in a Noisy World* (New York: Portfolio/Penguin, 2019).

Erik Peper and Richard Harvey, with Nancy Fass, *Tech Stress: How Technology Is Hijacking Our Lives, Strategies for Coping, and Practical Ergonomics* (Berkeley, CA: North Atlantic Books, 2020).

Gary Small and Gigi Vorgan, *iBrain: Surviving the Technological Alteration of the Modern Mind* (New York: HarperCollins, 2008).

Alex Soojung-Kim Pang, *The Distraction Addiction: Getting the Information You Need and the Communication You Want, Without Enraging Your Family, Annoying Your Colleagues, and Destroying Your Soul* (New York: Little, Brown & Company, 2021).

Catherine Steiner-Adair and Teresa H. Barker, *The Big Disconnect: Protecting Childhood and Family Relationships in the Digital Age* (New York: HarperCollins, 2013).

Sherry Turkle, *Alone Together: Why We Expect More From Technology and Less From Each Other* (New York: Basic Books, 2011).

Sherry Turkle, *Reclaiming Conversation: The Power of Talk in a Digital Age* (New York: Penguin Press, 2015).

Conclusion: The Spiritual
Side of Our Approach

Taoism:

A. C. Graham, trans., *Chuang Tzu: The Inner Chapters* (Indianapolis, IN: Hackett Publishing Company, 2001).

Chad Hansen, *A Daoist Theory of Chinese Thought: A Philosophical Interpretation* (Oxford and New York: Oxford University Press, 2000).

Chad Hansen, Chad Hansen's Chinese Philosophy Pages (webpage). Available at philosophy.hku.hk/ch/. Accessed on September 19, 2021.

Chad Hansen, *Tao Te Ching on the Art of Harmony* (New York: Shelter Harbor Press, 2017).

Thomas Merton, trans., *The Way of Chuang Tzu*, 2nd ed. (New York: New Directions, 2010).

Red Pine, trans., *Lao-tzu's Taoteching*, 3rd rev. ed. (Port Townsend, WA: Copper Canyon Press, 2009).

Burton Watson, *The Complete Works of Zhuangzi* (New York: Columbia University Press, 2013).

Alan Watts, *The Tao of Philosophy* (North Claredon, VT: Tuttle Publishing, 1995).

Western philosophy:

Julian Baggini, *What's It All About: Philosophy and the Meaning of Life* (Oxford and New York: Oxford University Press, 2007).

Douglas E. Harding, The Headless Way (website): headless.org. Accessed September 19, 2021.

Douglas E. Harding, *Look for Yourself: The Science and Art of Self-Realization* (Encinitas, CA: Inner Directions Publishing, 1998).

Rom Harré, *One Thousand Years of Philosophy* (West Sussex, UK: Wiley-Blackwell, 2000).

Alva Noë, *Out of Our Heads: Why You Are Not Your Brain, and Other Lessons from the Biology of Consciousness* (New York: Hill and Wang, 2009).

Richard Rorty, *Philosophy and the Mirror of Nature*, 30th anniversary ed. (Princeton, NJ: Princeton University Press, 2009).

Scott Soames, *Philosophy of Language* (Princeton, NJ: Princeton University Press, 2010).

Ludwig Wittgenstein, *Philosophical Investigations*, G. E. M. Anscombe, P. M. S. Hacker, and Joachim Schutte, trans., rev. 4th ed. (West Sussex, UK: Wiley-Blackwell, 2009).

Buddhism:

Stephan Batchelor, *Verses from the Center: A Buddhist Vision of the Sublime*, reissue ed. (New York: Riverhead Books, 2001).

The Dalai Lama, *The Dalai Lama's Book of Wisdom* (London: Thorsons, 1999).

Jay L. Garfield, trans., *The Fundamental Wisdom of the Middle Way: Nāgārjuna's Mūlamadhyamakakārikā* (Oxford and New York: Oxford University Press, 1995).

Greg Goode and Tomas Sander, *Emptiness and Joyful Freedom* (Salisbury, UK: Non-Duality Press, 2013).

Antonia Macaro, *More Than Happiness: Buddhist and Stoic Wisdom for a Skeptical Age* (London: Icon Books, 2018).

Tarthang Tulku, *Dimensions of Time and Space: Transcending Limits of Knowledge* (Berkeley, CA: Dharma Publishing, 1994).

Dharma Seed (dharmaseed.org) is a website that provides free audio talks and guided meditations by Buddhist teachers on Buddhism and meditation practice.

Shamanism:

Serge Kahili King, *Urban Shamanism* (New York: Simon and Shuster, 1990).

Roger Walsh, *The World of Shamanism: New Views of an Ancient Tradition* (Woodbury, MN: Llewellyn Worldwide, 2007).

Sufism:

Robert Frager and James Fadiman, eds., *Essential Sufism* (New York: HarperOne, 1999).

Idries Shah, *The Sufis*, 7th ed., (London: ISF Publishing, 2018).

Poetry:

John Brehm, *The Dharma of Poetry: How Poems Can Deepen Your Spiritual Practice and Open You to Joy* (Somerville, MA: Wisdom Publications, 2021).

David Hinton, trans., *Classical Chinese Poetry: An Anthology* (New York: Farrar, Straus and Giroux, 2010).

Denis Maloney, ed., *Finding the Way Home: Poems of Awakening and Transformation* (Buffalo, NY: White Pine Press, 2010).

Stephen Mitchell, ed., *The Enlightened Heart* (New York: Harper Perennial, 1993).

Rumi, *The Essential Rumi*, Coleman Barks, trans., new expanded ed. (New York: HarperOne, 2004).

Ryokan, *One Robe, One Bowl: The Zen Poetry of Ryokan*, John Stevens, trans. (n.p.: Weatherhill, 2006).

Jonathan Star, ed., *The Inner Treasure* (New York: Tarcher, 1999).

Appendix: Nonverbal Communication

Paul Ekman, *Emotions Revealed: Recognizing Faces and Feelings to Improve Communication and Emotional Life* (New York: Owl Books, 2003).

Paul Ekman Group, "Nonverbal Communication" (article online, no date). Available at paulekman.com/nonverbal-communication. Accessed on September 19, 2021.

Also see the rest of Paul Ekman's website, paulekman.com, for more articles and training materials for learning to recognize emotions in facial micro expressions.

Kathleen M. Galvin, "Elements of Non-Verbal Communication," chap. 8 in *Making Connections: Readings in Relational Communication*, 5th ed. (Oxford and New York: Oxford University Press, 2011).

Edward T. Hall, *The Hidden Dimension* (Garden City, NY: Doubleday, 1966).

David Matsumoto, Mark G. Frank, and Hyi Sung Hwang, *Nonverbal Communication: Science and Applications* (Los Angeles: SAGE Publications, 2013).

Acknowledgments

We give enormous thanks to our outstanding editor, Amy Rost, for helping us shape and organize our ideas. Her ability to think critically helped us clarify and hone both what we wanted to say and how we said it. Her encouragement and editing skills were invaluable during challenging times.

Many thanks to our family, friends, colleagues, and all those who inspired, encouraged, and supported us along the way.

We're indebted to the following people for providing many helpful suggestions and feedback. Much gratitude goes to Steven Kaplan, Deanne Stone, and Bob Morrison. They helped us move forward in so many ways, especially when we reached an impasse. We'd also like to acknowledge the support we received from Joseph Goldstein, Dan Harris, Djuna Odegard, Jane Ross, Kathryn Lee, Wes Nisker, Rachel Cooper, John Ford, Annie Popkin, David Lang, Marlys Mayfield, Mark Whitehill, Cynthia Bebee, Ruth Anne and Michael Grove, Perry Garfinkel, Robert Fraser, Aidan Fraser, Mushim Patricia Ikeda, Sarah Nielsen, Robert Perinbanayagam, Lauren Vanett, Richard Gelbard, Robin Burton, Rob Foster, Bea Deering, Jeff Greenwald, and Dana Mackey.

We want to thank our daughter, Rose, and her husband, Paddy, for their invaluable feedback about diversity and digital communication and for sharing their other illuminating insights.

Thanks also to David Brown and Gregory Ghent for their friendship and for providing wonderful places for our writing retreats.

Much appreciation to the students we've worked with for many years. Their participation in ongoing groups has helped shape our methodology. Together we've created a vibrant communication community.

Mudita thanks the women in her communication-based support groups. Their kindness and skillfulness are inspiring. A special shout-out to Jane Baraz, who helped Mudita launch her women's groups in the early days. Dan thanks his students at Golden Gate University and UC Berkeley Extension. Their curiosity, diverse experiences, and love of learning are inspiring.

Thanks to Rachel Lehto for her wonderful marketing and logistical support.

Thanks to Hugh McLean for his unique, wise, and, at times, radical approach to communication.

Last, we appreciate how much we've learned from each other. These skills have been a gift for nurturing our love.

About the Authors

Mudita Nisker is a licensed marriage family therapist (LMFT), coach, and trainer. She works with couples and individuals in her private practice in Oakland, California. A strong advocate of lifelong learning, she's led women's communication-training groups for more than thirty-five years. She also offers training and coaching to private, public, government, and nonprofit organizations. She's a strong proponent of applying critical thinking to practical, compassionate communication. Her articles in the Buddhist publications *Tricycle* and *Inquiring Mind* explore the Buddhist idea of "right speech" in daily life. Mudita is a musician and founding member of Gamelan Sekar Jaya, a sixty-four-member company of musicians and dancers specializing in the performing arts of Bali. She has contributed her communication expertise to GSJ's members and officers since its inception. Parenting her daughter has been one of the great joys of her life. Mudita received her B.A. and M.A. in psychology from the University of Minnesota.

Dan Clurman is a coach, trainer, and professor. Over the past thirty years, he has provided communication training and coaching to individuals and organizations in the private, public, government, and nonprofit sectors. He is on the faculty of the psychology department in the Edward S. Ageno School of Business at Golden Gate University in San Francisco. He teaches courses in team dynamics, conflict resolution, and coaching, emphasizing the interplay of critical thinking and communication. He also teaches business communication at UC Berkeley Extension. Dan received a B.A. in anthropology from Columbia University and an M.A. in psychology from Sonoma State University. He is a guild-certified practitioner of the Feldenkrais Method of somatic education and conducts workshops on the

Feldenkrais Method and mindfulness meditation at Spirit Rock meditation center, Natural Dharma Fellowship and Esalen Institute. Dan's publications include *Conversations with Critical Thinkers*; *Floating Upstream: Poems and Drawings*; and a book of cartoons, *You've Got to Draw the Line Somewhere.*

CPSIA information can be obtained
at www.ICGtesting.com
Printed in the USA
LVHW071654120623
749428LV00023B/496